D0868758

A PEOPLE DIVIDED

Judaism in Contemporary America

Jack Wertheimer

BasicBooks
A Division of HarperCollins*Publishers*

The poem/liturgy by Rabbi Sherwin T. Wine found on page 79 is reprinted with permission of the publishers of *Meditation Services for Humanistic Jews* (Farmington Hills, Mich.: Society for Humanistic Judaism). Copyright ©1976 by the Society for Humanistic Judaism. The author would also like to thank R. Stephen Warner for permission to use material quoted from "The Place of the Congregation in the Contemporary American Religious Configuration" (James Lewis and James P. Wind, eds. *The Congregation in American Life* [Chicago: University of Chicago Press, forthcoming]) on page 152 and from "Change and Continuity in the U. S. Religious System: Perspectives from Sociology" found on page 307.

Copyright © 1993 by BasicBooks, A Division of HarperCollins Publishers, Inc.

All rights reserved. Printed in the United States of America. No part of this book may be reproduced in any manner whatsoever without written permission except in the case of brief quotations embodied in critical articles and reviews. For information, address BasicBooks, 10 East 53rd Street, New York, NY 10022-5299.

Designed by Ellen Levine

Library of Congress Cataloging-in-Publication Data

Wertheimer, Jack
   A people divided : Judaism in contemporary America / Jack Wertheimer.
     p. cm.
   Includes bibliographical references and index.
   ISBN 0-465-00165-3 (cloth)
   ISBN 0-465-05464-1 (paper)
   1. Judaism—United States. 2. Judaism—20th century. 3. Jews—United States—Identity. 4. Orthodox Judaism—Relations—Nontraditional Jews.
I. Title.
BM205.W46 1993
296.'0973'0904—dc20   92-54514
                                               CIP

94 95 96 97 RRD(H) 10 9 8 7 6 5 4 3 2

In Honor of My Parents

CONTENTS

PART III
THE FRAGMENTING WORLD OF
ORGANIZED JUDAISM

PREFACE

Even though formal research for this book commenced only five years ago, my exploration of American Judaism began as a personal odyssey already in the early 1960s. Educated in Orthodox day schools, I was exposed to one form of Judaism and knew virtually nothing of the substance let alone contributions of the other branches. My awakening came in high school when I stumbled upon such major Jewish journals as *Judaism*, *Commentary*, and *Midstream*, and some of the official publications of rabbinic groups. Suddenly the larger, more diversified world of American Judaism opened before me. It was a pleasant homecoming to reread the same journal issues some twenty-five years later, as I embarked upon my research.

My educational journey continued at a number of institutions of higher learning that exposed me to engaged Jews and Christians of varying outlooks. First, I enrolled in undergraduate courses at the Jewish Theological Seminary of America, the educational center of the Conservative movement. I could not have known at the time that this would become my academic home for decades to come. During my years as a doctoral student at Columbia University, some of my classmates were activists in the nascent Havurah movement and among the most thoughtful proponents of feminist Judaism. In later years I spoke at Reform temples and taught at the Reconstructionist Rabbinical College. An opportunity to serve on the advisory committee of the Congregational History Project housed at the divinity school of the University of Chicago brought me into contact with some of the finest interpreters of American Protestantism and Catholicism. These institutions and the many colleagues I encountered along the way enriched my understanding of both contemporary American Judaism and the broader world of American religion. Through them I was able to observe firsthand a diversity of religious perspectives and practices.

I am indebted to a number of individuals who offered specific guidance as I worked on this book. David Singer and Ruth R. Seldin first commissioned me to write a lengthy essay, entitled "Recent Trends in American Judaism," for the 1989 *American Jewish Yearbook*. Their constructive suggestions and diligent editing vastly improved that essay, and I continued to draw upon their insights as I wrote this book. I thank Ruth and David and the sponsors of the *American Jewish Yearbook* for offering me the first opportunity to explore the themes central to this book.

I have been fortunate to work with a strong editor at Basic Books, Steven Fraser. Steve's quick decision to offer me a book contract raised my morale and confidence. He provided firm guidance as well as valuable criticism and also displayed patience and fairness as my work encountered the inevitable snags.

Many colleagues have given me much encouragement and guidance. I am particularly grateful to Benjamin Gampel, who has graciously served as a sounding board and sophisticated editor of my prose since our years together as graduate students. Benjy has endured many lunches with fork in one hand and red pen in the other. Upon the appearance of my essay in the *American Jewish Yearbook*, a number of colleagues took the time to share their responses with me. These included David Ellenson, Donald Feldstein, Alfred Gottschalk, Charles Liebman, Jonathan Sarna, Charles Raffel, and Alan J. Yuter. I thank Paul Ritterband and Barry Kosmin of the North American Jewish Databank for making available the Nine and Ten City Samples utilized in chapter 3. With his customary collegial generosity, Paul aided and encouraged my utilization of these data; in many hours of conversation, he has been an invaluable guide to the field of American Jewish sociology. Help of a different kind came from my friend and rabbi Yehoshua (Isidoro) Aizenberg, who lent me his office for two summers; I deeply appreciate his foresight in planning extended trips to Israel at precisely the times I most needed a quiet office close to home!

Meetings of the Congregational History Project, with their fast-paced discussions about American religious history and sociology, energized me; I often found myself scribbling furiously to get down a record of the new avenues suggested by our conversations. My thanks to the codirectors of the project, James W. Lewis and James P. Wind, for inviting me into this wonderful circle of colleagues, and to my fellow participants for their ongoing friendship—Dorothy Bass, Don Browning, Jay Dolan, Carl Dudley, DeAne Lagerquist, E. Brooks Holifield, Langdon Gilkey, Martin E. Marty, and R. Stephen Warner. Closer to home, my horizons were broadened by the erudition and model of Robert T. Handy, the dean of American church historians. In his last years before retirement, Bob generously invited me to meet with his students at Union Theological Seminary, thereby exposing me to the rich diversity of that religious institution.

The Jewish Theological Seminary of America has contributed tangibly to this book through summer and sabbatical grants from the Abbell Faculty Research Fund. The Seminary's environment of scholarly and religious engagement and its unparalleled library have provided a wonderfully conducive setting for research and writing. I am indebted to Ismar Schorsch, chancellor of the Seminary, for his warm encouragement and friendship over the course of more than two decades. Our conversations about modern Jewish history and contemporary American Judaism have enriched my perspective immeasurably. My encounters with students both in the classroom and in casual conversation further informed my understanding of American Jewish religious life. It has been a pleasure to acknowledge in the notes to this book several class papers written by my students.

My family has provided me with the most personally meaningful setting for the exploration of Judaism. As we strive to transmit a strong Jewish identity to our sons, Joshua and Daniel, and through them experience the joy of Jewish continuity, my wife, Rebecca, and I are spurred to further define our own places in the world of American Judaism.

In dedicating this book to my parents, I wish to honor the memory of my mother and pay tribute to my father. Survivors of the darkest era in Jewish history, they have inspired their children—and now their grandchildren—through their steadfast faith in the religious teachings and historical destiny of the people Israel.

INTRODUCTION

In the fall of 1988 the unity of the Jewish people in the United States was seriously undermined by bitter recriminations over seemingly minor political maneuverings across the ocean in the State of Israel. Seeking to form a new coalition government, the leaders of Israel's two major political blocs expressed a willingness to support demands by several small religious parties to amend Israel's Law of Return, the law that expresses the essential Zionist conviction that every Jew has the right to immediate citizenship upon settling in the Jewish state. Religious parties in Israel had lobbied for many years to have the Orthodox rabbinate granted exclusive authority to determine "who is a Jew" for the purposes of that law. With the political leverage they had won in the 1988 elections, their goal seemed within reach. Had they succeeded, anyone converted to Judaism by a non-Orthodox rabbi would have become ineligible for Israeli citizenship under the Law of Return. In time—and after considerable lobbying by American Jewish groups—Israeli political leaders forged a government that was not committed to support of the amendment.[1]

Until the matter was resolved, the question of "who is a Jew" threw the American Jewish community into disarray. The General Assembly of the Council of Jewish Federations, often called the parliament of North American Jews, devoted much of its agenda to the issue, particularly because community leaders feared that passage of an amendment to the Law of Return would seriously impair fund-raising in behalf of domestic and international Jewish needs.[2] The Jewish press carried an ongoing stream of reports on this issue, including interviews with converts and debates among rabbis over the implications of the impending Israeli move. And leaders of the major branches of American Judaism hurled insults and threats, each blaming the other for causing irreparable damage to the unity of the Jewish people.

A fair-minded observer might have wondered at the strange imbalance between the degree of rancor and the tiny population that would have been directly affected had the amendment passed. Surely, a creative solution could have been devised to resolve the status of the handful of non-Orthodox converts who immigrate to Israel annually. More important, why was the fabric of Jewish life in the United States ripping apart over a law that directly affected only a few Jews settling in Israel? Clearly, the issue had little practical importance but extraordinary symbolic significance for American Jews. From the perspective of non-Orthodox groups, the amendment could have only one purpose—the delegitimation of non-Orthodox rabbis. The true issue then was not so much "who is a Jew?" as "who is an authentic rabbi?"[3]

Much like an earthquake that releases pent-up pressures simmering beneath the earth's crust, the explosive "who is a Jew" controversy represented the eruption of bitter animosities between different factions of American Judaism that had been repositioning themselves and colliding with intensified force for several decades. The earthquake of the "who is a Jew" controversy left deep rifts in the Jewish world. Close observers of American Jewry, however, would have noticed a series of smaller fissures developing already in the years prior to the explosion of 1988.

Item: Before the Jewish High Holidays in 1984, readers of Jewish newspapers were exhorted in advertisements placed by the Union of Orthodox Rabbis of the United States and Canada "not to pray in a Reform or Conservative Temple, . . . whose Clergy have long rebelled against numerous sacred laws of the Torah and mislead thousands of innocent souls." Readers were urged to "pray at home even on Rosh Ha-shano and Yom Kipur," rather than spend the High Holidays in such a setting.[4]

Item: A conversion ceremony conducted by Conservative rabbis at a Chicago *mikveh* (ritual bath)* in the mid-1980s was interrupted by the shouts of an Orthodox Jew using a bullhorn to warn the prospective convert that the rabbis converting him were not rabbis and that his conversion ceremony was a sham. Charges of harassment were filed, and Conservative and Orthodox rabbis were prepared to testify against one another at the court hearings.[5]

Item: The Reform rabbinate's Committee on the Cultic Proselytiza- tion of Our Youth debated but ultimately tabled a resolution denounc- ing the outreach program of Lubavitch Hasidim, a program aimed solely at Jews.[6]

Item: After functioning harmoniously for a number of years, rabbis in Denver who had cooperatively supervised conversions on a community- wide basis dissolved their *Beit Din* (religious court) in 1983. The Orthodox, Conservative, Reconstructionist, and Reform rabbis on the conversion board could no longer find ways to reconcile their dif- ferences.[7]

These incidents make plain that relations between the factions of American Judaism were already deteriorating in the five years before the "who is a Jew?" controversy erupted. American Judaism was frag- menting over questions of religious authenticity, the nature of reli- gious reform, and different conceptions of *what* Judaism is. Little has happened in the intervening years to suggest that a harmonious reso- lution is imminent.

The acrimony displayed during the controversy also exposed another truth about American Judaism, namely, that Jewish religious divisions were sufficiently severe to disrupt the functioning of the larger American Jewish community. When major donors on either side of the divide threatened to withhold funding from the large fund-

* A glossary of Jewish religious terms and institutions is appended to this volume.

raising agencies, the official community took notice. Religious divisions could no longer be dismissed as solely a turf struggle between rabbis. It is increasingly evident that religious polarization affects the entire Jewish community of the United States.

In recent years religious questions have attracted the attention of the broader Jewish community for yet a second reason. Survey research on American Jews has found a direct relationship between religious commitment and support for Jewish communal institutions. One study in the late 1970s actually correlated the number of religious observances a Jew performed with the amount of money the individual donated to Jewish philanthropy. More ritually observant Jews contributed a greater amount of dollars per capita than did less observant Jews.[8] This was confirmed in the National Jewish Population Survey of 1990, which found that identification with Judaism is the critical variable for Jewish continuity in America. According to one leading demographer, "Jews by religion are more traditional and involved in their community" than secular Jews.[9] The health of American Judaism thus has a direct impact on the viability and unity of the Jewish people in America.

What, then, is the condition of American Judaism? What do we know about the vitality and meaning of religion for American Jews? There is no shortage of reports on the subject, but the message they present is a confusing one. With much enthusiasm, the general press presents evidence of Jewish religious revival: *Time* magazine features an essay on the religious gatherings of rural Jews in Vermont, and the *New Yorker* publishes a three-part report on the appeal of life in the Lubavitch Hasidic community.[10] Yet readers are left wondering whether these expressions of a vibrant Judaism represent the new vogue or merely the offbeat and the exceptional. Jewish periodicals, by contrast, suggest that American Judaism is racked by religious warfare, filled as they are with reports of vituperative denunciations, predictions of doom, and triumphal exclamations emanating from partisans of different religious factions. Academic observers, in turn, weigh the results of survey research and prognosticate about the future of American Judaism: whereas a decade ago, several outspoken sociologists were decidedly optimistic, today, after the latest national survey, most academic observers tend toward extreme pessimism.

The confusion is magnified when seemingly contradictory reports appear almost in tandem. In the spring of 1992 the press was full of upbeat coverage. The magazine of the *New York Times* ran a celebratory cover story on the Lubavitcher rebbe, a charismatic figure of venerable age whose followers expected him to announce at any moment that he was the Messiah. Without adducing any quantitative evidence, the article claimed that the Rebbe was "lionized by his nearly 200,000 followers" and declared his movement "a missionary juggernaut."[11] About the same time, *Moment*, a leading Jewish popular journal, printed a cover story on the turn to spirituality among Reform Jews. The article described the reappropriation of previously abandoned religious rituals and the formation of new religious groupings within Reform congregations. A leading Reform rabbi observed: "What we are seeing is the embrace of religious rituals, once discarded as 'unnecessary,' as a means of giving expression to a rising level of spirituality."[12] Simultaneously, a journalist reported on his cross-country travels in search of Jewish religious schools that "break the mold." Beginning his journey with a bleak assessment of such schools, he returned with greater hope because he found schools across the land with "a vision . . . of what they wanted their children to learn about being Jews."[13]

Just a few months before the appearance of these glowing reports, the General Assembly of the Council of Jewish Federations gathered under the dark cloud of a recently released survey of the American Jewish community. According to the 1990 National Jewish Population Survey, Jews were marrying non-Jews with ever-increasing frequency, so that by the late 1980s, more than half of Jews getting married entered into mixed marriages. The study provided evidence of increased estrangement from Judaism and Israel within the American Jewish community. And it indicated that there were more born Jews defecting to other religions than converts coming to Judaism. Understandably, when the leaders of American Jewry's most powerful organizations and communities met, they struggled to respond to the bad news.[14] A baffled observer may wonder how to reconcile reports of religious revival with contrary evidence of religious apathy among large sectors of American Jewry.

There are also conflicting interpretations of how to gauge the significance of polarization among Jews who do take their religion seriously. Reacting to the increasing frequency and hostility of religious confrontations, some observers have voiced concern that American Jewry will soon be riven into contending camps that do not recognize each other's legitimacy as Jews. Others remark that such a polarization has already come to pass, that a deep divide separates Orthodox from non-Orthodox Jews, with only a relatively small population of Modern Orthodox and right-wing Conservative Jews seeking to bridge the divide. And still others view the present confrontations as merely passing tempests in the continuing evolution of a distinctly American version of Judaism.[15]

To make sense of contemporary Jewish religious life, this book intends to go beyond the headlines. Certainly, one must evaluate the significance of the confrontations between religious factions; but the deeper trends within American Judaism—the rapid and massive changes in American Jewish religious life—also need to be identified and considered. How do patterns of religious observance today compare with those of the recent past? What are the major concerns of the Jewish laity? And how have rabbinic elites responded to those concerns? Which new rituals and religious forms have captured the imagination of Jews in recent decades? And how do patterns within American Judaism correlate with broader trends within American religious life?

As Martin E. Marty, one of the preeminent historians of American religion, has noted: "Observers of American religion regularly need to map the terrain. Its bewildering pluralism, they soon learn, resists a single or permanent outline."[16] This book maps the terrain of contemporary American Judaism and seeks to capture its bewildering diversity by examining Judaism against the backdrop of the larger American environment. And thus it aims to speak to readers interested in the controversial and ever-changing role of religion in contemporary America.

Fundamentally, this book is addressed to those concerned about the condition of American Jewish life. Its focus on the *religion* of American Jews sets it apart from the many discussions primarily concerned with Jews as an *ethnic* group. These works pose questions about changes in the size of the Jewish population, geographic and occupational trends, rates of fertility, friendship and marriage patterns, and associational behavior.[17] All of these can serve as a basis for judging the vitality of Jewish ethnicity, but they tell us little about the religious dimension of

American Jewry. This study, by contrast, focuses sharply on contemporary American Judaism, examining religious behavior and public discussion about Judaism.

A People Divided exposes the deep fissures in American Jewish religious life today, a division fundamentally between a growing majority of American Jews for whom religion plays a minimal role and an increasingly passionate minority that has created dynamic programs for religious revival. The latter have been inspired—and challenged—by a resurgent Orthodoxy, but they may be found across the religious spectrum of American Judaism. The committed minority can be found in each of the official religious movements, as well as in groups that reject denominational labels. Indeed, even as transdenominational groupings have flourished, thereby bringing different types of Jews together, each of the movements of American Judaism has been racked by internal dissension. As a result, the Orthodox, Conservative, Reform, and Reconstructionist movements each consists of coalitions that periodically threaten to break apart over issues of theology and religious policy.

It is not accidental that American Judaism has fragmented since the 1960s. This has been an era of deep division in American society and religion in general; the discord within Jewish denominations has its counterparts in the worlds of American Protestantism and Catholicism. Many—though not all—of the issues that have precipitated what one sociologist has characterized as an American "culture war" polarize religious Jews as well. Similarly, the triumphalism of the religious right in America and the declining attraction of liberal religion find their analogues in the Jewish community.

American Judaism, however, must also contend with some uniquely Jewish dilemmas. Certainly, the most divisive issue in contemporary American Judaism reflects the pattern of the larger American scene—the explosive growth of intermarriage in virtually all sectors of American society. But the despair and confusion of American Jewry in the face of this crisis has no parallel in other religious communities. Nor can the religious apathy of so many American Jews be ascribed to American society; ironically, the most assimilated American Jews differ from their Christian neighbors by virtue of their religious indifference.

The world of American Judaism is thus divided along a variety of grids: there is a yawning chasm between the religiously committed and the indifferent; the four major denominations are in conflict with each other and each is divided internally; there are Jews who choose to remain on the margins of official Judaism and reject all denominational religion; there are issues that unite some Jews across denominational lines to join in ideological combat against other Jews; finally, the international unity of the Jewish people is threatened by growing religious differences between American and Israeli Jews. To some observers, these polarities suggest vitality—a Jewish community that takes its religion seriously. Where debate attests to passionate, albeit conflicting, commitments, the absence of discord would signal apathy. By emphasizing the fragmentation, this book sides with those who fear that polarization will weaken the Jewish community and erode the unity needed by the shrinking Jewish minority in the United States.

Nevertheless, this book is not written as an alarmist tract that denigrates Jewish religious creativity in America or warns of impending decline. American Judaism, as we shall see, suffers from many weaknesses but also displays much vitality. From a numerical standpoint, the religiously apathetic vastly outnumber the religiously engaged, but from a qualitative perspective, American Judaism continues to display innovativeness and dynamism. It would be foolhardy to write off American Judaism at a time when many synagogues, educational institutions, summer camps, and retreat programs that promote Judaism are thriving and when individual Jews in the large centers and in rural enclaves continue to pour their energies into the creative exploration of their religious traditions. A stark black or white assessment cannot do justice to the colorful kaleidoscope that is American Judaism in the late twentieth century. One hopes, however, that each reader may come away from this book with information to form a judgment about some of the most controversial questions of modern Jewish history: Can Judaism weather the corrosive effects of modern societies? How effectively can a diaspora Jewish community promote religious continuity? And how well is the largest diaspora Jewish community sustaining itself?[18]

Our inquiry spans the half century between World War II and the early 1990s. American religious life at midcentury serves as a benchmark for measuring change: it was a time when institutional growth was virtually limitless and religious communities basked in a comfortable optimism. In the 1960s, however, the placid mood gave way to turbulence and self-doubt. Radically new ideologies and perspectives challenged comfortable assumptions, including fundamental religious presuppositions. Traditional religions were assaulted by radically new conceptions of gender roles, sexual morality, and the nature of individual autonomy. Ascribed characteristics transmitted from one generation to the next further lost their allure: where modern society had earlier challenged the natural transmission of occupational and social roles from one generation to the next, it now attacked ascribed religious identities and gender roles. The initial result was much confusion and experimentation. In time, as these new perspectives were internalized, they profoundly altered the way that Jews and Christians assessed religious issues, and they eventually shaped highly individualized religious options, which in turn heightened religious fragmentation. To set into bolder relief the far-reaching shifts of the recent past, we begin with a brief consideration of Jewish religious life in the middle decades of the twentieth century, a time of seeming consensus when religious divisions were partially submerged beneath the surface.

PART I

Postwar Judaism:
An Era of Stability,
a Decade of Conflict

1

Expansion and Respectability at Midcentury

AN ERA OF INSTITUTIONAL GROWTH

The dominant characteristic of Jewish life between 1940 and 1965 was numerical growth and physical expansion. Jews participated with the American population at large in a postwar revival. As the Great Depression eased and veterans returned from World War II, Americans married in record numbers and began families. For Jews, this boom was propelled by the children and grandchildren of immigrants from Eastern Europe who had come to America in ever-swelling numbers between 1880 and the outbreak of World War I. Never before in the history of American Jewry had such a vast age cohort begun families within so short a time span. Simultaneously, large numbers of these young Jewish families joined the general American exodus to suburbia, an uncharted territory bereft of Jewish institutions.[1] Their relocation represented not only a move from city to suburb but also a departure from Jewish neighborhoods to settings populated mainly by Gentiles. Others moved to geographic regions of the United States that previously had only small Jewish communities, most notably Southern California and other more temperate zones. These twin developments—a burgeoning population and a major geographic shift—account for the growth of Jewish institutions needed to provide communal services and educational programs to a new generation residing in suburbia.[2]

But these factors alone do not explain the rapid numerical growth of synagogues. For the young families moving to suburbia in the 1940s and early 1950s often had had only scant exposure to synagogue life prior to their move. Overwhelmingly second- and third-generation descendants of East European Jews, they had grown up either in homes where Judaism was taken for granted and Americanization had been given highest priority or in socialist homes that rejected most religious practices. To be a Jew was primarily a matter of association with fellow Jews, not an act of affiliation with a synagogue, let alone a commitment to paying membership dues.[3] This changed in the 1940s, for several reasons. First, when Jewish veterans returned from the war, they were eager to participate in the same kind of Americanized religious services they had encountered in military chapels—services that were led by an American-trained rabbi who spoke their language and that were based on a liturgy that incorporated both traditional and English readings. Hence, returning Jewish veterans were receptive to the program of evolving suburban synagogues.[4] Second, after moving to suburbia, transplanted urbanites found themselves lonely for Jewish companionship. They discovered a need for a synagogue to anchor them on the suburban frontier and provide a network of Jewish friends and peers. Jewish suburbanites, observed one contemporary writer, embarked on "a new adventure in Jewishness, expressing itself in formal affiliation for the first time in their lives with a Jewish community institution."[5] In the city one did not have to work at finding a Jewish peer group; in suburbia the synagogue was a surrogate for the Jewish neighborhood. As one promotional leaflet stated: "The community needs a place for our children and we adults need some place to carry on our social lives. What better place can there be than our synagogues?"[6] Third, in the absence of a Jewish neighborhood where youngsters were socialized in Jewish customs and behaviors through an unconscious osmotic process, it became necessary for parents to affiliate with a synagogue that would serve as a surrogate agent for education.[7] Fourth, involvement in building a synagogue and sending children to a synagogue school were means for these Jews to participate in the larger revival of institutional religion that characterized midcentury America. Ironically, by participating in seemingly parochial activities within their synagogues, these Jews were playing the part of quintessential midcentury Americans.[8]

As a result, the quarter century from 1940 to 1965 was a boom period in the establishment and construction of new Jewish religious institutions. Suburbia proved especially conducive to the building of new synagogues: the United Synagogue of America, Conservative Judaism's organization of synagogues, increased its affiliates from approximately 350 at the conclusion of World War II to 800 by 1965, with as many as 131 new congregations joining in a two-year period of the mid-1950s.[9] Similarly, the Reform movement's Union of American Hebrew Congregations boasted three hundred more member congregations in 1966 than in 1948 (664 versus 334). In the mid-1950s, 50 new congregations joined the UAHC within a two-year period.[10] Orthodox synagogues, too, experienced a period of growth, as Young Israel and other modern Orthodox congregations sprang up in newly emerging urban and suburban settlements.[11]

Not only were hundreds of new congregations established, but existing ones experienced unparalleled growth. It now became common for synagogues to serve thousands of members. In 1937 the largest Reform temples numbered five to eight hundred families and only a half dozen had passed the thousand-family mark. By 1963, twenty such temples boasted over fourteen hundred families and a few exceeded twenty-five hundred families. As Jacob Shankman noted of Reform temples during the heyday of synagogue growth, "In May 1937, the suburban congregation of Glencoe [IL] had 327 families, that in New Rochelle [NY] 250 families, Great Neck [NY] 150 families, and White Plains [NY] 115 families; today each one of them has more than 1300 families and one of them is approaching the 2000 family size." Although Conservative and especially Orthodox synagogues rarely attracted such large membership bases, they too expanded dramatically.[12]

The explosive growth of synagogues was matched by an equally dramatic expansion of synagogue schools: in 1940 approximately 190,000 children attended Jewish schools; this figure rose to 231,028 in 1946 and then doubled to 488,432 by 1956; finally, by the early 1960s enrollments peaked at approximately 590,000. In short, the number of young Jews attending Jewish schools tripled between the early 1940s and early 1960s. The vast majority of these children attended synagogue-based schools (only 8 percent were enrolled in intercongregational or noncongregational schools by 1962).[13]

There were important variations in the type of schooling adopted by the major religious movements. The Reform movement continued its earlier policy of emphasizing Sunday school, that is, one-day-a-week education. In the peak years of the early 1960s, 60 percent of Sunday schools were under Reform auspices, 25 percent under Conservative auspices, and fewer than 10 percent under Orthodox auspices. By contrast, Conservative synagogues invested heavily in Hebrew school education, that is, schools that required attendance several times a week, usually on three separate days. In 1962 half of the Hebrew schools were in Conservative synagogues, almost a quarter in Orthodox ones, and 13 percent in Reform Temples. Within the Orthodox movement, the pattern was more complex. These figures illustrate that Orthodox synagogues continued to sponsor both Sunday schools and Hebrew schools; but in the postwar era, growing numbers of Orthodox Jews opted for education outside the synagogue, in intensive, all-day schools. The shift was especially dramatic outside of New York City: day schools there grew from barely a handful in 1940 to 107 in 1959. Significantly, 85 percent of all day schools in America were under Orthodox auspices by 1962, even though close to one-third of their pupils were drawn from non-Orthodox homes.[14]

There were several important consequences to this rapid growth of synagogue and educational establishments. First, there were insufficient numbers of personnel to staff them. It was estimated in 1962 that some three thousand additional rabbis and educators were needed to meet the growing institutional needs of American Jews.[15] One can only speculate as to the consequences of this shortage, but it is not difficult to imagine that the dearth of trained rabbis and educators limited the effectiveness of synagogue and educational programs at a time when Jews were joining institutions in record numbers. Second, the massive growth in the population of children shaped the priorities of synagogues: large percentages of synagogue budgets were devoted to schooling; in Conservative synagogues, for example, education absorbed over a quarter of synagogue budgets, an allocation second only to the cost of salaries.[16] This represented a dramatic change from earlier models of synagogue life, in which children played little role and where most activity was focused on the needs of adult men. Now the synagogue was viewed as the primary vehicle for the socialization and education of young people in the ways of Judaism. The rabbi and teachers—and by extension, the synagogue—were assigned a role in loco parentis, as substitute agents of Jewish socialization.[17] Third, synagogues used their schools as a means of increasing membership. Often, congregations did not even charge tuition but rather financed their schools through membership dues. In the short run, the strategy compelled parents to join congregations if they wished to educate their children and have them celebrate a Bar or Bat Mitzvah; but over time it also resulted in parents dropping their membership once their youngest child had completed his or her Jewish education.[18]

THE RELIGIOUS MOVEMENTS

Conservative Judaism

The expansive growth of religious institutions benefited all of the major Jewish religious movements, with the Conservative movement appearing as the greatest beneficiary. Not only did the number of Conservative congregations double in this period, but Conservatism was also the preferred religious self-identification of a plurality of American Jews.[19] This was not necessarily a matter of ideological commitment, as the most astute sociologist of the time noted already in the early 1950s; rather, it reflected a decision to opt for a compromise between the extremes of Orthodoxy and Reform.[20] Jewish men serving in the military during World War II had been exposed to an essentially Conservative worship service, even though most Jewish chaplains were not Conservative rabbis: such a service was deemed most appropriate to the spectrum of Jews in the military. When these veterans returned to found new synagogues in the suburbs, they generally opted for Conservative synagogues as a compromise solution.[21] As one synagogue organizer put it: "We figured that the Conservative [synagogue] was 'middle of the road,' and would not offend any group in the community. So we called it a Conservative congregation."[22]

While only a minority of synagogue members adhered to the religious commitments of the Conservative movement, significant numbers were attracted to specific Jewish programs offered by Conservative synagogues. These were, principally, the more intensive schooling offered by Hebrew schools as compared with Sunday schools; a worship service that combined a high degree of fidelity to the traditional liturgy with innovations deemed appropriate to midcentury America; and a lavish panoply of social and recreational programs that Conservative synagogues sponsored more readily than their Reform or Orthodox counterparts.[23]

The heady growth of the United Synagogue's congregational base spurred the Conservative movement to take a number of important institutional steps. To meet the needs of Conservative youth, the Jewish Theological Seminary, the educational center of Conservative Judaism, in conjunction with other arms of the movement, founded the Ramah summer camp program in 1948.[24] During the 1950s and 1960s the Conservative movement began to invest systematically in day-school education, creating a network of fifteen Solomon Schechter schools by 1965.[25] It was symptomatic of Conservative Judaism's self-confidence that it established an international arm (the World Council of Synagogues) in November 1957 and in the 1960s developed a rabbinical seminary (the Seminario Rabinico Latinoamericano) to serve Latin American Jewry.[26]

The movement also took steps to clarify its ideological posture. The Rabbinical Assembly, the organization of Conservative rabbis, endorsed a *Sabbath and Festival Prayer Book* for the first time, in 1946.[27] Two years later relations between the Rabbinical Assembly and the Jewish Theological Seminary of America were revamped in a manner that gave wider latitude to the Conservative rabbinate's Law Committee. Within a short period, the Law Committee began to issue rulings on halakhah (Jewish law) that departed significantly from Orthodox interpretations, such as a ruling in the early 1950s concerning the permissibility of driving to a synagogue on the Sabbath.[28] Conservative leaders issued a series of volumes designed to disseminate information about the movement, such as Mordechai Waxman's *Tradition and Change*, a compilation of ideological statements by prominent Conservative thinkers, Moshe Davis's history of the origin of Conservative Judaism, Evelyn Garfiel's guide to the prayer book, and various guides to the dietary laws and other observances written by Seymour Siegel and Samuel Dresner.[29] Gradually, the movement managed to achieve a significant measure of uniformity in the practices of its congregations. Guidelines issued by the United Synagogue for congregational programs and practices such as mixed pews, mixed choirs, and Bat Mitzvah ceremonies for girls gained wide, if not universal, currency.[30]

Hence, the middle decades of the twentieth century were a time of self-confidence for the Conservative movement. New synagogues mushroomed and membership grew dramatically. The movement pioneered new educational programs. Overall it seemed perfectly attuned to the prevalent mood of the postwar era: religious life gravitated to the center. As the historian Robert Wuthnow wrote of this period in American religious history: "Pressures from outside as well as conscious efforts to hew to the middle ground forged an unusually strong coalition that largely avoided the divisive tendencies of extreme liberal or extreme conservative orientations."[31] As the advocate of religious centrism, Conservative Judaism benefited most from the moderate tone of American religion at midcentury.

Reform Judaism

The same decades were a period of significant institutional growth for the Reform movement as well.[32] Throughout the postwar era the Union of American Hebrew Congregations (UAHC) reported annual gains in new affiliates. Some of this growth resulted from deliberate efforts taken by the Reform movement to expand its membership base. Thus, in the late 1940s it launched an intensive campaign to "win the unaffiliated," a shift away from the policy of social exclusiveness that had characterized recruitment policies earlier in the century.[33] The UAHC relocated from its former headquarters in Cincinnati to New York City, a move designed to place the organization within the heartland of the American Jewish population.[34] And the Hebrew Union College, the rabbinical seminary of Reform Judaism, expanded to reach new populations, merging with the Jewish Institute of Religion to create a New York school, establishing a Los Angeles branch in 1954, and opening a Jerusalem campus in 1963 both to train rabbinical students and to establish a base in Israel. Under the leadership of Rabbi Maurice Eisendrath from 1943 to 1973, the Union of American Hebrew Congregations invested heavily in programs to improve American society through social action. Eisendrath summed up his position in a 1959 interview given when he received an award as clergyman of the year. Social action, he declared, "that's religion. The heart of religion concerns itself with man's relation to man." The Reform movement gave tangible expression to this concern when in 1961 it established its Social Action Center, later renamed Religious Action Center, in Washington, D.C. In the practical sphere, Reform rabbis assumed a leadership role in the movement to desegregate the South.[35]

Simultaneously, the Reform movement underwent important shifts in its approach to Jewish rituals. A survey conducted by the UAHC in the late 1940s found that virtually all responding congregations claimed to have moved toward "increased ritualism."[36] In a reversal of long-standing policies, congregations gradually permitted men to wear a head covering if they so chose; and in a shift that had a broader impact, the Bar Mitzvah ceremony was reintroduced in virtually all temples. (It had earlier been rejected in favor of confirmation services for older adolescents.) Congregations that had ushered in the New Year with trumpet blasts reverted to the traditional *shofar* (ram's horn); and cantors were hired to replace or supplement non-Jewish choirs. Studies of home observance indicated as well that members of Reform temples were more receptive to rituals such as candle lighting on Friday evenings and Hanukkah and the celebration of the Passover seder.[37] Much of the impetus for such changes emanated from the ranks of the new Reform laity, which in the postwar era had been recruited from the children and grandchildren of more observant East European immigrants. As the historian Michael A. Meyer observed of this period, "Reform's link with traditional Judaism was once again biological, as it had always been at its points of origin and growth."[38] Joining the Reform camp, the descendants of East European immigrants carried with them an attachment to traditional ways and thereby tempered some of the radical innovations of American Reform Judaism.

This renewed interest in once-abandoned rituals engendered considerable soul-searching among the rabbinic elite of the Reform movement. In part, rabbis resented the pressure to reintroduce rituals that apparently appealed to folk sentiments, for example, the Bar Mitzvah ceremony—formerly rejected by Reform rabbis on grounds of principle—now dominated the Sabbath morning service. Equally important, the new turn to ritualism was regarded by many rabbis as a rejection of Classical Reform Judaism, which had attempted to purge Judaism of anachronistic ceremonies that contemporary Reform Jews felt could no longer "elevate and sanctify" their lives.[39] Some Reform rabbis voiced resentment over "the reintroduction of medieval nostrums into the synagogue."[40] Typical of this view were remarks by Professor Jacob R. Marcus of the Hebrew Union College in a speech delivered in 1959: "There are today too many Reform Jews who have ceased to be liberals. Their Reform, crystallized into a new Orthodoxy, is no longer dynamic. Shocked by the Hitlerian catastrophe, many have turned their backs on the future to seek comfort in the nostalgia of a romanticized Jewish past which never existed. We cannot lead our people forward by stumbling backward."[41] By the late 1950s there was a palpable sense of unease among many Reform leaders concerning the future direction of their movement.

Orthodox Judaism

The crucial factor shaping Orthodoxy at midcentury was an infusion of new energy and leadership brought about by the immigration of refugees from Nazi Europe. The newcomers arrived from diverse Jewish environments, ranging from the rationalist yeshiva world of Lithuania to the Levantine Jewish society of the Balkans, from the Westernized, acculturated Orthodox *Gemeinden* of Germany to the insulated, self-segregating communities of Hungary. For the first time in American Jewish history, a significant group of Jewish traditionalists immigrated. The group included rabbinic elites, as well as their followers: German separatist rabbis and their devoted flock; Lithuanian scholars and their students; Hasidic rebbes and their disciples. They came not out of a desire for self-advancement in the American *Goldene Medina* (Golden Land) but because their communities had been decimated by the Nazi death machine. They were filled with nostalgia for the rich Jewish lives they had known in the Old World, and they were intent on re-creating much of that life on American soil. Some built segregated enclaves in urban settings or rural environs, such as Boro Park and Williamsburg in Brooklyn and New Square in Rockland County, N.Y.; some insisted on wearing distinctive garb and communicating mainly in Yiddish; and most regarded American innovations in religious life with contempt. They saw themselves as the embodiment of the destroyed European Judaism, the only Judaism, they insisted, with a claim to authenticity.[42] Gradually, the new immigrants assumed important roles within all sectors of Orthodox society, serving as rabbinic authorities,[43] charismatic holy men, teachers, ritual functionaries, and organizers.

The arrival of a strong traditionalist element prompted a more combative and exclusive Orthodox posture in this period. The new assertiveness was signaled at a meeting of Orthodox rabbis in 1945 devoted to the banning and public burning of Rabbi Mordecai Kaplan's *Sabbath Prayer Book*, a Reconstructionist siddur.[44] By the mid-1950s the rabbis who had immigrated from Eastern Europe began to push for Orthodox self-segregation, much as it had existed in Europe. In a widely reported edict issued in 1956, eleven *roshei yeshiva*, heads of rabbinic academies of advanced study, joined by the leader of the Hasidic Lubavitch movement, issued a ban on Orthodox participation in rabbinic organizations that included non-Orthodox rabbis. This ban was designed to place pressure on American-trained rabbis, particularly alumni of Yeshiva University and the Hebrew Theological College, to withdraw from umbrella organizations such as the Synagogue Council of America and local boards of rabbis.[45] The Rabbinical Council of America, the organization of modern Orthodox rabbis, was thrown into turmoil by the decision: its president supported the ban, but the majority of the rank and file rejected it.[46] (They could do so because the revered leader of the modern Orthodox rabbinate, Rabbi Joseph B. Soloveitchik, refused to sign the ban.) The issuance of the ban was symptomatic of the intention of the traditionalist leadership to pursue a separatist policy vis-à-vis the non-Orthodox community, a policy pioneered by Orthodox Jews in Germany and Hungary in the 1860s and 1870s.[47]

The Modern Orthodox community also assumed a more combative posture in these years. Rabbis affiliated with the Rabbinical Council of America joined in a concerted effort to stem the massive tide of defection by Orthodox congregations into the Conservative camp. In legal challenges fought before state supreme courts, Orthodox leaders sought to prevent congregations that had previously relegated men and women to separate synagogue precincts from introducing mixed seating, a change that signified a congregation's defection from Orthodoxy to Conservatism. Yeshiva University also pressured its rabbinic graduates not to serve in congregations that permitted mixed seating or the use of microphones on the Sabbath.[48] In the late 1950s rabbis espousing the Modern Orthodox position established a new journal, *Tradition*, as a vehicle for conveying their own point of view as well as for combating their non-Orthodox rabbinic counterparts. Early issues of the journal were replete with hard-hitting critiques of Reconstructionist ideology, Conservative halakhic rulings on the *ketubah* (the marriage document) and mixed seating, and the Reform movement's liturgical innovations.[49]

Orthodox groups of all stripes invested heavily in this period in the establishment of day schools and yeshivas. In 1944 the Torah U'Mesorah movement was established to link all Orthodox day schools. It oversaw the growth of day schools from approximately thirty before World War II to over three hundred by the mid-1960s. Simultaneously, rabbinic figures who had recently arrived from Europe founded academies of higher study to support the continuing education of adult men—even after their ordination.[50] The latter institutions, *kollelim*, would produce the future leaders of right-wing Orthodoxy and provide teachers for the day schools.

Even with the emphasis on separate schooling, Orthodox Jews made important strides toward Americanization in these years. During the middle decades of the century, Orthodoxy ceased to be the province of relatively poor immigrant Jews, as its adherents participated in the upward mobility that brought affluence to large segments of American Jewry. Orthodox Jews now founded their own vacation resorts, as well as summer camps for their youth. Perhaps even more important, they capitalized on changes in the marketing of American foodstuffs to convince manufacturers that it paid to carry kosher certification: growing numbers of non-Jewish food manufacturers carried kosher labeling for the first time in a direct pitch to the market of observant Jews concerned with dietary laws. This development symbolized the growing financial clout of Orthodox Jews and also made it more attractive and manageable to adhere to Orthodoxy.[51]

Despite these strides, Orthodoxy appeared to be a marginal phenomenon in the middle decades of the century. Contemporary observers preoccupied with the widespread Jewish effort to integrate successfully into postwar America saw Orthodoxy as a relic of past Jewish separatism. There was, moreover, also objective evidence of Orthodox weakness, as hundreds of congregations that had been counted as Orthodox in the decades prior to World War II either folded or shifted their allegiance to Conservative Judaism. And many of those Jews who continued to identify as Orthodox were merely residual members of the movement: when they attended a synagogue, it had to be Orthodox; but they did not observe Jewish religious laws with any thoroughness.[52] Even parents who sent their children to the expanding network of day schools did not practice consistently or meticulously.[53] As for their role in Jewish communal life, Orthodox Jews did not have a great impact on policy or philanthropy. Writing at midcentury, Marshall Sklare contended that "Orthodox adherents have succeeded in achieving the goal of institutional perpetuation to only a limited extent; the history of their movement in this country can be written in terms of a case study of institutional decay."[54] Though this assessment proved incorrect in the long term, it accurately identified the more visible trend in Orthodox life at the time.

The mushrooming of synagogues across the American landscape, the rising demand for Jewish education, and other such symptoms of religious vitality were not viewed by all observers as signs of hope. Mordecai Kaplan, for example, expressed skepticism concerning the institutional and numerical growth of American Judaism. Addressing his colleagues in the Rabbinical Assembly in 1959, Kaplan described "Jewish spiritual life in America [as] only skin deep. Jewish life is social, rather than spiritual. . . . One half of Jewish identity is the product of Gentile exclusiveness and the other half is the product of Jewish association."[55] Will Herberg, perhaps the most famous critic of the American religious revival at midcentury, questioned the depth of religiosity of those who were so eager to affiliate with churches and synagogues, characterizing their involvement as "religiousness without religion, . . . a way of sociability or 'belonging' rather than a way of orienting life to God."[56]

The notable rise in synagogue affiliation among Jews was not matched by a rise in synagogue attendance, however. Survey research consistently found that Jews lagged far behind Catholics and Protestants in weekly attendance at a worship service.[57] Hence, although Jewish religious life at midcentury showed important *quantitative* gains for synagogues, Jewish schools, and each of the major Jewish denominations, observers concerned with the *quality* and depth of religious commitment, as measured by synagogue attendance and ritual observance,[58] had reason to be skeptical.[59]

JUDAISM ENTERS THE MAINSTREAM

Although the skeptics proved correct regarding the commitment of Jews to religious practices and beliefs, Judaism unquestionably assumed a new prominence in American public life during the 1940s and 1950s. A *Time* magazine cover story about Louis Finkelstein, chancellor of the Jewish Theological Seminary of America, symbolized the new respectability of Judaism in America. Appearing shortly after the High Holidays in 1951, the story emphasized Finkelstein's—and by extension American Jewry's—pivotal role in the emerging interfaith movement. The essay reported with approval Finkelstein's hope that "U.S. Jews will more and more observe the Law's injunction to make 'peace between man and his fellow': . . . When someone asks me why we Jews should bear the burden when other groups don't seem interested in doing anything, I consider it an impious question. Jews must see themselves as God intends them to be—His servants and the servants of mankind."[60] Finkelstein's visible presence on the cover of a major magazine with national circulation and deep roots in the American Protestant establishment was dramatic evidence that Judaism had arrived.

A few years later, Will Herberg's *Protestant, Catholic, Jew: A Study in American Religious Sociology* broadcast a vision of Judaism as a normalized religion on a par with the major Christian faiths.[61] Herberg perceived an America that homogenized its population into a "triple melting pot":

> However important the ethnic group may have been in the adjustment of the immigrant to American society, and however influential it still remains in many aspects of American life, the perpetuation of ethnic differences . . . is altogether out of line with the logic of American reality. The newcomer is expected to change many things about him as he becomes American—nationality, language, culture. One thing however he is *not* expected to change—and that is his religion. And so it is religion that . . . has become the differentiating element and the context of self-identification and social location.[62]

Remarkably, Judaism, whose adherents constituted no more than 3.5 percent of the American populace, had become integral to mainstream American religion. This new respectability may be attributed in part to public guilt about the Holocaust,* but it also reflects the significant strides taken by the Americanized children of East European Jewish immigrants. Certainly, the activism of individuals such as Louis Finkelstein and Maurice Eisendrath helped build bridges between Judaism and other religious communities. Most important, Judaism benefited as religion itself assumed a new significance in American public life.

Herberg's book documented the way in which religion bound Americans of diverse national backgrounds into a coherent whole. All religious communities in midcentury America shared common values and supported the prevailing American way, and American leaders acknowledged the unifying role of religion in a heterogeneous society. As Herberg put it: "Americans believe in religion. . . . The primary religious affirmation of the American people, in harmony with the American Way of Life, is that religion is a 'good thing' for the individual and the community."[63] Evoking the new "piety on the Potomac," President Dwight Eisenhower declared in 1954: "Our government makes no sense unless it is founded on a deeply felt religious faith— and I don't care what it is."[64] In conforming to the national mood at midcentury, American Judaism facilitated the acceptance of American Jews. Ironically, the more Jews contributed to the parochial activities of building synagogues and Jewish religious schools, the more they participated in a universal enterprise endorsed by the nation's leadership.

Jews in suburban America often built their new institutions in the same architectural style their Protestant and Catholic neighbors used for their churches. Jews paid lip service to the American credo—"the family that prays together stays together"—even though they attended services with far less regularity than Catholics and Protestants.[65] And

---

* It appears that such an outpouring of goodwill was the only visible consequence of the Holocaust in the fifteen years after the conclusion of World War II. Neither the Holocaust nor the creation of the State of Israel in 1948 had a direct and tangible impact on American Judaism until the 1960s. These gaps in consciousness seem incomprehensible in light of subsequent developments in American Jewish life, but they must be understood as a delayed response to cataclysmic events abroad by an American Jewry preoccupied with the need to redefine its place at home, within American society.

they substituted a child-centered religion for the adult-centered religion of the immigrant period.[66] By midcentury American Jews had surmounted the strains of immigrant adjustment, the trauma of discrimination and anti-Semitism at home and the Holocaust abroad, and divisive communal battles over Zionism. Like their Christian neighbors, they sought respite. As the historian Martin E. Marty has observed: "After the American religious depression of the 1930s and the preoccupation of World War II, it became clear that around 1950 many Americans were in a settling-down mood. They needed a means of justifying their complacencies, soothing their anxieties, pronouncing benedictions on their way of life, and organizing the reality around them. Millions turned to religion." In a highly public, though superficial display, American Jews also turned to their religion at midcentury.[67]

2

The Turbulent Sixties

The decade of "sober serenity," as one historian dubbed the 1950s,[1] gave way to the turbulent 1960s. And just as Jewish religious institutions enjoyed a boom period during the American religious expansion of the postwar era, they were buffeted by the upheaval that shook American society during the tumultuous 1960s. The historian Sidney Ahlstrom has described the latter decade as a time when "the foundations of national confidence , patriotic idealism, moral traditionalism, and even of historical Judeo-Christian theism, were awash. Presuppositions that had held firm for centuries—even millennia—were being widely questioned."[2] Despite the postwar expansion of religious institutions, Ahlstrom concluded, "Jews like other Americans, would discover that the religious revival had provided very feeble preparation for the social and spiritual tumult of the 1960s."[3] Arising from a range of circumstances both endemic to the Jewish condition and generic to the American and even international mood at the end of the twentieth century, new movements reshaped the agenda of religious institutions and individual Jews. The convulsions of the 1960s transformed the midcentury contours of Jewish religious life.

THE IMPACT OF PROTEST MOVEMENTS

The most visible symptoms of social dislocation in the 1960s were new movements of protest—the civil rights struggle, the antiwar move-

ment, the battle for women's equality, and the so-called counterculture.[4] Each profoundly challenged American society at large and religious institutions in particular. In criticizing the status quo in the name
of idealism and morality, these movements trod on turf properly considered the domain of religious communities. Churches and synagogues became staging grounds for pitched battles, as civil rights and
antiwar activists recruited supporters for their causes. From within
sanctuary pews, advocates of women's rights and countercultural values issued demands for reform. And religious leaders such as the Rev-
erend Martin Luther King, Jr., Father Daniel Berrigan, and Rabbi
Abraham Joshua Heschel led tens of thousands of marchers in protest
demonstrations, thereby thrusting religion into the maelstrom of the
American social upheaval.

The emerging prominence of religious institutions in the public
arena was first displayed in late November 1963, during the national
outpouring of grief for the fallen president, John F. Kennedy. Via the
relatively new medium of television, the entire nation attended a
Catholic funeral mass. For many Americans this was the first sustained
exposure to Catholic religious ritual. It served to educate them about
Catholicism and opened American society to greater tolerance of religious expression outside of mainline Protestantism—a process already
advanced by the election of the first Roman Catholic president. It also
made manifest the intertwined relationship of organized religion and
American politics.

With the assassination occurring on a Friday afternoon, stunned
Jews flooded into their synagogues in search of solace at Sabbath services. A contemporary observer estimated that more Jews attended
services that weekend than during the High Holidays a few weeks earlier. An estimated six thousand worshipers attended services at New
York City's Temple Emanu-El; and in White Plains, N.Y., the same
number of Jews attended synagogues, comprising half the Jewish community in that suburban city.[5] Those mournful days foreshadowed the
heightened involvement of synagogues and other religious institutions
in the social upheaval of the 1960s.

As the civil rights and antiwar movements spread, some Jewish
religious leaders jumped into the fray. At the forefront of Jewish
activists were the official leaders of the Reform movement, who
defined social justice as central to their agenda. Under Rabbi Maurice Eisendrath, the Religious Action Center and the Union of
American Hebrew Congregations moved far more boldly to the left

on social issues.[6] In southern cities individual Reform rabbis, such as Jacob Rothschild of Atlanta, threw their energies into the civil rights movement. And to the dismay of many Jews in the South, rabbis from the North proudly traveled South to march in civil rights demonstrations. It was, of course, the local Jews who paid the price for their virtuous coreligionists: southern synagogues were fire-bombed and Jews in the South were held accountable for the deeds of Jewish visitors from the North.[7]

Reform rabbis were also in the vanguard of Jewish antiwar activities. Addressing the General Assembly of the Union of American Hebrew Congregations in 1965, Eisendrath declared: "We transgress every tenet of our faith when we fight on another's soil, scorch the earth of another's beloved homeland, slay multitudes of innocent villagers." The assembly passed a resolution urging a cease-fire and negotiated peace in Vietnam, a position that in 1965 was not yet popular with either the American public or American Jewry. Even the Reform movement, however, was not spared the divisiveness that characterized American life during the Vietnam War. When Eisendrath published an open letter to President Lyndon B. Johnson in 1967 comparing the president to Antiochus Epiphanes, the tyrant of the Hanukkah account, twenty-five Reform congregations joined with New York's Temple Emanu-El to secede from the UAHC for more than a year in protest over Eisendrath's extreme position.[8]

The protest movements over civil rights and the war in Vietnam brought religious leaders unprecedented public exposure. For the first time since the establishment of the State of Israel, rabbis had fighting causes to galvanize the laity of the staid synagogue precincts. A Reform rabbi in Boston confessed that his congregants took him more seriously since his arrest in antiwar demonstrations: "My actions, more than all the sermons I had preached, got my point across."[9] Rabbis across the religious spectrum threw themselves into the new social activism. To cite two examples: the Massachusetts board of rabbis declared California grapes not kosher because they were picked by oppressed laborers. Their counterparts in Philadelphia voted to provide draft counseling in some of their synagogues.[10] Jewish religious leaders, along with their Christian counterparts, would eventually recognize, however, that social protest might energize the laity in the short term, but over time it would also blur the boundaries between society and congregation—to the detriment of the latter.

THE CHALLENGE OF FEMINISM AND
THE COUNTERCULTURE

Even as public attention was focused mainly on civil rights and antiwar activists, more subtle and profound challenges to religious institutions were mounted by other, newly emerging movements. By virtue of their unusually high levels of educational attainment, Jews were particularly receptive to the new movements promoted by feminists and the counterculture. To be sure, Jews initially drawn to these movements were generally indifferent to religious life and did not expect to introduce their revolutionary agendas into Judaism. But by the late 1960s, more committed Jews took the first steps toward bridging the worlds of Judaism and of feminism and the counterculture.

The so-called second wave of American feminism is generally traced to the publication in 1963 of *The Feminine Mystique* by Betty Friedan. Arguing that this mystique kept women trapped in a life of emptiness and frustration, tied to their suburban homes, and dependent upon men for financial support, Friedan also accused religious institutions of restricting women and imposing a male worldview upon women's religious expression. Friedan's book inspired American women to reconsider their lives and spawned a vast literature of feminist protest, much of it written by women of Jewish background.[11] With the incorporation of the National Organization for Women (NOW) in October 1966 and the emergence of a women's liberation movement out of the New Left in 1967, a new phase of American feminism had begun.[12]

Influenced by these new movements, Jewish women concerned about inequality in Jewish life began to organize and speak out. Initially, their goals were meliorative: they sought equal opportunities for women in the synagogue service and as religious leaders—as rabbis, cantors, educators, and synagogue board members; they fought stereotypes of women and girls in Jewish educational materials; and they demanded due recognition by the Jewish community for the critical role women played as volunteers who sustained synagogues and communal institutions. Gradually, in the early 1970s, some knowledgeable Jewish women also questioned whether women's sensibilities were given adequate attention and influence in the shaping of liturgy, rituals, and other forms of religious expression. Two particularly influential essays posed these challenges directly: Trude Weiss-Rosmarin's

"The Unfreedom of Jewish Women" denounced "the unfairness of Jewish marriage laws to divorced and abandoned women"; and Rachel Adler's "The Jew Who Wasn't There" "contrasted male and female models of traditional Jewish piety" and called for greater sensitivity to the religious experience of females.[13]

In September 1971 a group composed mainly of Conservative Jewish women in Manhattan founded Ezrat Nashim to discuss the status of women in Judaism.[14] The following March they held a "countersession" at the national convention of the Conservative rabbinate and issued a series of demands for the full acceptance of women as the religious equals of men.[15] One year later the first National Jewish Women's Conference drew an audience of five hundred.[16]

All the movements of American Judaism were challenged by the new Jewish women's movement, and all began to search for ways of bridging the gap between their conception of Judaism and the demands of Jewish women. It was symptomatic of the heightened awareness of women's protest that in 1969 Rabbi Aaron Soloveitchik addressed the Union of Orthodox Jewish Congregations on the "Attitude of Judaism toward the Woman." In early 1974 the Young Israel movement, another Orthodox synagogue body, held a conference to consider the status of Jewish women.[17] By 1972 the (Reform) Hebrew Union College ordained Sally Preisand as the first American woman rabbi. And the following year, the Conservative movement's Committee on Law and Standards issued a *takkanah* (legislative enactment) empowering each pulpit rabbi to decide whether women may be counted as part of a prayer quorum (minyan) of his synagogue.[18] Although most of the major strides of women in the religious sphere took place in the 1970s, profound changes in outlook were already occurring in the 1960s, during the early years of the feminist revolution.

Virtually simultaneously, a Jewish offshoot of the American counterculture emerged among college and graduate students.[19] As products of the "youth movement," the self-proclaimed "new Jews" espoused the political ideology of the time. They adopted the rhetoric of the New Left and supported the general critique of American society and especially of the Vietnam War.[20] But what distinguished this group from so many other young American Jews was their involvement with Jewish concerns. For even as they criticized established Jewish institutions, they were engaged in the process of remaking Jewish life, rather than rejecting it wholesale.[21] Alan L. Mintz, the first editor of *Response*, the most prominent journal of the Jewish counter-culture, wrote: "A most startling discovery has been made that Judaism does not have to be identical to the scheme of middle-class values. . . . A new consciousness of the past has brought us to believe that a more fundamental and nourishing Judaism existed, was discussed, and did not need a middle-class life style and its constellation of values."[22] Some set out to reform existing Jewish institutions, while others formed alternative Jewish communities.

Although a few prominent gurus were drawn from the older gener-ation, the Jewish counterculture was primarily created by and for Jew-ish baby boomers who came of age in the 1960s. Many were third-generation Americans whose parents had participated in the exodus to suburbia after World War II. Now they openly rebelled against their parents' style of living, the tedium and complacency of suburbia, and the desiccated Judaism practiced in suburban synagogues. As Hillel Levine, a prominent activist, wrote: "We woke up from the American dream and tried to discover who we really were. For many of us this now means turning our concerns inward into the Jewish community because we are disenchanted with the crass materialism of the larger society. Yet where can we find inspiration in the multimillion dollar Jewish presence of suburbia?"[23]

The Jewish counterculture scorned Jewish organizational life and criticized in particular the misguided priorities of the Jewish commu-nity. The youthful critics could find nothing worthwhile in suburban synagogues that touted the values of "success, wealth, and rote reli-gious performance" above all else. Suburban Judaism, wrote one activist, was "a spiritual Hiroshima which had been the setting for the transformation of the Hebrew spirit into an increasingly dispensable appendage of middle-class culture." Nor could the family offer Jewish meaning. The young activists bitterly denounced the Jewish family as yet another institution fostering Americanization and assimilation. In place of the middle-class family, they called for "real community" and "real intimacy."[24]

And so they appropriated the ancient rabbinic havurah (fellowship) for radically new ends. In the fall of 1968 Havurat Shalom, "the first countercultural Jewish community," was founded in Somerville, Mass-achusetts.[25] Begun as an alternative seminary, it was soon transformed into an experimental community that encouraged ritual innovation and sought to avoid having a single authority or rabbi. Within a short time the New York Havurah was formed, and not long afterward, young Jews formed the Farbrangen in Washington and a minyan in Germantown, Philadelphia.[26] By the early 1970s new groups proliferated at major universities. For the most part, these early havurot were closed to nonmembers. They were run democratically and generally included some program of communal study, as well as regular communal meals and occasional weekend retreats.[27]

The havurah was intended as an alternative to suburban Judaism. According to one of the founders, members "wanted to create a participant community rather than to be in a large impersonal institution in which culture or religion was dished out to us. We didn't want to be an audience, we wanted to be the *kahal* (community)." If the large suburban synagogue was a gargantuan, impersonal creation, the havurah would offer a "Judaism of scale," where Jews could pray and study in intimate fellowship.[28] The havurah model appealed because it offered its members the opportunity to form small intimate fellowships for study, prayer, and friendship that seemed impossible in the large, decorous, bureaucratized synagogues of their youth. It allowed individual participation and spontaneity, whereas established synagogues were dominated by professionals who "led" formal services. The founders of Havurah Judaism sought a religious community that would alter "the relationship between the individual and society, between making and consuming, between membership and community, and between instrumentality and authenticity."[29]

The goal, however, was not only to alter the setting of religious interaction but also to construct a different type of Judaism. Although they appropriated traditional forms and even fancied themselves neo-Hasidim, adherents of Havurah Judaism fundamentally rejected a normative approach to Judaism and sought instead to experiment and improvise. The anthropolgist Riv-Ellen Prell notes astutely: "The countercultural aesthetic that shaped the *havurah* depended on expressive individualism that featured the activism of all participants. Expressive individualism in turn was the product of the American culture that gave rise to American Judaism and promoted Jewish secularism."[30] Despite their superficial adherence to traditional forms of behavior, the early havurot created a framework that was not normative.

Although they felt alienated from the official Jewish community and regarded themselves as outsiders, the new havurot were nevertheless taken seriously by the Jewish religious establishment virtually from the start. True, some scorned the innovations of Havurah Judaism, but they never ignored the movement:[31] it was impossible to avoid the challenges posed by the havurot, particularly because members constituted the vanguard of committed Jewish youth. Writing in the house organ of the Conservative rabbinate, Stephen Lerner declared in early 1970, just a year and a half after the founding of Havurat Shalom:

> If the *havurah* does nothing else, it should remind Jewish leaders that . . . religious creativity, fervor, and a sense of community have not passed from this earth. . . . Rabbis will have to surmount their own inertia, the resistance of synagogue boards and ritual committees, and get youth involved in every aspect of synagogue life. They must make sure that services provide at least some modicum of informality, youthful participation and creative study.[32]

Within a decade some aspects of Havurah Judaism were adopted by many synagogues and in time havurah members assumed positions of influence in the Jewish community. But the outlook of Havurah Judaism was broadcast widely even earlier, with the appearance of the first *Jewish Catalogue* in 1973. The catalog and its successors became Jewish best-sellers,[33] further testament to the growing influence of this movement. Originating in the American counterculture of the 1960s, Havurah Judaism and its sometime ally, the Jewish feminist movement, challenged the established institutions and movements of American Judaism to rethink their priorities and reshape their religious programs in the concluding quarter of the twentieth century.

CHANGES IN AMERICAN RELIGIOUS LIFE

Judaism in America was also affected by the general turmoil in American religious life during the 1960s. Like their Christian counterparts, Jewish religious groups were both inspired and confused by the protest movements. The antiwar movement, for example, provoked mixed feelings, particularly after the Six-Day War of 1967, when concerns arose that a weakened military in America would be unable to provide the Israeli army with effective weaponry.[34] Whereas in the past religious institutions had routinely supported the troops and conferred their blessings on American policies, some religious groups now rethought their relationship to the American government and its policies—but not without much turmoil and soul-searching. Similarly, religious leaders were forced to respond to the growing influence of the provocative sexual and interpersonal mores promoted by the counterculture. Not only did religious institutions confront the programs of these movements, but they also had to assess the consequences of taking any position. How would support for the antiwar movement affect congregational or denominational unity? And how would taking any stance on public policy redefine the mission of a religious institution? The 1960s, in short, pushed religious leaders to rethink the role of religion in society.

This mood of self-doubt was stimulated as well by new patterns within American society that profoundly affected the fate of religious institutions more generally. Although the impact of these changes on Jewish religious life became clear only in the mid-1970s, the process of restructuring had already begun in the 1960s. We will briefly trace the broader patterns of change and then in later chapters analyze their impact on Jewish religious life.

Perhaps the most troubling new pattern was the declining involvement of young people, the baby boomers, in religious life. Beginning in the mid-1960s, liberal Protestant churches began to hemorrhage—with the oldest and hardiest Protestant denominations losing the most members: in the decade after 1965 Episcopalians, Methodists, Presbyterians, and other so-called mainline groups sustained a drop of over 10 percent in membership.[35] Among Catholics, there was a perceptible decline in mass attendance by the well-educated young.[36] And in the Jewish community similar declines were noted in synagogue membership. This was confirmed in a 1971 national survey, which indicated that less than half the Jewish population was affiliated with a synagogue.[37]

The crisis within Protestant mainline churches was sufficiently clear by the late 1960s to prompt the publication of a book by Dean M. Kelley, *Why Conservative Churches Are Growing*, the first in a series of studies examining the failure of liberal churches and the resurgence of conservative forms of religion. Kelley contended that religious groups most identified with mainstream American culture were declining, while those that challenged the prevailing American way were growing.[38] The historian Martin E. Marty explained this phenomenon by noting that established, mainline churches flourish when "the official culture is secure and expansive . . . [but suffer] in times of cultural crisis and disintegration, when they receive blame for what goes wrong in society. . . . So they looked as good in the 1950s as they looked bad by the 1970s."[39] Kelley went further, however, and traced the problem not to Zeitgeist but to ideology: the more a denomination blurred its boundaries with the surrounding society and the more it deferred to ecumenism and denied the particularity of its outlook, the greater the chances it would fail to retain members.[40] Although the circumstances would differ within American Judaism due to peculiarly Jewish concerns, liberal forms of Judaism suffered similar declines, while more traditional versions held their own.

The sociologist Robert Wuthnow has argued persuasively that rising levels of educational attainment were the critical factor in the declining rates of religious participation. An expanding proportion of young Americans attended college in the postwar era. In the decade of the 1960s, alone, the proportion of eligible young people who actually attended college rose from 22.3 percent to 35.2 percent. Survey research at the time indicated the profound impact of higher education upon the attitudes of young people regarding sexual mores, divorce, the status of women, and government support for social programs. Concomitantly, attendance at religious services declined among the better educated. According to Wuthnow, church attendance among the college educated fell by 6 percent between 1969 and 1970 alone, but levels remained constant among those without college education. When asked whether religion could answer all or most of society's problems, 26 percent fewer people who had some college education answered affirmatively in 1974 as compared with 1957.[41] Jews, a population with a disproportionately high level of educational attainment, followed these patterns as well, with consequences we shall yet examine.

The expansion of higher education was a central factor in the increasing levels of tolerance in American society that also marked the 1960s. The civil rights movement, the new ethnic consciousness that grew out of the black power movement, the election of a Catholic president, and the enormous respect and goodwill accorded to Pope John XXIII, as well as many other factors, opened American society to heterogeneity. Americans learned to tolerate diversity and the offbeat, such as new hair styles, innovative dress, experimental musical and artistic expression—and unconventional religious behavior. Eastern religions made inroads, as did religious cults and experimentation with forms of mysticism. Due to the activism of black religious leaders,

African-American churches and their distinctive religious services came to public attention. Similarly, Catholic liturgy and rituals became more accessible to the American public during the Kennedy presidency. Whereas the dominant liberal churches of Protestantism had once defined proper religious decorum and self-presentation, the decline of an official American religion and the loosening of cultural norms opened a vast new space for traditional religious groups. This opening of American society enabled more traditional versions of religion—including varieties of Jewish Orthodoxy—to flourish.[42] It was symptomatic that in this era, as never before, observant Jewish males were comfortable wearing a yarmulke in public rather than going bareheaded or wearing a hat.

Paradoxically, greater toleration for nonconventional groups also created new lines of religious division, for as traditional rivalries and animosities between Protestants and Catholics and between Christians and Jews gave way, new polarities formed. As one observer put it: "Increasingly, Fundamentalist, Evangelical, and Conservative Christians realized that the real enemy was not the Roman Catholic or Jew but the smiling, flexible, civil Protestant modernist who wrote them off as 'religious fanatics' unwilling to take the rough edges off their beliefs and practices and glide along smoothly with others in the prosperity of post-war America."[43] As new rivalries developed in the 1960s, the stage was set for heightened religious polarization within each religious tradition.

THE JEWISH PREOCCUPATION WITH SURVIVALISM

Although affected profoundly by broader trends in American society and religion, American Judaism reoriented itself in the 1960s for reasons internal to Jewish life as well. A palpable shift in the outlook of Jews affected communal priorities and morale. The social scientists Steven M. Cohen and Leonard J. Fein characterized the reorientation as a move from a preoccupation with accommodation to survivalism: "Jewish survival—that is, the survival of Jews as a distinct ethnic/religious group—has become a major priority of at least equal, and perhaps greater, concern to many Jews and, more particularly, to the agencies and institutions that determine the collective agenda of the Jewish community."[44]

The communal agenda shifted in the late 1960s from universalistic concerns to a preoccupation with Jewish particularism and threats to Jews, as fears for the physical safety of the Jewish people surfaced after lying dormant for almost a generation. The trauma of the Holocaust, buried in the American Jewish psyche since 1945, erupted into public consciousness. First came the rediscovery of the murdered six million with the Israeli abduction and trial of Adolf Eichmann. The capture of Eichmann had been intended to serve a pedagogic purpose: "We want the nations of the world to know," declared Israel's prime minister, David Ben-Gurion. Even he, however, could not have anticipated the educational impact of the trial on Jewish consciousness in Israel and throughout the world. In short order new books on the Holocaust appeared—Raul Hilberg's *The Destruction of the European Jews* in 1961, Hannah Arendt's provocative assessment of the Eichmann trial, *Eichmann in Jerusalem*, in 1963, and one year later Rolf Hochhuth's *The Deputy*, a scathing indictment of Pope Pious XII for his indifference and moral failure during the Holocaust. Then in 1967 Arthur Morse published *While Six Million Died*, a controversial work of journalism that brought the Holocaust home to the American Jewish community through its critical evaluation of Franklin Roosevelt, the hero of most American Jews.[45] Symptomatic of the new personalized involvement with the Holocaust was the self-critical question posed in a review of the Morse book: "The indifference and insensitivity of those non-Jews who stood by *While Six Million Died* doing nothing when 'They Could Have Been Saved' has been exposed and documented. But what did American Jews do in the years of the holocaust?"[46] That question haunted American Jews and inspired a new commitment to Jewish survival, succinctly expressed in the newly coined Jewish credo—"Never Again!"

In the spring of 1967 American Jewish fears were rekindled by Arab threats to the State of Israel. Describing those frightening days, Abraham Joshua Heschel linked the trauma of the recent past with fears for the future: "Terror and dread fell upon Jews everywhere. Will God permit our people to perish? Will there be another Auschwitz, another Dachau, another Treblinka? The darkness of Auschwitz is still upon us, its memory is a torment forever. In the midst of that thick darkness there is one gleam of light: the return of our people to Zion. Will He permit this gleam to be smothered?"[47] Despite their relative safety during the Holocaust years, American Jewry came to identify with the collective insecurity of Jewish victims. All over the country Jews turned to their synagogues in record numbers, with attendance on the Sabbaths before and after the Six-Day War approaching that on Yom Kippur. "Before the war, Jews went to pray for the survival of Israel, and afterwards, to give thanks."[48]

The war also converted American Jewry to Zionism. Whereas American Jews had demonstrated sympathy in the past, Israel now was incorporated into the very structure of American Jewish identity. As the fighting raged, surveys found that "ninety-nine out of every hundred Jews expressed their strong sympathy with Israel."[49] For many the new-found identification with Israel was a conversionary experience. As one Jewish woman wrote in the left-wing *Village Voice*: "Two weeks ago, Israel was they; now Israel is we. . . . I will not intellectualize it; I am Jewish; it is a Jewish we. Something happened. I will never again be able to talk about how Judaism is only a religion, and isn't it too bad that there has to be such a thing as a Jewish state. Roots count."[50]

The war transformed religious institutions as well. At the Jewish Theological Seminary of America, which in 1948 had banned the playing of "Hatikvah" (the Israeli national anthem) at its commencement, Professor Saul Lieberman, the rector and most influential faculty member, issued a statement on June 5, 1967, to

all Jews in the world and, in particular, the members of the Rabbinical Assembly and the congregations of the United Synagogue: the people of Israel have the privilege to give their lives to preserve the very exis-tence of the nation. The best we Jews in America can do is to support them with our money. This day is our great opportunity, one that may never repeat itself, to save *Klal Yisrael* [the Jewish people].[51]

The Six-Day War also signaled the virtual dismantling of the Reform offshoot, the American Council for Judaism, a Jewish anti-Zionist organization. Its leading spokesmen broke ranks and con-tributed to the Israel Emergency Fund, while other members resigned.[52]

The intense identification with Israel transformed Jewish religious education in America. Since 1967 it has become more common for Jewish adolescents to spend summers in Israel, sometimes at the expense of local federations of Jewish philanthropy. Israel figures prominently in the curriculum at Jewish schools. And it has now become almost universal at all but Orthodox synagogues and schools to use the Sephardic pronunciation of Hebrew, as is popular in Israel. To cite a minor but symptomatic change, the traditional Ashkenazic Sabbath greeting *gut shabbos* has given way to the Israeli *shabbat shalom*.

The war also inspired a greater political activism in behalf of Jewish causes. Most notably this translated into lobbying activity in support of Israel and the freeing of Soviet Jews. In addition, as we shall see, religious groups within American Judaism felt freer to lobby for their own agendas. The new activism energized congregations and other religious institutions,[53] but it also diverted attention from more narrowly religious concerns, such as ritual practice, prayer, and observance of the commandments, a development captured by the quip that American Jews were "reverse Marranos"—Jews in the streets but not in their homes.

The turn to more parochial Jewish interests was prompted not only by self-confidence engendered by the Israeli victory and a commitment to Jewish survival but also by alienation from former allies in the struggle for a better society. In the weeks prior to the Six-Day War, Jews who had nurtured interfaith ties were shocked at the indifference to Israel displayed by their partners in religious dialogue. For the most part, Christian clergy could not fathom the attachment Jews felt to Israel. Many Christian leaders remained neutral as Arab armies arrayed themselves against Israel. Even more disturbing, liberal clergy criticized Israel for its handling of the war. Perhaps the most savage attack came from the former president of the Union Theological Seminary, a leading seminary of liberal Protestantism. In a letter to the *New York Times*, Henry P. Van Dusen wrote:

> All persons who seek to view the Middle East problem with honesty and objectivity stand aghast at Israel's onslaught, the most violent, ruthless (and successful) aggression since Hitler's blitzkrieg across Western Europe in the summer of 1940, aiming not at victory but at annihilation—the very objective proclaimed by Nasser and his allies which had drawn support to Israel.[54]

Samuel Sandmel, a professor at the Hebrew Union College and frequent participant in interfaith dialogue, voiced the disappointment of Jews:

> We Jews and you Christians had co-operated on the national level in many enterprises, such as civil rights [and] many Jews assumed that the

same outpouring of sympathy for the beleaguered Jews that animated next-door Christian neighbors would be reflected in the organized Christian Bodies. . . . To the consternation of these Jews, such support was not forthcoming. . . . In the dismay at the Christian neutrality, some Jews felt completely abandoned by precisely those Christians with whom they had so much affirmative cooperation.[55]

Indeed, some Jewish leaders active in the ecumenical movement considered the dialogue silenced, if not dead. David Polish, a Reform rabbi, wrote in the *Christian Century* that in light of the Christian "moral failure, the much-touted Christian-Jewish dialogue is revealed as fragile and superficial."[56]

Jews also felt rebuffed by the separatist and anti-Israel positions adopted by the black power movement. Jewish religious groups that had been active in the civil rights movement noticed a dampening of interest among their members, a state of affairs lamented by Maurice Eisendrath in the early 1970s: "Wounded by anti-Semitic public statements of some lunatic-fringe blacks; bruised by the apparent indifference of non-Jews to the 1967 war in Israel; hurt by those blacks who . . . turned sour on interracial amity and cooperation, a considerable number of Jews have withdrawn from all such outstretch of hand and heart."[57] Eisendrath tried to convince his group to continue programs of social action that had worked earlier in the decade; he even called for a major campaign similar to the United Jewish Appeal in order for the Jewish community to pay its share of reparations to American blacks. But the UAHC refused to support him.[58]

As they recoiled from the hostility or indifference of former allies, American Jewish groups also confronted an emerging threat to Jewish survival from within—the rising rate of intermarriage. The mid-1960s brought unmistakable evidence of a significant increase in the number of Jews taking non-Jewish spouses.

Item: As early as 1960 a leading sociologist engaged in research on intermarriage cited findings of the U.S. Bureau of the Census indicating a national intermarriage rate for Jews of 7.2 percent in 1957 and compared it with surveys in Iowa and the San Francisco area, which indicated rates ranging from 17–32 percent. Erich Rosenthal warned:

If we accept the findings of the [Federal census] and if, at the same time, we assume that the statistics for Iowa and San Francisco are merely regional variations of the overall rate, we can probably be justified in defending the current survival formula as adequate for the preservation of the Jewish group. If we assume, however, that the findings for Iowa and San Francisco are the first indications of the future over-all rate of intermarriage, then the efficacy of the survival formula must be seriously doubted.[59]

Item: A survey published in the *National Review* found that perhaps as many as one-third of Jewish collegians declared themselves as not opposed to intermarriage.[60]

Item: By 1970 Marshall Sklare, the dean of American Jewish sociologists, sounded the tocsin: "If by 1965 one in five young Jewish couples in Boston constituted a case of intermarriage, we can safely assume that the figure is now approaching one in four. And if that is true in so conservative a city as Boston, it must mean that intermarriage has reached large-scale proportions throughout the country as a whole."[61] Based on admittedly sketchy evidence, Arthur Hertzberg placed the intermarriage rate in the mid-1960s at 15 percent, a figure borne out by the National Jewish Population Study of 1971.[62]

Fears of increased intermarriage were further fueled by new evidence that the American Jewish population was no longer growing. Survey research conducted in the early 1970s confirmed what Jewish institutions—especially synagogues and religious schools—had encountered already in the mid-1960s: the end of the baby boom. A survey conducted under the auspices of the Council of Jewish Federations in the early 1970s indicated that American Jewry had entered an era of demographic stagnation: Jews were having fewer children relative to the American population; immigration had virtually ceased; and rates of intermarriage had been spiraling since the mid-1960s.[63] Demographers of American Jewry vied with one another to issue gloomy prognostications, with one author contending that by the year 2076, American Jewry could shrink to one-fifth its size or even less if current rates continued.[64] Demographic stagnation coupled with rising levels of intermarriage demoralized community leaders and affected the tone of Jewish public discourse about the future of American Judaism. The new pessimism was captured in a feature essay published by *Look* magazine entitled "The Vanishing American Jew."[65] Little wonder, then, that Jewish survival at home and abroad became the new preoccupation, as self-absorption and doubt replaced the buoyant mood of the 1950s.

THE MALAISE IN ORGANIZED JEWISH RELIGIOUS LIFE

The organized movements of American Judaism were particularly hard hit. Whereas Jewish philanthropic federations experienced a resurgence because of their close involvement with fund-raising for Israel, and Jewish communal agencies threw their energies into lobbying in behalf of beleaguered Jews at home and abroad, synagogues lost their luster. Oriented toward programming for youth, they suffered as the numbers of young Jews dwindled. But the malaise in organized Judaism also reflected a loss of bearing about the proper role of synagogues in Jewish life and a loss of faith in the ability of organized Judaism to respond to the new world created by the 1960s.

Much as in the Christian world, liberal religious movements suffered the most. As the standard-bearer of American Judaism at mid-century, Conservative Judaism was especially hard hit by the upheaval of the 1960s. In contrast to the earlier, frenetic pace of synagogue growth, not one new Conservative synagogue was founded between 1965 and 1971.[66] Congregational membership began to decline as many Conservative families left their synagogue once the youngest child had celebrated a Bar or Bat Mitzvah. A 1965 survey by the United Synagogue found that during the previous three years the primary reason members left a congregation other than death or geographic relocation was that a "son had completed Bar Mitzvah or Hebrew School."[67] Now that their children had completed their studies, some parents no longer felt any need to retain their membership. Congregational schools suffered a consequent decline in enrollments and were forced to cut back or eliminate their programs. By the 1970s, numerous Conservative congregations were forced to merge their schools and even synagogues because their membership bases could no longer sustain programs.[68]

The Conservative movement also suffered the loss of its left wing in the 1960s, when the Reconstructionists broke away to form their own movement. Since the 1920s Rabbi Mordecai M. Kaplan had led proponents of change within the movement by preaching the need for a new "Copernican revolution" that would substitute the Jewish people for God as the center of the Jewish universe. "Torah," wrote Kaplan, "exists for the sake of the Jewish people." Kaplan understood Judaism as a "religious civilization" encompassing "language, folkways, patterns of social organization, social habits and standards, spiritual ideals, which give individuality to a people and distinguish it from other peoples." The radical import of Kaplan's revolution was to dethrone God as a being above nature and deprive the Jewish people of its "chosenness," for Kaplan believed that all people regard themselves as chosen. Kaplan was a radical within Conservative Judaism, because he viewed Jewish laws as folkways that could be altered by the will of the people, just as they had been created by the will of the people.[69]

Kaplan and his disciples had preached the ideology of Reconstructionism since the appearance of his most important work, *Judaism as a Civilization*, in 1934, but they had taken few steps to create a fourth religious movement. On the contrary, Kaplan believed that Reconstructionism would eventually become the dominant religious movement of American Jews. He steadfastly refused the entreaties of his followers to institutionalize his movement and focused instead on disseminating his views through a journal of opinion, *The Reconstructionist*, and a synagogue in New York, the Society for the Advancement of Judaism. Kaplan remained firmly within the Conservative camp, presenting his viewpoint to generations of rabbinical students at the Jewish Theological Seminary and arguing for change before his colleagues in the Rabbinical Assembly.[70]

In 1963, at the age of eighty-two, Kaplan retired from the Jewish Theological Seminary. This freed him to support his followers' desire to expand Reconstructionism from an ideological movement to a distinct denomination within Judaism. Plans were made to establish the Reconstructionist Rabbinical College, which opened in 1968.[71] And even before that, a federation of Reconstructionist congregations was founded to unify like-minded synagogues, as well as to bring more groups into the fold.[72] Although the movement was poised for growth by the late 1960s, it was still only a fringe phenomenon of a few thousand adherents, overshadowed by Reform, Conservative, and Orthodox Judaism.[73] The secession of Reconstructionists, however, created the need for an internal realignment within the Conservative movement, a restructuring that threw the movement into turmoil for more than fifteen years.

All the uncertainty and self-doubt in the Conservative movement surfaced in the early 1970s, with the publication of a critical article by Marshall Sklare. Updating his classic study of the Conservative movement, Sklare "offered a thesis that the Conservative movement at the zenith of its influence, has sustained a loss of morale," attributable to "the emergence of Orthodoxy, the problem of Conservative observance, and the widespread alienation among Conservative young people."[74] According to Sklare, the festering crisis of morale in the movement had been brought on by the defection of young people who left the movement in order to join the nascent havurot, coupled with the perception of rabbis that they had failed to persuade the laity to live as observant Jews. In the journals of the Conservative movement and at national gatherings of its leaders, rabbis vented their frustration: "We are touching only the periphery of Jewish life. We are failing in those areas that concern us most," lamented Rabbi William Lebeau.[75] Others voiced their concern that the movement "had become less identifiable" and was in danger of "los[ing] its force and becom[ing] of less and less consequence on the American Jewish scene."[76] The Conservative mood was aptly captured by one rabbi who remarked to his colleagues that "self-flagellation appears to be the order of the day for the leadership of Conservative Jewry."[77]

Reform Judaism fared no better. Summing up the shocks of the 1960s, the increasingly influential Reform theologian Eugene Borowitz wrote: "The crisis in American society, the peril to the state of Israel, the new appreciation of ethnicity all seemed to call for a reexamination of Reform Jewish principles. . . . The style of synagogue life which seemed so fresh a few years previous, seemed somewhat stale and in need of invigoration."[78] Unlike the other movements of Judaism, Reform undertook two major surveys in this period to take the pulse of rabbis and lay people. The findings were hardly encouraging.

Based on research conducted at a dozen representative congregations, the authors of *Reform Is a Verb* found that members of Reform temples were thoroughly alienated from temple life: the majority of respondents, both young and old, saw the temple as peripheral to their concerns. Youth were even more indifferent to their Judaism than their elders and found nothing wrong with intermarrying.[79] A second study conducted by Theodore Lenn confirmed these bleak findings. According to Lenn, "The vast majority of Reform congregants *do not consider themselves religious.*"[80] Moreover, "on every issue of Jewish identity on which they were queried, Reform youth seem to be more detached from Judaism and Jewishness than their parents." Rabbis in particular expressed their concern: over 50 percent of rabbis and congregants surveyed felt that "Reform Judaism was in the midst of a crisis—a situation that will become worse, many felt, before it becomes better."[81]

The Lenn study highlighted the confusion of Reform rabbis: they believed they had lost their aura of authority and felt unappreciated as orators. Moreover, Reform rabbis were under intense pressure to officiate at mixed marriages. The Lenn study found that more than one in three congregants aged twenty to twenty-four was married to a spouse who was born non-Jewish. One in four of this age group was married to a spouse who had not converted. By the early 1970s, 41 percent of rabbis in the sample officiated at mixed marriages with no prior conversion; and of those who did not, half referred couples to such rabbis.[82] Indeed, by 1969 a list of colleagues who officiated at mixed marriages was circulated to all members of the CCAR.[83] Simultaneously, and in a seemingly contradictory fashion, 43 percent of the same rabbis wished to incorporate more traditional beliefs and practices into Reform Judaism.[84] Reform was in serious need of reorientation after the crises of the 1960s, as articulated by Rabbi Richard N. Levy:

> The American Reform synagogue is in trouble. It has generally defaulted on all three of its traditional functions. . . . There are few Reform synagogues where prayer is a regular and significant event for the majority of members; even fewer where there is a serious study of Jewish literature and ideas . . . ; and as Reform congregations grow in size, meetings in any sense beyond occasional social affairs where few members know each other, have become equally rare."[85]

As by far the smallest of the wings of Judaism in the postwar era, Orthodoxy had been written off as a vestige of the immigrant past. With no more than 11 percent of American Jews identifying themselves as Orthodox as compared with 33 percent for Reform and 42 percent for Conservative Judaism, Orthodoxy seemed peripheral.[86] Moreover, there was little reason to anticipate anything other than further decline in their numbers, since studies of local communities found Orthodox Jews to be the oldest segment of the Jewish population with the highest percentage of foreign born.[87] Remarkably, however, in the 1960s Orthodoxy showed itself to have unanticipated staying power. Writing in 1965, Charles Liebman argued the need for a second look:

"The only remaining vestige of Jewish passion in America resides in the Orthodox community," he declared. "There is a recognition and admiration for Orthodoxy as the only group which today contains within it a strength and will to live that may yet nourish all the Jewish world." Liebman also noted the growing isolation of Orthodox Jews from the rest of the community and the rising power of sectarian Orthodoxy over modern elements, patterns that would accelerate in the coming decades.[88] Thus, despite their continuing numerical decline, Orthodox Jews did not experience the same malaise as did other movements in American Judaism during the 1960s.

The growing importance of Israel in American Jewish consciousness by late in the decade increased the self-confidence of Orthodoxy. In Israel, after all, Orthodox leaders helped govern the country and monopolized Jewish religious expression. As ties between American and Israeli Jews strengthened, Orthodoxy acquired a new legitimacy in the American Jewish community, as well. By contrast, as non-Orthodox groups increased their involvement with Israel, they encountered a religious establishment intolerant of all except Orthodox versions of Judaism. An incident in 1968 was symptomatic of the problem. The World Union of Progressive Judaism (Reform) held its international convention in Jerusalem to express its solidarity with the people of Israel and announced plans to conduct a prayer service at the Western Wall with men and women seated together. The announcement set off a vitriolic debate on the floor of the Knesset, Israel's parliament. Describing Reform Jews as "traitors to their people, their land, and their God," the newspaper of one religious party, Agudat Yisrael, suggested they "build a wall near one of their temples and go pray there with their wives and mistresses."[89] By virtue of their monopoly on Jewish religious expression, Orthodox groups in Israel felt no compunctions about giving full vent to their animosity toward non-Orthodox forms of Judaism.

This kind of rhetoric spilled over into the American Jewish community, where tensions had anyway been building for a while over a range of issues. At a private meeting designed to thrash out differences, rabbis from the three major movements could not reach a consensus. They could agree only on support for the civil rights movement and the war on poverty; they were deeply divided over internal Jewish matters, especially the issue of Jewish-Christian dialogue.[90] With Israel now assuming a central role in American Jewish consciousness, with growing concerns over intermarriage, and with new pressures on all of the movements to respond to new social and religious developments, American Judaism was poised for changes that would intensify religious polarization.

In this regard as well, developments within Judaism paralleled those in the Christian world. A contemporaneous study of American religion noted the growing rift in Protestantism:

> It has become fashionable to speak of the "common religion" of Americans and to believe that denominationalism is now based upon organization rather than theological considerations. . . . While the old differences may have passed away . . . new ones have appeared virtually unnoticed. . . . Perhaps at no prior historical moment have the Christian denominations been so divided over basic tenets."[91]

The organized movements of American Judaism were about to discover that they too were on a collision course as they responded to dramatically new trends in Jewish popular religion.

PART II

Popular Religion: Apathy *and* Renewal

3

The Drift toward Religious Minimalism

Since the 1960s the landscape of American religious life has been altered in significant ways. Robert Wuthnow, writing about the condition of American religion in the late 1980s, comments to this effect: "The mosiac of denominational pluralism that analysts described a generation ago no longer provides a useful image of the main contours of our faith. The tiles that made up the mosaic have been torn from the foundations. Some have been broken, and others have been scattered to form new patterns."[1]

Most striking is the reemergence of religion as a powerful force after the onslaughts of the 1960s. Survey research conducted during that turbulent decade had found Americans assigning decreasing importance to the role of religion in their lives and a concomitant exodus from organized religious life. By the 1980s many who had abandoned churches had returned, and religion was assuming a central role in public discourse. A fundamental transposition in outlook had occurred, noted the historian Martin E. Marty: "Secularists are in disarray, while religionists have regrouped."[2] Whereas for much of the modern era, religion was on the defensive and secularism triumphant, by the waning decades of the twentieth century, the certitudes of secularists had given way and religion received a more respectful hearing.

The resurgence of religion has occurred in a highly complex and contradictory fashion. On the one hand, large majorities of Americans aver a belief in God and claim to attend religious services regularly; on the other hand, some important segments of the population, such as baby boomers, have kept their distance from congregational life. On the one hand, high percentages of Americans claim that religion plays a major role in their lives; on the other hand, many identify with a highly private form of religion and eschew formal affiliation—they are religious without a community. Even as large majorities of Americans agree on the rising significance of religion in their own lives and the life of the nation, religious questions polarize and divide adherents of every denomination.

Organized religion in America is buffeted by these contradictory trends. Some denominations are thriving; others are in decline. Yet even among the Christian and Jewish denominations that are losing support and power, many of the affiliated local congregations are robust. "The congregation," writes the sociologist Stephen Warner, "is not the denomination writ small."[3] "What counts," according to one report, "if a church or synagogue is to attract its share of the baby-boom market, is not the name on the door, but the program inside."[4] Religion in America, in short, has many consumers—perhaps more than ever before; but they shop with care to meet highly individualized needs.

Underlying these contradictory trends is a fundamental shift in perspective that occurred in the 1960s: the application of American individualism to the religious sphere. In their probing examination of contemporary American religion, the sociologists Wade Clark Roof and William McKinney highlight the importance of this new perspective:

> Of all the recent religious changes in America, few are more significant, or more subtle, than the enhanced religious individualism of our time. Americans generally hold a respectful attitude toward religion, but also they increasingly regard it as a matter of personal choice or preference. Today choice means more than simply having an option among religious alternatives; it involves religion as an option itself and opportunity to draw selectively off a variety of traditions in the pursuit of the self. . . . Foremost is the individual's choice of whether to pursue a "religious matter"; then come whatever commitments of a personal or communal sort, if any, a person may choose to make."[5]

The deeply entrenched American values of individualism and voluntarism have been transferred to the religious sphere, leaving each individual free to pick and choose as he or she sees fit.

Such selectivity produces diversified religious options. For some, it has led to a rejection of formal religion in favor of a more privatized spirituality. In their meditation on what they regard as the "cancerous" growth of individualism in America, the multiple authors of the widely remarked study entitled *Habits of the Heart* paint a portrait of such a perspective. An interviewee named Sheila Larson described her faith as "Sheilaism": "I believe in God. I'm not a religious fanatic. I can't remember the last time I went to church. My faith has carried me a long way. It's Sheilaism. Just my own little voice."[6] Research on the baby-boom generation has led some sociologists to conclude that such religious privatism is widespread, particularly among Jews.[7]

Religious individualism may also lead to a rejection of ascriptive loyalties and externally imposed norms, two essential building blocks of traditional Western religions—especially Judaism. Americans value the right to choose their own religious preference, rather than having to rely on its automatic transmission from one generation to the next. Indeed, they regard with disdain the unthinking assumption of an ascribed religious identity.[8] Moreover, they have come to question the right of outside institutions to define norms of behavior. These assumptions about the virtues of expressive individualism are promoted by a variety of cultural outlooks that go under labels such as "the therapeutic sensibility, the culture of narcissism, the pursuit of self-fulfillment, and civic privatism."[9]

Although expressive individualism may lead to a rejection of religion, it can also lead to an affirmation of religious identity, albeit a self-chosen one. Large percentages of Americans now "switch" their religious allegiances from the denomination of their birth to another affiliation, a state of affairs that fosters competition among congregations and denominations. The new voluntarism in religious life also leads some Americans to opt for highly traditional forms of religion. The rejection of ascription encourages some to choose conservative religion, which provides certainties in the unstable climate of contemporary religious life. Indeed, the more conservative forms of religious expression have been some of the biggest winners in numerical terms. Paradoxically, the new individualism also sanctions the creation of tightly knit religious communities designed to meet the personal needs of their members.

All of these approaches to religion in America have profoundly transformed Jewish religious life. Since midcentury Jewish patterns of affiliation and religious participation have shifted; new expressions of popular religion have emerged; and the fortunes of formal institutions of American Judaism have seen dramatic changes. The contradictory patterns in American religious life in general have their counterparts in American Judaism: there are Jewish variations of "Sheilaism," rampant Jewish religious switching, movements of return to tradition, and much experimentation with the selective reappropriation of religious traditions to meet individualized needs. Nevertheless, American Judaism since the 1960s is its own distinctive mosaic, one that differs from its midcentury pattern and that assumes contours different from those of American Christianity.

MEASURING JEWISH RELIGIOUS BEHAVIOR

Population studies and surveys are the main sources of quantitative data on the religious behavior of American Jews. Between 1977 and 1987, more than fifty local federations of Jewish philanthropies sponsored demographic surveys for the purpose of compiling profiles of the populations they served. Virtually every large Jewish community has been surveyed, as have numerous midsize and small communities.[10] In addition, the Council of Jewish Federations, the national umbrella organization for local federations, commissioned two national surveys of American Jewry, one in 1971 and the other in 1990.[11] All of these surveys include a series of questions pertaining to religious life: synagogue membership and attendance, selected measures of ritual observance, denominational affiliation, and patterns of intermarriage. Taken together, the national and the local surveys complement one another to suggest broader trends and variations from one locality to the next. Unfortunately, only a few comparable studies were undertaken at midcentury, which limits our ability to trace change over time.

Our analysis is hampered as well by the shallow quality of survey research. For the most part, studies measure observances and preferences in a few areas of religious life that, in the view of sociologists, stand for larger patterns, but they offer little information on either

the context or content of religious behavior. Accordingly, we know
about frequency of synagogue attendance but have no information
about private prayer or attendance to say Kaddish (the mourner's
prayer) for the dead. We have data on the percentages of Jews who
fast on Yom Kippur but know virtually nothing about why they deem
it important to do so. Most glaring is the almost total absence of
research on the quality of religious behavior. Even when we can measure the incidence of participation in a ritual, we do not know how
the ritual is performed, let alone what it signifies to the participant.
Hence, when we learn that high percentages of Jews attended a
Passover seder, we are unable to judge whether such an activity
served a religious purpose, whether it included any reflection on the
bondage of the ancient Israelites in Egypt, and whether participants
read from the religious text of the Passover Haggadah, let alone
whether they observed the special dietary restrictions for the holiday.
Bearing in mind these limitations, we begin our examination of
American Jewish popular religion with existing quantitative measures
of religious behavior.

SYNAGOGUE MEMBERSHIP AND ATTENDANCE

Synagogue membership serves as a tangible, although relatively pas-
sive, measure of religious participation. Membership rates around the
country show considerable variation. In communities as diverse as the
Twin Cities, Seattle, and Nashville, close to 80 percent of Jews claim
current synagogue membership; by contrast, in Los Angeles and
Phoenix, synagogue membership is confined to a quarter and a third of
the Jewish populations, respectively; and in cities as diverse as Washington, D.C., Philadelphia, New York, Denver, and Boston, synagogue
membership hovered at about 40 percent in the mid-1980s.

A recent study identified four variables that help determine rates of
synagogue membership within communities.[12]

1. Marriage rates: communities with a high proportion of married
heads of household have a higher rate of synagogue membership; conversely, the larger the population of divorced or single adults, the
lower the rate of affiliation. This conforms with a widely reported
finding that American Jews generally join synagogues when they

become parents and that divorce often leads to a lapse of synagogue membership.[13]

2. Age structure: the higher the percentage of Jews in their twenties and thirties, the lower the rate of affiliation; since younger Jews are less likely to have children, they do not join synagogues in appreciable numbers.

3. Place of birth: transients are less likely than Jews rooted in a community to invest in synagogue membership; where most Jews in a community are born locally, rates of synagogue membership are high. Thus, it is not an accident that in cities in the North synagogue membership is common, whereas in places like Phoenix it is relatively low.

4. Denominational identification: in communities where one of the religious movements is dominant, it becomes socially important to join a synagogue. In Minneapolis-St. Paul, for example, the high rate of affiliation is related to the great strength of local Conservative synagogues.

The most recent surveys suggest that synagogue affiliation is declining nationwide. Compared with the 48 percent of American Jews found to have been synagogue members in the 1971 national survey, a Gallup poll conducted in 1987 found that only 44 percent of Jews surveyed claimed synagogue affiliation.[14] Low membership rates reported in the largest Jewish population centers also suggest a decline in rates of synagogue affiliation during the 1980s. Indeed, the 1990 national survey found that only 41 percent of entirely Jewish households were currently members of synagogues and that other types of Jewish families had even lower rates of affiliation.[15]

How does synagogue membership translate into actual attendance at religious services? According to national surveys of American religious behavior, 24 percent of American Jews said they had attended synagogue during the previous month (a figure well below the rate of church attendance for the Christian population, as we shall see).[16] By contrast, surveys conducted under Jewish auspices in the 1980s found that in hardly any of the communities for which data are available do anywhere near this percentage of Jews claim to attend synagogue "frequently"—a response sometimes interpreted to mean weekly attendance and sometimes attendance at least once a month. Furthermore, in most communities, between one-third and one-half of all Jews attend religious services either never or only on the High Holy Days.

While there is ample evidence that synagogue attendance earlier in the century was quite low, it appears that in recent decades attendance at synagogue services is even lower. In Rochester, for example, 14 percent claimed to have attended services weekly in 1961, compared with 2 percent in 1980; attendance only on the High Holy Days rose from 19 percent to 45 percent. In Baltimore the proportion who attended synagogue only "a few times a year" rose from 37 percent to 52 percent between 1968 and 1985 (although levels for more frequent attendance also rose modestly in that period). In short, American Jews, never ardent synagogue goers, appear to be attending religious services less than ever.

RELIGIOUS OBSERVANCE

Since Judaism is so highly oriented to ritual performance, survey research has attempted to measure patterns of observance. Rather than ask about each of the myriad of rituals, social scientists have limited their inquiries to a select number of observances that they see as representative of broader patterns of behavior. Their task has been complicated by the range of attitudes within the denominations about which specific observances are still binding. Thus, the observance of the dietary laws is optional in the Reform movement but mandatory in Orthodox and Conservative Judaism; refraining from using transportation on the Sabbath is viewed as mandatory by Orthodox rabbis, whereas Conservative rabbis have sanctioned such travel if it is necessary to attend synagogue services. Moreover, as we have noted, quantitative data shed little light on the quality and meaning of religious experience. Still, for all their shortcomings, surveys of religious behavior provide important insights into religious life.

The national survey of American Jews conducted in 1990, as well as surveys of local communities that vary widely in size, geographic location, and social composition, consistently demonstrate the same patterns of religious observance. In every community, the most widely performed ritual is attendance at a Passover seder, followed by the lighting of Hanukkah candles, the presence of a mezuzah on the front doorpost, and fasting on Yom Kippur. It is indeed noteworthy that over two-thirds of all Jews in community surveys claim to observe these rituals. Moreover, it appears that in recent decades the observance of these four rituals has become more widespread than it was at midcentury.[17]

How do we explain the popularity of these four rituals and the relatively low rate of observance of other rituals? The sociologist Marshall Sklare identified five criteria that help explain why certain rituals are retained by American Jews, even as others are discarded. A ritual is most likely to be retained, he said, if it can be redefined in modern terms; does not demand social isolation or the adoption of a unique life-style; accords with the religious culture of the larger community while providing a Jewish alternative when such is felt to be needed; is centered on the child; and is performed annually or infrequently.[18] The widespread observance of the seder and Hanukkah meets all five criteria, while fasting on Yom Kippur fits in with the first and last.[19] Affixing a mezuzah to a doorpost certainly conforms to the last criterion but may also reflect the present eagerness of Jews to display their religious and ethnic identification in public.

Sklare's criteria also help to explain the relatively low levels of observance of the dietary laws and Sabbath prohibitions. In both cases, the rituals set Jews apart from their neighbors and require ongoing, rather than infrequent, attention. While observance of the dietary laws and the Sabbath had already suffered decline earlier in the century, there is some evidence of even further attrition in recent decades. In Baltimore in 1985, 23 percent of Jews surveyed claimed to light the Sabbath candles weekly, compared with 39 percent in 1968; in 1985, 24 percent of Baltimore Jews claimed they always purchased kosher meat, compared with 36 percent in 1965. In Boston, 31 percent of Jews in 1985 claimed they lit Sabbath candles regularly, compared with 62 percent in 1965; and 17 percent claimed to have a kosher home in 1985, compared with 27 percent who bought kosher meat and 15 percent who kept two sets of dishes in 1965.[20] Nationally, the 1990 survey found that only 17 percent of Core Jews* always or usually lit candles

---

* The 1991 national survey differentiated between categories of Jews: (1) born Jews who claimed their religion was Judaism; (2) Jews by Choice (converts to Judaism); (3) born Jews claiming no religion—that is, secular Jews. Together, these Jews were defined as the Core Jewish Population. In addition, the survey included: (4) individuals born and/or raised Jewish who converted to another religion; (5) adults of Jewish parentage with another current religion; (6) children under the age of eighteen being raised with another religion; (7) Gentile adults living with Jews. The Core Jewish Population was estimated to number 5,515,000 individuals; the rest numbered a bit over 3,000,000 individuals. Unless noted otherwise, this chapter will solely examine the Core Jewish Population.

on Friday night and only 13 percent claimed to have separate dishes to comply with dietary rules.[21] Clearly, the observance of traditional religious rituals that require ongoing attention is in steep decline.

By contrast, rising numbers of Jews are incorporating the Christian symbol of the Christmas tree into their households. According to the 1990 national survey, over one-third of Core Jewish households always or usually have a Christmas tree. Certainly, these numbers are inflated by the presence of intermarried families. But even in households where both spouses were born Jewish, about 10 percent have Christmas trees. The survey did not ask whether families viewed such trees as religious or national symbols, and so we do not know what motivates Jews to bring them into their households. From the perspective of *all* the normative movements of American Judaism, however, there is no justification for such a practice.[22]

DENOMINATIONAL PREFERENCES

Identification with the denominations of American Judaism offers yet further information about the religious makeup of American Jews. It is now demonstrable that in the aggregate denominational self-identification predicts the intensity of Jewish involvement and religious behavior. The claims of the sociologist Paul Ritterband about the Jewish population of New York hold true nationally as well:

> The Orthodox report the most pro-Jewish behavior followed by the Conservative followed by the Reform. The indicators include the proportion of friends who are Jews, intermarriage, conversion where there is an intermarriage, living in a Jewish neighborhood, giving more to Jewish than to non-Jewish charities, and number of visits to Israel. Orthodox Jews expend more of their temporal and material resources in living their lives as Jews than do Conservatives who in turn outstrip Reform.[23]

We must therefore analyze the denominational preferences of American Jews and consider what they portend for the future of American Judaism.

Recent population studies indicate that the majority of American Jews continue to identify with one of the major denominations of American Judaism, albeit at varying rates. In the national survey of

1990 approximately four-fifths of the adult Core Jewish population identified with one of the religious denominations: among those who identified as Jews by religion, only 9 percent eschewed a denominational label; and all but 8 percent of Jews by Choice (converts to Judaism) identified with a denomination. (Not surprisingly, three-quarters of secular Jews did not identify with any Jewish denomination.)[24] Identification with Orthodox, Conservative, Reform, or Reconstructionist Judaism does not necessarily translate into synagogue membership or religious observance, but it indicates that the majority of American Jews still accept some kind of religious label. However, compared with the National Jewish Population Study of 1971,[25] which found that only 11 percent of American Jews eschewed a denominational preference, it appears that a rising percentage of Jews do not identify with any of the religious movements.

For the most part, it is only in smaller Jewish communities that approximately 85 percent of Jews accept a denominational label. By contrast, in the larger centers of Jewish population it is far more common for Jews to see themselves as "just Jewish" or without a religious preference. The rejection of a denominational label by 23 percent of New York Jews, 28 percent of Los Angeles Jews, 30 percent of Miami Jews, 20 percent of Chicago Jews, and 22 percent of Philadelphia Jews is particularly noteworthy, given that these are the five largest Jewish communities in the United States and encompass close to 60 percent of the national Jewish population.

The most recent national survey of American Jews provides evidence of a massive shift in denominational identification during the past generation. According to a national survey conducted in 1990 the adult Core Population of Jews stated its identification as follows: Reform 38 percent, Conservative next with 35 percent, Orthodox 6 percent, Reconstructionist slightly over 1 percent. This represents a major departure from the findings of the previous national survey twenty years earlier, namely, that the plurality of American Jews—42 percent—identified themselves as Conservative, 33 percent identified as Reform, and 11 percent identified as Orthodox.[26] This current denominational breakdown seems to defy the pattern of Christian denominations whereby liberal Protestant groups have sustained serious losses while conservative Christian groupings have grown; among Jews, the two most liberal factions—Reconstructionism and Reform— are gaining relative to the other groups, while the more traditional movements—Conservative and Orthodox Judaism—are sustaining a relative decline. And finally, it suggests that despite the triumphalist rhetoric of Orthodox leaders, the percentage of American Jews who identify with the Orthodox label continues to drop relative to the other movements.

Upon closer examination, these data reveal a more complex state of affairs. To begin with, the self-identification of Jews does not translate into actual patterns of affiliation. Of Jews who actually join a synagogue, 43 percent join Conservative congregations, 35 percent join Reform Temples, 16 percent join Orthodox synagogues and 2 percent join Reconstructionist ones.[27] In contrast to those who selected the Reform label, Jews who identify with the other movements are more likely to invest their money in synagogue membership. Thus, in cities such as Boston, Philadelphia, and Phoenix, barely a third of Jews who identify as Reform join congregations, compared with more than half of those identified with the other movements; in Los Angeles, with its notoriously low rates of affiliation, fewer than a quarter of the identified Reform Jews bothered to take out temple membership, compared with 45 and 42 percent of Jews who identified with Conservative and Orthodox Judaism, respectively. The sharply lower affiliation rate of Jews who identify as Reform is one of many pieces of evidence that the Reform label is now utilized by many Jews who are not necessarily committed to the movement.

The increased popularity of the Reform label does not come solely at the expense of the other movements. Historically, religious "switching" has accounted for the rise and decline of Judaism's denominations. It is therefore noteworthy that currently almost half the Jews by Choice (converts) identify themselves as Reform, as do more than half of the mixed Jewish and Gentile households who identify with any of the Jewish religious movements.[28] Thus, Reform gains have derived in part from new Jewish populations, rather than solely from those rejecting the other movements.

The greatest loser in denominational switching has been the Orthodox label. Among the estimated one million Jewish adults who reported they were raised in Orthodox homes, 73 percent are no longer Orthodox; by contrast about a half million born Jews reported a Reform upbringing out of nearly 1.2 million who now claim a Reform identity. The Conservative movement has remained virtually stationary, maintaining slightly over one and a half million self-identified adherents; and the sharpest relative growth was sustained by the Reconstructionists, who grew by 200 percent and now number an estimated forty-six thousand adults.[29]

The popularity of each denomination fluctuates from one part of the country to the other, so that each of the major movements can claim great strength in particular communities.[30] A high level of identification with Orthodoxy is confined largely to New York City and its environs. But even in New York, Orthodox allegiance is concentrated mainly in the boroughs of Brooklyn and the Bronx and is relatively weak in Manhattan. (Twenty-seven percent of heads of Jewish households in Brooklyn identified as Orthodox compared with 8 percent in Manhattan.)[31] The numerical strength of Orthodoxy in the largest Jewish community of the United States gives that movement a visibility that belies its actual size. Most community surveys outside of New York found a self-identification with Orthodoxy limited to somewhere between 4 and 10 percent of the Jewish population, with Baltimore at 20 percent and Seattle at 16 percent as notable exceptions.

Identification with Conservative Judaism continues at a high level in every Jewish community, but the dominance of the movement is now challenged by Reform in quite a number of localities. In some areas, such as Philadelphia and Minneapolis-St. Paul, Conservatism has maintained formidable strength: in the mid-1980s, 53 percent of Jews in Minneapolis, 55 percent of Jews in St. Paul, and 41 percent of Jews in Philadelphia identified with Conservative Judaism. It also holds the allegiance of a high percentage of Jews in the Sunbelt communities, both in areas where older Jews retire, such as southern Florida, and in burgeoning communities, such as Atlanta.

Reform continues to exhibit great popularity in its traditional areas of strength—the Midwest and South—but is gaining many new adherents throughout the nation. A plurality of Jews in Los Angeles, Boston, and Cleveland now identifies with Reform. Just as the middle decades of the century witnessed dramatic numerical gains by the Conservative movement, the closing decades of the century are a period of particular growth for Reform Judaism.

To refine our figures and project likely trends for the near term, it is useful to examine patterns among age groups. A dozen studies of Jewish communities during the 1980s provided data on the identification of various age groupings within each of the religious denominations. Among Jews who identify themselves as Orthodox, a consistent pattern emerges: higher percentages of Orthodox Jews are in the eighteen- to thirty-four-year-old group than in middle-age groupings; but the highest percentages of Orthodox Jews in any age category are over age sixty-five. This suggests both a source of future strength and future weakness for Orthodoxy. Unlike the other denominations, Orthodoxy is retaining the allegiance of most of its young and even showing a modest increase in attractiveness to younger Jews. By contrast, surveys conducted shortly after World War II repeatedly found that younger Jews from Orthodox homes intended to abandon an Orthodox identification. As a denomination with more adherents in the childbearing years than in middle age, Orthodoxy can expect an infusion of new members through the birth of children to its younger population. But even as it maintains its attractiveness to its youth, Orthodoxy will have to contend with ongoing losses through the death of its older population, a group that is considerably more numerous than its young population.[32] In virtually every community for which data are available, with the notable exception of New York, between two and three times as many Orthodox Jews are over age sixty-five as are between ages eighteen and forty-five. Thus, despite higher birthrates, Jews who identify as Orthodox are not likely to increase in the near future.

Adherents of Conservative Judaism follow a different pattern. Self-identification with Conservatism is stronger among middle-age groups than among younger or older groups. In some communities the largest segment of Conservative Jews is aged thirty-five to forty-four and in others forty-five to sixty-four; but the percentage of Conservative Jews aged eighteen to thirty-five is smaller than in either of the other two age categories. The apparent attrition among younger members constitutes the greatest demographic challenge facing the Conservative movement. It is unclear at present whether the movement has been unable to retain the allegiance of many of its youth, or whether children who grow up in Conservative families defer identifying with the movement until they have children of their own, in which case population studies conducted in the 1990s should reveal a rise in the percentage of Conservative Jews in the younger categories.[33] Depending on which of these explanations holds true, the Conservative movement will either age or retain a youthful character.

Of all the denominations, Reform maintains greatest stability across the age spectrum, with the exception of the oldest age cohorts. In virtually every community there are approximately as many Reform Jews in the younger age grouping (eighteen to thirty-five) as in middle-age groupings. This would indicate the success of the movement either in retaining its youth or in recruiting younger Jews from the other denominations.

The most recent national survey of American Jews provides tantalizing evidence, according to the demographer Sidney Goldstein, that "the pattern [of denominational self-identification] may be altering again."[34] Among those between the ages of eighteen and twenty-four at the time of the survey in 1990, Reform accounted for only 35 percent, Orthodox 10 percent, and Conservative 44 percent; this translates into gains for the Orthodox and Conservative and losses for the Reform movement among the youngest age cohort surveyed as compared with the twenty-five to forty-four-year-old age cohort. Goldstein speculates that younger Jews raised as Reform may be opting for a secular identification, thereby giving a larger share to the Orthodox and Conservative camps.

Future surveys conducted during the 1990s will shed more light on the self-identification of young Jews with the major religious movements. In the meantime, it is possible to project ahead by examining the denominational choices of Jews by their generation in America. Among first-generation Jews, 30 percent claim to be Orthodox, 35 percent Conservative, 17 percent Reform, and 18 percent other. Among the second generation, 10 percent claim the Orthodox label, 43 percent Conservative, 32 percent Reform, and 15 percent other. Among third-generation Jews, 3 percent identified themselves as Orthodox; 35 percent as Conservative, 43 percent Reform, 19 percent as other. And among fourth-generation Jews surveyed, 3 percent identified as Orthodox, 23 percent as Conservative, 57 percent as Reform, and 17 percent as other.[35] The passing of the generations is therefore characterized by a progressive shift to identification with the Reform label.

THE IMPORTANCE OF DENOMINATIONAL IDENTIFICATION

Changing trends in denominational preference are critical because the label a Jew selects generally predicts the degree of Jewish involvement.

On a range of measures of Jewish behavior, the folk wisdom holds remarkably true: Jews who identify as Orthodox, Conservative, and Reform represent a spectrum of Jewish involvement, with the former most intensively Jewish, the latter least, and the Conservative group in the middle, sometimes closer to Orthodox patterns and sometimes closer to Reform patterns.[36]

Item: Synagogue membership is claimed by 73 percent of Jews who identified themselves as Orthodox, 53 percent as Conservative, 37 percent as Reform.[37]

Item: Synagogue attendance twelve or more times annually is claimed by 55 percent of self-identified Orthodox Jews, 21 percent of Conservatives, and 12 percent of self-proclaimed Reform Jews. By contrast, 45 percent of the Orthodox claimed to attend synagogue once or more a week, compared with only 8 percent of Jews who identified themselves as Conservative and 2.5 percent who identified as Reform.[38] Moreover, when we include generation as a variable, we find that only among the Orthodox does regular synagogue attendance rise from the third to the fourth generation; among Conservative and Reform identifiers the trend is to attend synagogue with less frequency with the passing of each generation.[39]

Item: Ritual performance such as fasting on Yom Kippur, lighting candles on Friday evenings, not handling money on the Sabbath, and keeping kosher are observed regularly by Orthodox Jews, followed by Conservatives, followed by Reform. For rituals requiring less attention such as participating in a seder, lighting Hanukkah candles, and affixing a mezuzah, rates of observance among Conservative Jews approximate the levels of the Orthodox; Reform Jews, by contrast, observe these rituals at far lower rates.[40]

Even in matters of Jewishness where religion plays no direct role, the spectrum from Orthodox to Conservative to Reform holds. When asked, for example, about the *religion of their best friends*, 90 percent of Orthodox Jews reported all their best friends were Jewish, followed by 78 percent of Conservative Jews and 64 percent of Reform Jews. *Visits to Israel* conform to the same pattern: 71 percent of Orthodox Jews have been to Israel at least once, compared with 41 percent of Conservative Jews, 30 percent of Reform Jews, and 31 percent of secular Jews.[41] And *parochialism in charitable giving* follows the same pattern: of those reporting charitable gifts to non-Jewish causes the figures are 57 percent of the Orthodox, 67 percent of Conservatives, 75 percent of Reform Jews, and 85 percent of secular Jews. Interestingly, Conservative Jews have the highest rate of giving to the local Jewish federation campaign: when asked whether they gave to the federation, 57 percent of the Orthodox said yes, compared with 63 percent of the Conservative Jews, 52 percent of the Reform Jews, and 36 percent of self-identified secular Jews. Orthodox Jews tend to give largely to their own institutions, whereas Conservative Jews are the most pan-Jewish in their philanthropy.[42] Finally, *rates of intermarriage* also conform to the denominational spectrum: in a sample of ten Jewish communities of varying sizes surveyed in the 1980s, fewer than 1 percent of Orthodox Jews claim to be in mixed marriages, compared with 2.4 percent of Conservative and Reconstructionist Jews, 9.4 percent of Reform Jews and 17.8 percent of secular Jews.[43]

The denominational label a Jew selects therefore tells us much about his or her Jewish commitments. We must stress that the denominations do not sanction many of these patterns of behavior and are often dismayed by what self-professed adherents do in the name of the denomination. For the purpose of assessing the condition of Jewish religious life in American, however, it is of more than passing interest that the Reform label has now become the most popular and the Orthodox and Conservative labels have suffered relative declines. There has been a progressive shift in the denominational self-identification of Jews from the popularity of the Orthodox label in the early decades of the century to the reflexive identification with the Conservative label by midcentury to the contemporary popularity of the Reform label. For many Jews today the reflexive identification with Reform bespeaks a drift toward religious minimalism.

INTERMARRIAGE

Intermarriage is generally defined as the marriage of a born Jew to a person who was not born Jewish. Some intermarriages result in conversionary marriages, where one spouse converts to the religion of the other; others result in mixed marriages, where the two partners formally remain members of two separate religions. Strictly speaking, intermarriage does not provide a measure of religious behavior because one can be married to a non-Jew and continue to practice Judaism.[44] Intermarriage is important in our context for several reasons, however: it blurs religious boundaries between Jews and Christians; it serves as a potential source for new Jews if the non-Jewish spouse converts; it has a profound impact on the religious identity of children; and it raises serious questions of Jewish religious law and policy that bedevil the Jewish community today in an unprecedented manner. Our focus here will be on the quantitative aspects of intermarriage.

Intermarriage has exploded on the American Jewish scene since the mid-1960s, rapidly rising in incidence to the point where more than half the Jews who married between 1985 and 1990 wedded a partner who was not Jewish. The National Jewish Population Study of 1971 was the first survey that drew attention to the changing dimensions of this phenomenon. When married Jews in the national sample were asked whether they were wed to someone who had not been born Jewish, roughly 2 to 3 percent who had married in the decades from 1900 to 1940 answered in the affirmative; the figure rose to 6.7 percent for those who had married in the 1940s and 1950s; jumped to 17.4 percent for those married between 1961 and 1965; and soared to 31.7 percent for those married between 1966 and 1970.[45] Recent population studies make it clear that intermarriage rates have remained high and dramatically exceed the rates of twenty years ago. Summarizing results of the 1990 survey, demographer Sidney Goldstein put matters baldly: since the mid-1980s, "for every new couple consisting of two Jewish partners, there were approximately two new couples in which only one of the partners was Jewish."[46]

Intermarriage rates vary considerably from city to city: in surveys conducted during the 1980s anywhere from 17 to 37 percent of Jewish households consisted of intermarried families. A critical variable in these differential rates is the density of Jewish population. Just as rates of mixed marriage among American Protestants and Catholics and various ethnic groups correlate with population density,[47] so too Jewish rates of mixed marriage are dramatically lower in the area of densest Jewish population—New York City—than in cities with smaller Jewish communities. In fact, according to the 1991 survey of New York Jews, the intermarriage rate is half that of the rest of American

Jews.[48] Rates of intermarriage also rise in communities with young Jewish populations, since younger Jews are more apt to intermarry than were their elders: the proportion of intermarried Jews in San Francisco and Dallas was 20 percent higher than in northeastern cities.[49]

The dimensions of the problem are further highlighted by the age distribution of Jews involved in mixed marriages. There are data from eight communities on the age composition of married couples who indicated that one spouse was an unconverted Gentile. In comparing couples in three age categories—18–29, 30–39, 40–49—it becomes evident that the younger the couple, the more widespread is marriage to a non-Jewish partner. It may be that a certain percentage of these marriages will still become conversionary. Egon Mayer found that one-quarter to one-third of intermarriages eventually lead to the conversion of the non-Jewish spouse, but those findings were based on research conducted in the late 1970s and the early 1980s.[50] During the 1980s conversion to Judaism by the non-Jewish partner declined further in each age cohort, and the percentage of mixed households rose.[51] Despite a range of outreach efforts and the willingness of some Reform and Reconstructionist rabbis to officiate at mixed marriages in the hope that their participation will bring the couple closer to the Jewish community, converts to Judaism constitute a declining proportion of the mixed couples, decreasing from 28 percent in 1970 to 13 percent in the 1980s.[52] Thus, intermarriage rates among younger Jews are accelerating, while conversions to Judaism are declining.

Only limited data are available on the incidence of intermarriage among adherents of the various denominations, but they help clarify why the Reform movement has been most active in formulating new responses in this area. In a survey conducted in 1985 at the biennial convention of the Union of American Hebrew Congregations, the congregational body of Reform Judaism, 31 percent of lay *leaders* of Reform temples reported having a child married to a non-Jewish spouse.[53] In the three communities for which data are available on the parental background of Jews who intermarried in the 1980s—Richmond, Philadelphia, and Cleveland—rates were highest among the offspring of those who identify as Reform, lower among those who identify as Conservative, and lowest among the Orthodox.

If all intermarriages resulted in the conversion of the non-Jewish partner, the matter of intermarriage would still raise important religious issues for American Jews, but they would revolve around the proper manner of integrating the converts into Jewish society. In most communities, however, the percentage of households where no conversion has occurred—the mixed-marriage category—is far larger than the percentage of conversionary households. The issue is thus not only how to deal with converts but also how to cope with the far larger population of Jews who choose to marry a non-Jew and still identify themselves as Jewish and raise their children as Jews.[54]

The religious status of such children has become a bone of contention in the Jewish community. In the present context, attention needs to be paid to the religious outlook and behavior of children whose parents are mixed married. The most extensive analysis of this question appears in research conducted by Egon Mayer.[55] Among his conclusions are the following: children of conversionary marriages are more than three times as likely as children of mixed marriages to identify as Jews; 69 percent of children in conversionary families definitely or probably want to be Jewish, compared with 26 percent of children of mixed marriages. According to Mayer, 81 percent of teenagers in mixed-married families never attend a synagogue, compared with 15 percent of teenagers in conversionary families; and only 14 percent of children of mixed marriages celebrate their Bar or Bat Mitzvah, compared with 73 percent of children of conversionary marriages.[56] The most recent national survey has confirmed the pattern noted by Mayer in the early 1980s: it found that in households where children under eighteen live with one parent who belongs to the Core Jewish Population and one parent who is not Jewish, only 25 percent were being raised as Jews, 30 percent were being raised with no religion, and 45 percent were being raised in another religion. By contrast, virtually all the children in homes where the Gentile-born spouse converted to Judaism were being raised as Jews.[57] It remains to be seen whether children accepted as Jewish under the new patrilineal definition will conform to the patterns of conversionary or mixed-married children.

The overall impact of intermarriage upon Jewish religious involvement is not in dispute. Where such a marriage leads to the conversion to Judaism of the spouse who was not born Jewish, the household participates in Jewish ritual and religious life as actively as, if not more actively than, born Jews. Where a household remains mixed, however, its Jewish identifications and behaviors are slight. A recent analysis of intermarriage and its impact arrives at the following stark conclusion:

Despite the hopes and assumptions, Jewish identification does not fare well in mixed marriages. . . . Overall, the chances of a mixed marriage resulting in a single-identity household at any level of Jewish identification are extremely slim, and the chances of it resulting in a single-identity household at a high level of Jewish identification are infinitesimal. Under these circumstances, the likelihood of creating an unambiguous Jewish identity, should such indeed be the intention or the desire, is virtually nil.[58]

HOW AMERICAN IS JEWISH RELIGIOUS BEHAVIOR?

When Jews discuss the weakening of religious and communal commitments that has characterized the modern Jewish experience, they invariably invoke the term "assimilation."[59] According to the conventional wisdom, Jews are imitating and seeking entry into the larger society by absenting themselves from religious services, by intermarrying with Gentiles, and by abandoning religious rituals. Upon closer examination, however, it is not so apparent that the drift to religious minimalism on the part of large percentages of American Jewry renders Jews like their Christian neighbors. In some ways, their religious indifference sets them apart, even if it does not prevent their eventual disappearance into the larger American society. In order to clarify the significance of the patterns we have traced, we conclude this chapter by placing Jewish behavior within the broader American religious setting.

When it comes to intermarriage, Jews clearly are behaving more and more like their neighbors. As the historian Jonathan Sarna has noted astutely: "Religious differences in America are no longer a socially acceptable barrier to marriage, nor are ethnic differences, nor even racial differences. Where once . . . Jews and other American groups held congruent views on intermarriage, views strongly supportive of endogamy, *[Jewish leaders] today are all alone in their views, separated from the pro-intermarriage mainstream by a huge cultural chasm.*"[60] Since approximately half of all Jews who have married recently selected non-Jewish spouses, it appears that Jews are joining the mainstream trend toward out-marriages. Only about one in five baby boomers of Italian, Irish and Polish ancestry are marrying someone of their own ethnic group, a finding that suggests the melding of white ethnicity.[61] Marriages between Catholics and Protestants, as well as across Protestant denominational lines, are also soaring. Already by the 1970s half of young Catholics were marrying Protestants.[62] And in the same period more than two-thirds of Methodists, Lutherans, and Presbyterians were marrying Christians of other denominations.[63] Like some of their Jewish counterparts, Catholic and Protestant clergy consecrate intermarriages routinely. Thus, when Jews intermarry, they are embracing the American way.

The same cannot be said regarding some other aspects of religious behavior. In comparing Jews with Christian groups, George Gallup, Jr., somberly concluded that "religion is a relatively low priority for American Jews." To support this analysis, Gallup and others cite a number of glaring divergences between Jews and Christians. In the mid-1980s 40 percent of the general American populace claimed attendance at religious services on a weekly basis, compared with less than half that percentage of American Jews. Thirty-five percent of Jews stated that "religion is not very important" in their lives, compared with 14 percent of the general population.[64] We may add still other divergences: the percentages of Jews who never attend synagogue are greater than the percentages of Christians who claim never to attend church.[65] And whereas approximately six out of ten Americans affiliated with a church in the 1970s, among Jews four out of ten are members of synagogues.[66]

The comparison between Jewish and Christian religious patterns gets more difficult when other measures are used. We have only to note that survey research on American religion relies heavily upon measures of religious belief, whereas surveys of Jews generally fail to ask about such matters. Conversely, in light of Judaism's emphasis upon ritual performance, surveys of Jews ask questions about religious practices that have no analogue in Christianity, for example, concerning the use of two sets of dishes or not handling money on the Sabbath. Still, there are a few suggestive studies that provide a basis for some comparison.

In a 1989 survey the sociologist Steven M. Cohen asked a sample population of Jews about their belief in God and received skeptical responses from nearly one in five respondents; by contrast, in the general American population, over nine out of ten affirm a belief in God.[67] Cohen also found that 30 percent of Jews viewed religion as not very important in their lives, whereas Gallup polls find only 14 percent of the larger populace answering this way.[68] And several measures of belief in a personal God indicate significantly lower levels among Jews than among Christians.[69] Some of these divergences may be attributed to the valence carried by belief in the religious demands of Judaism as opposed to Christianity: action has traditionally been far more important than credal belief in Judaism. But we have seen that ritual performance has dropped precipitously in the Jewish community. For perhaps as much as half the Jewish population, religion in both its credal *and* its ritual form plays a minimal role.

Such is not the case in American society at large. Survey after survey has found that the American population is overwhelmingly religious and that there has been remarkable stability in Americans' religious behavior. Belief in "basic doctrines, church attendance, organizational affiliation and activity, [and] religious experience ... have not changed," according to Andrew Greeley and other students of American religious life.[70] The vast majority of Americans, unlike citizens of other countries, continue to attend religious services and accept religious beliefs.

In an effort to understand why Jews differ, some observers contend that the nature of Jewish religious expression has been transformed rather than abandoned. Steven Cohen, perhaps the most forceful proponent of this position, has concluded that American Jewry consists of three populations:

> To one side ... are a collection of more highly involved Jewish groups ... amount[ing] to about one-quarter of American Jewry. Many in this group are Orthodox, but most are not. The intensively active include those Conservative and Reform Jews who take their respective movements' normative positions quite seriously.... At the other end of the spectrum are those ... with only tenuous connections with the formal community.... Between the more intensive group and the more peripheral group lies about half the Jewish population, the moderately affiliated.[71]

It is this moderately affiliated group that continues to involve itself in religious life, albeit on nontraditional terms. According to Cohen:

> The vast majority believes God exists, but only a narrow minority believe God is active and personal. The vast majority think that knowing the fundamentals of Judaism is important for them and their children, but only a small minority believe day schools, text study, and

adult Jewish education are important. The great majority are committed to observing certain holidays and practices, but very few attach great importance to ritual observance or obeying Jewish law.[72]

Cohen's is a nuanced portrait of the religious attachments and commitments of large numbers of Jews. And it certainly clarifies the nature of the target population for outreach programs designed to enrich Jewish living.

The question remains, however, why are Jews less religiously inclined than the rest of the American population? To answer that Jews are primarily an ethnic or cultural group, a view shared by large majorities of Jews, begs the question:[73] Whereas other ethnic groups that have assimilated into American society have retained if not intensified their religious commitments, Jews have not. Many Jews in fact fail even to grasp the intensity of American religiosity and its pervasiveness throughout American history. Perhaps this is what the demographer Barry Kosmin meant when he warned that American Jews "have been assimilated into a mythical . . . America that is only inhabited by a few Episcopalians and Unitarians."[74] Other than when they are concerned about right-wing groups that wish to Christianize America, many Jews are convinced that Americans are apathetic about religion; that is, they project their own religious indifference upon the rest of American society. By contrast, outside observers from Alexis de Tocqueville and Max Weber to contemporary sociologists have been struck by the *pervasiveness* of religiosity in American society. There is a remarkable irony in the drift toward religious minimalism that characterizes a significant population of American Jewry, aptly captured by Paul Ritterband: "As Jews have become more American (and less Jewish) in their style of life, they have on another level, the religious plane, become less American."[75]

4

Expressions of Popular
Religious Revival

Despite the slide toward religious minimalism on the part of large segments of American Jewry, a passionate minority of Jews has invested a lot of energy in creating and nurturing innovative programs that encourage religious renewal. Observers of the American Jewish community cannot fail to note the remarkable juxtaposition of a serious erosion in Jewish commitments on the part of a significant proportion of the populace with a religious energy and dynamism perhaps unmatched in any earlier era of American Jewish history. Even as large numbers of Jews choose to offer their children little or no Jewish education, Jewish religious programs in synagogues, day schools, and summer camps are thriving. Even as many Jews attend synagogue only a few times a year, others have either successfully refashioned existing congregations to reflect their own needs or established alternative Jewish religious communities. Even as American Jews have rejected institutional Judaism as fossilized and irrelevant, others have infused traditional rituals with powerful contemporary meaning. In the last decades of the twentieth century, then, American Judaism is suffering a staggeringly high rate of defection and indifference, even as it simultaneously experiences a creative renaissance and return to tradition by Jews across the spectrum of Jewish life.

Much of the impulse for this renewal has originated outside, and sometimes in conscious rejection of, organized American Judaism. True to the spirit of individualism that characterizes American society at large, Jews—often unassisted by professional leaders—have created innovative religious programs. During the past twenty years American Jews have experimented with new forms of religious communities, innovative liturgies that express contemporary concerns, and nontraditional settings for Jewish study. In time, some of these programs were integrated into or tacitly supported by established religious institutions. But much of the impulse and energy for innovation has come from individual Jews seeking new ways to express their religious commitments.

THE HAVURAH MOVEMENT

The most striking and influential attempt to foster religious renewal through the establishment of an alternative to established synagogues was made by the Havurah movement. As we saw in chapter 2, havurot were initially vehicles of revolt for young Jews who viewed the established community as self-satisfied, staid, and impersonal. Havurah members sought a more intimate communal experience than the conventional fare offered by midcentury synagogues.

Their quest for a meaningful religious life led them to rediscover and reappropriate aspects of the tradition that had been downplayed in American Judaism and also to experiment with new forms of social organization. Riv-Ellen Prell has emphasized the generational aspirations and aesthetic implications of the Havurah movement:

> The entire *Havurah* movement was an exercise in the construction of the meaning of third generation Judaism. . . . Its participants sought their ethnicity within the cultural forms of traditional Judaism, but continually re-created those hallmarks of European Jewish life within the context of the youth-dominated America of the 1970s. Indeed the decorum developed by *Havurah* members acted as a counter-decorum to normative Judaism. . . . They established a new generational rendering of Judaism built upon a new aesthetic and new organizations more suitable in their view to the creation of Jewish community.[1]

The Havurah outlook of this period came to wider attention with the publication of *The Jewish Catalogue* (1974) and *The Second Jewish*

Catalogue (1976), which along with a third Jewish catalog eventually sold over half a million copies. Modeled after the popular *Whole Earth Catalog*, the Jewish volumes contained a wide range of entries written by several dozen contributors—almost all associated with the Havurah movement. The first volume promoted a do-it-yourself approach aimed at "enabling the individual Jew to build his own Jewish life."[2] The volume emphasized "the physical aspects of Jewish life, and provided a guide for the construction of Jewish objects."[3] By contrast, the second catalog was more concerned with "proper ways to act rather than the simple how-to of doing Jewish things—more attention to the community, less to the self."[4] Surveying the Jewish life cycle, study, synagogue, prayer, and the arts, the second catalog offered a "mix of personal advice with *halachic* and other traditional sources, together with ideas, suggestions, illustrations, photographs, general information, and small-print commentary."[5] Both volumes featured an encounter with traditional Jewish sources and a concern with halakhah, coupled with experimentation and eclecticism.

By the mid-1970s this approach came under attack from within. Some longtime members of the Havurah movement grew impatient with what they saw as a casual, highly subjective approach to Jewish tradition, summed up by the remark of one insider: "We are a *havurah* so we examine halakhah (traditional Jewish law), then decide what *we want* to do."[6] Describing his early years in the Havurah movement, Alan Mintz noted sardonically, "In those days my Judaism was a delicate flower of the Diaspora, a kind of aesthetic religion based on values and symbols which sacralized personal relations."[7] Mintz and others sought a more normative approach to Judaism. By contrast, William Novak challenged Havurah Judaism to stake out an alternative approach to Jewish tradition: "Is it not time," he asked, "that those who find the Halakhah an inadequate surface begin to pave a more systematic alternative?"[8]

In the 1980s these issues began to recede, as the Havurah movement underwent important transformations. All of the non-Orthodox versions of American Judaism expressed a new openness to the Havurah form. Reconstructionism enrolled havurot as constituents in its Federation of Reconstructionist Congregations and Havurot; and Conservative and Reform congregations organized synagogue-based havurot. The latter were designed to offer synagogue members intimate fellowships, alongside their simultaneous participation in the life of a larger congregation and in the wide range of programs that only a large congregation can support. In an influential essay, Rabbi Harold Schulweis urged his colleagues "to offer the searching Jew a community which does not ignore his autonomy":

> We are challenged to decentralize the synagogue and deprofessionalize Jewish living so that the individual Jew is brought back into a circle of Jewish experience. . . . I see one of the major functions of the synagogue as that of the *shadchan*—bringing together separate, lonely parties into *Havurot*. In our congregation, a *Havurah* is comprised of a minyan of families who have agreed to meet together at least once a month to learn together, to celebrate together and hopefully to form some surrogate for the eroded extended family.[9]

Schulweis advocated the creation of synagogue havurot as the ideal means for coping with the loneliness, ambivalence, and insecurity felt by many contemporary Jews. Over sixty havurot were established in his own congregation.[10]

Although definitive statistics are not available on the number of synagogue-based havurot, it is clear that the model proposed by Schulweis has been adopted by a significant number of congregations. A survey conducted by a Reform commission headed by Rabbi Saul Rubin in the early 1980s found that at least 129 Reform temples sponsored havurot, with the largest numbers in the Northeast and on the West Coast. Most contained between ten and nineteen people and revolved mainly around educational activities, social programming, holiday observances, and Jewish family life.[11] Similar data are unavailable for Conservative synagogues, but the attention devoted to synagogue havurot at conventions of the Rabbinical Assembly suggests the proliferation of such fellowships in Conservative congregations.[12] Research conducted in the second half of the 1970s found that "the synagogues most likely to have *Havurot* are large, non-Orthodox, suburban, founded after the Second World War, and with a predominant membership of adults aged between 40–59 years." Synagogue-based havurot were most evident on the West Coast.[13]

The introduction of fellowships into larger synagogues has provided some adherents of Havurah Judaism with the opportunity to reestablish their ties with the American synagogue. Whereas havurot once represented a break with establishment Judaism, they now serve as a bridge linking former members of the student movement with the

larger Jewish community. This linkage was made especially evident by
the formation in 1979 of a national organization of havurot that brings
together both the independent and the synagogue types.[14] The distance between Havurah Judaism and the establishment it once
opposed has been lessened by the interdependence of both communities: the established community no longer views havurot as a threat but
has incorporated the fellowship ideal into some of its programs; in
addition, it has recruited members of the Havurah world to serve as
rabbis, administrators, and educators within the larger Jewish community. In turn, members of havurot rely on the larger community for
their children's Hebrew or day-school education, Jewish camping
experiences, and the social and recreational programs offered by Jewish community centers.[15]

A second dramatic change within havurah Judaism has been the
shift from a community focused on study and social interaction to one
primarily concerned with prayer services. In fact, many a Havurah has
signaled the shift by renaming itself a "minyan," a prayer quorum. To
some extent, this is a function of changes in the life situations of members. The undergraduate and graduate students who founded the
movement have taken on career, marriage, and family responsibilities
that leave little time for intensive communal experiences. At the same
time, the minyan may also represent a reaction to the loose, informal
structure of earlier havurot; the goal of the minyanim is to provide
structure for fulfilling a technical requirement of religious life—public
prayer.[16] The havurah and minyan are also distinguished by membership patterns. Minyanim are open to anyone who will participate regularly; as a result, "the typical *minyan* is larger than a *havurah*, and may
reach a membership of eighty to a hundred."[17] But the growing population of minyanim has also led to dissatisfaction among those who feel
that a large group works against spontaneity and brings newcomers
who lack the synagogue skills and havurah experience of veterans.[18]

A third important change in Havurah Judaism has been the introduction of gender equality as a fundamental principle. As the women's
movement developed in the 1970s, havurot incorporated egalitarianism as a basic ideal, albeit not without some strains. Since much of the
liturgy of the havurot was highly traditional, it took time for women to
be integrated into nontraditional synagogue roles as prayer leaders,
Torah readers, and so forth. The movement as a whole also debated
whether males of an Orthodox outlook, who insisted on praying in a

minyan that separated the sexes, could be included in Havurah Judaism.[19] The gradual evolution of egalitarian religious services within the Havurah movement not only transformed the prayer services of the movement but also served as a model for women in conventional synagogues. Moreover, with the intensification of their involvement in religious services, women in havurot began to experiment with new religious rituals and liturgies to express their separate concerns.

A quarter of a century after its founding, the Havurah movement can be credited with several important achievements. As Riv-Ellen Prell has observed, the Havurah movement is a vehicle for one segment of American Jewry's third generation, a group that came of age in the 1960s. Its egalitarian and democratic organizational structure, its informal attitudes toward synagogue decorum, and its aesthetic approach to Jewish living all distinguish it from the suburban Judaism of midcentury America. Havurah Judaism has also demonstrated a capacity for development, as is evident from the shifts to gender equality and from the communal to the minyan model. Within a decade of its emergence, Havurah Judaism already began to reshape the programs of the very institutions it so vehemently criticized, particularly the large synagogues of suburbia. Thus, the movement has demonstrated its vitality and ability to influence the broader Jewish community.

Havurah Judaism's relationship with the larger community is not entirely without challenges, however. Since its inception, the movement has been uncertain of its position vis-à-vis the established denominations. Does Havurah Judaism represent a "fifth" religious movement? Is it postdenominational and therefore separate from all movements? Or does it share many of the religious and ideological assumptions of mainstream Judaism—particularly of the Conservative movement, from which many of its members came? A second challenge pertains to the relationship of havurah members to other generations of American Jews. Ironically, the young Jews who founded havurot to express the needs of their own generation have persuaded their elders of the value of their program but have been far less successful with their juniors. Lamenting the absence of younger members, a Havurah founder observed: "No one beyond the generation that began the *Havurah* joined or created new ones. Where are the college aged students today? They are becoming Orthodox Jews. We could only speak for ourselves."[20] As the former members of America's "youth culture" make their way through their forties, they may find themselves without a successor generation for the Havurah movement.

FEMINIST JUDAISM

Jewish feminism has served as a second source of innovation outside of American Judaism's organized institutions.[21] Jewish feminists have created new ceremonies and liturgies, or reappropriated older forms to mark the particular life-cycle events of women. Though they communicate with each other in the pages of established journals, as well as in new publications such as *Lilith*, Jewish feminists appear to lack institutions to coordinate their activities. There are pockets of activists and small groups in many areas of the country but little centralized activity.[22] Moreover, Jewish feminists vary widely, running the gamut from Orthodox women who will work only within the parameters set by halakhah, to women who create nontraditional liturgies, to radical feminists who insist on breaking with the existing vocabulary of Judaism, claiming it is inherently distorted by patriarchal values and masculine religious categories. Due to the diffuse nature of feminist Judaism, it is difficult to assess just how many women are involved in its activities. But the proliferation of new liturgies and ceremonies attests to the creative engagement of those women who do participate in the movement.[23]

The initial focus of the Jewish women's movement within the religious sphere was to accord women a greater role in traditional ceremonial life. Hence, double-ring ceremonies were introduced at Jewish weddings so that brides could play a more active role; and the ceremony of *brit milah* was revised in order to accord mothers an opportunity to recite part of the liturgy at their son's circumcision. Once these hurdles were overcome, Jewish feminists shifted the focus of their attention to the celebration of women's life-cycle events.

The most widely practiced of these were undoubtedly birth ceremonies for baby girls. These have ranged from the *simchat bat*, or *shalom bat*, which includes remarks by the newborn's parents but no new liturgy or formal ceremony, to the *brit banot*, which not only models itself after the liturgy of the *brit milah* but in some instances also seeks a substitute for the act of circumcision in physical acts, such as immersing the baby in a ritual bath or washing her feet in water.[24] As noted by the anthropologist Chava Weissler, such ceremonies strive to achieve several ends: (1) to create an elaborate celebration that rivals the *brit milah;* (2) to develop a liturgy initiating the child into the covenant that binds Israel to its God; (3) to define an approach to sex-role differentiation.[25]

A wide range of ceremonies was developed to celebrate other milestones in the lives of women. These include the redemption of the firstborn daughter (*pidyon ha-bat*); weaning ceremonies; and special prayers that commemorate both pregnancy and miscarriage.[26] Further, an array of liturgies was created to mark the fertility cycle of women. The onset of menstruation is celebrated rather than perceived as a curse; it is designated as a "coming of age" to be proclaimed by daughter and mother in a public setting.[27] Jewish feminists have also created other ceremonies to reappropriate the monthly ceremony of ritual immersion in the waters of the *mikveh*, as well as to mark the onset of menopause.[28] The value of such rituals for feminists is that they grant recognition to the unique experiences of women and celebrate the milestones in their lives, rather than ignoring them or relegating them to private commemoration. For some feminists, however, the emphasis on women's biological functions represents a step backward. "Is the celebration of the recurrence of the menses feminism, or is it a ceremony honoring instrumentality?" asks Cynthia Ozick in a widely remarked essay. Feminism, she argues, must enable women to transcend biology; accordingly, Jewish feminism should seek to end the segregation of women.[29]

Feminist Judaism has found particular meaning for women in two Jewish holidays—Passover and the Festival of the New Moon (Rosh Chodesh). Passover has become central to feminist celebrations for a number of reasons: it is the most widely celebrated of all Jewish holidays; it is thematically focused on liberation; it has traditionally been a time when women shoulder the burden of preparation; and the Exodus narrative itself draws attention to the roles of women—Yocheved and Miriam, Shifra and Puah. Structurally, the twin seder evenings provide an opportunity to experiment with new liturgies on the second evening, even for those who prefer the traditional ceremony on the first. Not surprisingly, there has been an outpouring of feminist Passover liturgies. Here is a small sampling from a guide to the new seder services:

Women's Haggadah: "Any reference to God is changed to goddess, in even the translation of blessings. There is the addition of a 5th question—How is this seder different? Women have always been enslaved, now they participate."

The Stolen Legacy: A Women's Haggadah: "This Haggadah superimposes womanhood on tradition. It is angry at the forgotten legacy of Jewish women yet respectful of Judaism and tradition. Its overall tone is a plea for redemption of Jewish women."

A Jewish Women's Haggadah: "Questions of four women are asked alongside those of the four sons although the answers are directed to the women's questions. Jewish women's strength is shown throughout history."

The tension within these new Haggadot is between their exclusive concerns with women and the family-oriented nature of the traditional seder. Some women overcome this tension by holding a "third night feminist seder."[30]

Some Jewish feminists have also reappropriated the Festival of the New Moon by building upon its traditional association with women. Rabbinic texts have long enjoined women, as opposed to men, from engaging in their usual work routines on the New Moon (Rosh Chodesh); and some of those texts had in fact identified Rosh Chodesh as a reward to women, a time in the world to come when "women will be renewed like the New Moons."[31] The strong historical association of women with this monthly holiday commended Rosh Chodesh as a natural occasion for exploring the unique spiritual needs of women. Building upon traditional *techinot* (women's supplications), feminist liturgists have written new compositions to reclaim the celebration of the New Moon. Since the early 1970s, when these celebrations gained popularity, Rosh Chodesh groups have met throughout the country, usually during the evenings when the new moon has appeared, and have marked the occasion with "anything from a scholarly (or hagiographic) presentation on some aspect of Jewish women's history, to artistic renderings—verbal, musical, or plastic—of women's experience, to cooking of symbolic foods, to guided imaging and myth-writing."[32]

In all these activities Jewish feminists have grappled with the tension between developing opportunities for women to express their own religious needs and integrating women into all facets of Jewish religious life.[33] The former leads easily to liturgies and rituals that are exclusively for women; the latter seeks a voice for women in communal religious activities that are not gender specific. This issue is central to discussions of liturgical innovations: Is the goal of new liturgies to refer to God using pronouns that are feminine or using pronouns not associated with either gender? And if either approach is utilized, will Jews find meaningful a liturgy that departs radically from the hallowed prayers?[34]

Beyond these questions lie deeper theological and religious concerns. If contemporary feminists conclude that the experiences and religious aspirations of earlier generations of women are absent from Jewish texts, can they rest content with the reclamation of the few women who are mentioned, or will they find it necessary to create a new Jewish women's history? If women seek a substitute for the male imagery of the Bible, will it suffice to substitute female pronouns or will they also seek to change traditional Jewish conceptions of God? And if contemporary feminists elevate egalitarianism to a supreme value, will they see fit to reject the range of polarities known to Judaism, a religion that draws distinctions—between classes of Jews, between kosher and nonkosher, between the sacred and the profane? As one feminist put it, "We cannot just 'add women and stir': . . . If half of Judaism, as many argue, has been missing, no one is sure what Judaism will look like once it is reunited with its other half."[35]

RELIGION FOR JEWS ON THE PERIPHERY

The era of the 1970s and 1980s also witnessed the creation of new religious groups by Jews who felt neglected by the mainstream denominations. Some felt peripheral because they literally lived in geographically distant places where Jewish services were hard to find. But most of these groups were on the periphery by virtue of their unconventional social and religious outlook. We shall see that these Jewish groups are analogous to special-purpose groups on the American religious scene: parallel Christian groups undoubtedly inspired Jews, served as models, and also gave license for experimentation with new organizational forms. But internal Jewish preoccupations have also promoted the establishment of such groups, especially the desire to accommodate the needs of every type of Jew at a time when the Jewish community is fighting to stem the hemorrhage of unaffiliated and indifferent Jews. Herewith are some of the most noteworthy of the new groups created by Jews who have felt neglected by establishment institutions.

Gay Synagogues

In 1972 homosexual men and women organized Beth Chayim Chadashim in Los Angeles, the first gay synagogue. Since then approximately twenty additional congregations have been established, with the largest, Congregation Beth Simchat Torah in New York, claiming to have eleven hundred members and two thousand worshipers at High Holiday services.[36] When interviewed, members of these congregations describe their early education in yeshivas and Hebrew schools and their subsequent rejection of Judaism because of the conflict between their sexual preferences and traditional Jewish norms.[37] Gay synagogues provide these individuals with an opportunity to participate in Jewish life with men and women who share their way of life.

While much of the traditional liturgy is utilized at the services of gay synagogues, new prayers are added to "remove gender references to God, recognize the contributions of women as well as men . . . , and to reflect the experiences of lesbian and gay Jews." A new prayer included in the liturgy of Sha'ar Zahav in San Francisco expresses the hope: "Let the day come which is all Shabbat, when all people, all religions, all sexualities will rejoice as one family, all children of Your creation."[38] Gay synagogues also provide rites of passage unavailable at most synagogues, such as consecration, wedding, and affirmation services for gay and lesbian couples, baby-naming ceremonies for homosexual couples who adopt a child, and "coming out" celebrations. As the AIDS epidemic has ravaged the homosexual community, gay congregations also offer unique support and liturgical compositions to console both the sick and their loved ones.[39]

Communities of Rural Jews

Throughout American Jewish history, some Jews have resided in small rural communities, separated by vast distances from larger centers of

Jewish life. Rural Judaism declined in the middle decades of the twentieth century, as younger Jews sought higher education and settled in urban centers. In the late 1960s this process was briefly reversed, as small numbers of Jews involved in the American counterculture sought escape from their suburban homes in rural America as part of a "back-to-the-land" movement. In time, some confronted the isolation of their lives and particularly their loss of Jewish contacts. By the mid-1980s an annual Conference on Judaism in Rural New England was convened to connect Jews in Vermont, New Hampshire, and Maine, who live far from a synagogue; by the 1990s, it attracted over five hundred participants annually.[40] A klezmer band and bimonthly journal, *KFARI: The Jewish Newsmagazine of Rural New England and Quebec,* link these rural Jews.[41] And in Montpelier, Vermont, eighty families practice "new-age Judaism" in a nondenominational synagogue that functions without a rabbi.[42]

The Jewish Renewal Movement

The new-age Judaism of rural Jews is part of a larger movement that since the 1960s has sought to merge Eastern religion, the self-actualization movement, and the counterculture outlook with Jewish religious traditions, particularly with Jewish mysticism. Led by a charismatic rabbi named Zalman Schachter-Shalomi, this loosely organized movement has gradually evolved an institutional network known as the P'nai Or Religious Fellowship, which numbered eleven American affiliates in the late 1980s.[43] As stated in its promotional brochure:

> P'nai Or searches the inner meaning of Torah, Kabbalistic philosophy, Chasidic prayer, meditation, humanistic and transpersonal psychology, and *halakha* to gain a practical orientation to Jewish spiritual life. By understanding their intentions, the individual derives a new appreciation of Judaism as a path to inner balance and inter-connectedness with others, and with the world we live in.[44]

The founder of P'nai Or, Reb Zalman, as he is called by his disciples, has publicly spoken of his evolving Judaism, which began with intense study of Lubavitch Hasidism and later encompassed formal study of psychology, experimentation with LSD, and study with various masters of Asian religions.[45] An observer of Reb Zalman's performance at a renewal retreat described his impact on Jews searching for a means to reconnect with Judaism: "With his vestige of a European accent, his enchanting talents as a storyteller and his habit of referring to his students as *kinderlach*, he is the ultimate grandpa, the . . . *zayde* for the spiritually orphaned Jew."[46]

In light of its emphasis upon self-expression, the Jewish renewal movement is particularly concerned with prayer. Reb Zalman has developed what he refers to as a "Davenology," an examination of the Jewish prayer that "monitors each phase of the inner process and observes it in differing personality types." P'nai Or groups look to dance, song, and movement to invigorate their bodies and stimulate spiritual intensity.[47] A draft version of the new prayer book of P'nai Or entitled *Or Chadash* incorporates liturgies that reflect the range of interests in the renewal movement: a selection for "Active Davening for the Morning Blessings," which offers instruction on the appropriate stretching and yoga exercises to use as accompaniment to the recitation of traditional morning benedictions; formulations of benedictions that employ both male and female Hebrew pronouns for God; and a prayer to the patriarch Abraham, who mourns the continuing conflict between the descendants of his equally beloved sons, Isaac and Ishmael.[48]

Designed as a self-consciously experimental movement, which "welcomes all Jews, including those who have been disenfranchised by the Jewish establishment,"[49] the Jewish renewal movement has begun to grapple with questions of definition and boundaries. A recent issue of *New Menorah: The P'nai Or Journal of Jewish Renewal* featured a debate over the "content" of Jewish renewal. As articulated by Arthur Waskow, one of the more politically active leaders of the movement, there is a vast difference between "Jewish restoration" and "Jewish renewal." The latter continues to do what Jews always have done: "keeping women in their separate place; keeping gay and lesbian Jews invisible; imagining God always and only as Lord and King; saying 'all my bones will praise You' while sitting locked into pews where no bone can move a quarter-inch; reciting the second paragraph of the Sh'ma while taking no responsibility to end the acid rain that is destroying earth." Jewish renewal, according to Waskow, requires the rejection of all these positions.[50] As the movement coalesces into what some regard as yet a fifth Jewish religious movement,[51] it will be forced to decide whether it is a movement of "content" as well as of form. And as they re-create traditions, members will have to clarify the limits to religious syncretism and to each individual's autonomy to invent his or her own Judaism.

Humanistic Synagogues

In 1963 a Reform rabbi, Sherwin Wine, formed a secular humanistic Jewish congregation in Farmington Hills, Michigan, to provide a setting for Jews who rejected God but sought a communal structure to meet with fellow Jews. Wine's congregation now numbers five hundred families and has been augmented by twenty-five additional congregations affiliated with the Society for Humanistic Judaism. These congregations hold Sabbath and holiday celebrations, utilizing "nontheistic symbols (a *sukkah*, *lulav*, and *etrog*, for instance), folk songs and celebrations, such as a Purim carnival—independent of services." Rites of passage are commemorated in ceremonies that do not include blessings or Torah readings but do connect the life-cycle event to the larger tapestry of Jewish history. In general, congregational meetings consist of two parts: a period of time devoted to reading philosophical reflections, poetry, meditations, and songs; and a part devoted to a lecture or cultural program. The flavor of the former is conveyed by the following poem/liturgy by Rabbi Sherwin T. Wine:

> *Where is my light? My light is in me.*
> *Where is my hope? My hope is in me.*
> *Where is my strength? My strength is in me,*
> *And in you.*

Claiming to have an international membership of thirty thousand Jews, Humanistic Judaism seeks to reach out to Jews who are not interested in any religious observance but nonetheless identify with the Jewish people and its culture.[52]

Interfaith Synagogues

Perhaps the newest manifestation of a special-interest group is the interfaith congregation. The first of these groups, the Interfaith

Chavurah for Liberal Judaism, was founded in Hartford, Connecticut, during the summer of 1990. As described by its rabbi,

> members rejoice in the choices we have made and the lifestyles we have created within the context of interfaith marriage. Rather than bemoan the interfaith trends as a "catastrophe" or an "epidemic" as is often bandied about in the media, we seek creative responses to the issues interfaith families confront. We understand that to maintain ties with Jews who intermarry, our community must be accepting and understanding of the needs of their non-Jewish partners. . . . We must create a community in which Jews and non-Jews feel they can belong—*each in their own way.*

As members of a national organization called Parveh: The Alliance of Adult Children of Jewish-Gentile Intermarriage, the congregation strives to give equal time to both the Jewish and the Christian perspectives on issues affecting interfaith families—to the point of having a Methodist minister and a Catholic lay minister as adjunct advisers. Its rabbi proudly describes the cutting-edge quality of the enterprise, "whose ongoing mission is to boldly go where no congregation has gone before . . . [and] invites the entire Jewish community to accompany us."[53]

Although these groups have been created by Jews who feel peripheral to the mainstream, members of some of them interact with each other and engage in a multiplicity of Jewish activities. There is, in fact, considerable overlap in the populations of Jews who identify with several of the new and experimental movements. The Havurah movement, feminist Judaism, Jewish renewal, and, to some extent, gay Judaism often share a common outlook and draw upon similar constituencies. They also share a common belief that they are disenfranchised from establishment institutions and synagogues. In truth, members of these movements are frequently invited to address rabbinic and synagogue conventions, and they publish in the journals of the mainstream religious movements. Their experimentation with new liturgies and ceremonies is having a perceptible impact on denominational Judaism. To the extent that they absent themselves from the institutions of mainstream American Judaism, they deprive the establishment of important sources of enthusiasm and creativity. Conservative synagogues would take on a far more youthful and dynamic quality were they to regain the youth lost to havurot; and Reconstructionism would have greater momentum were the sympathies of its adherents not divided between it and the Jewish renewal movement. Leaving aside the problematic relationship of these movements to the established institutions of American Judaism,[54] the diverse activities we have surveyed provide further evidence of a renewed popular interest in religious life that also attracts Jews who have felt marginal.

JEWS BY CHOICE

The revitalization of popular Judaism has benefited from an infusion of new and newly involved Jews. Conversion to Judaism has occurred on a scale perhaps unmatched in any other era of Jewish history. And the movement of return by Jews from peripheral involvement to engaged commitment (*baalei teshuvah*) is unprecedented as well. Though numerically small compared with the vast numbers of Jews drifting toward religious minimalism, the converts and *baalei teshuvah* play an increasingly important role in Jewish life. By choosing to take Judaism seriously, they both add to the population of engaged Jews and attest to the compelling nature of Judaism in the contemporary world, thereby boosting the morale of all religiously engaged Jews.

There has been much speculation about the actual numbers of converts to Judaism. It was estimated in the early 1980s on the basis of no discernable evidence that some ten thousand Americans converted to Judaism annually.[55] Since there is no centralized office that coordinates conversions, estimates were largely based on guesswork. Nevertheless, it became clear in the 1970s to those overseeing conversions that for the first time since the Roman era large numbers of people were becoming "Jews by Choice," that is, converts. Circumstances had changed: converts no longer feared that society would penalize them for joining the Jewish people, and rabbis felt fewer inhibitions about accepting converts. As rates of intermarriage soared, some Jewish leaders even urged aggressive programs to convert the "unchurched" Gentile spouses of Jews.[56]

The National Jewish Population Study of 1990 provides detailed data on Jews by Choice, a group thought to number some 185,000 individuals.[57] On every measure of religious behavior, Jews by Choice were found to observe Judaism at the same or even higher rates as born Jews. In so-called conversionary households, a home where one spouse has converted to Judaism, there is a greater likelihood that rituals such as Friday night candle lighting and using separate dishes for meat and dairy foods will be observed, as compared with households where both spouses were born Jewish. Jews by Choice also attend synagogue far more regularly than born Jews.[58] The demographer Sidney Goldstein concludes that "Jews by choice more closely resemble those who are Jews by religion, whereas secular Jews operate closer to the margins of traditional behavior."[59]

There is little disagreement that most conversions in this period were initiated for the sake of a marriage, either before the actual wedding or at a later point when the married couple realized the need for the household to identify with one religion. Some Jews by Choice, however, claim that they were drawn to a Jewish spouse because of a prior interest in Judaism.[60] As for the actual conversion, it appears that pressure from a rabbi and family influence the decision to convert, but the major factor is the attitude of the Jewish-born spouse. According to a study by Egon Mayer and Amy Avgar, the Jewish partner's positive feelings about the Jewish heritage conveys an enthusiasm that encourages the non-Jewish partner to explore Judaism.[61]

Although rates of conversion to Judaism declined in the 1980s, the critical mass of converts is having a perceptible impact upon American Judaism—most overtly the converts who become rabbis, cantors, Jewish educators, and lay leaders. In truth, some observers also suspect more subtle influences that not all born Jews necessarily welcome: they question whether converts will push the Jewish community to emphasize its religious dimensions at the expense of Jewish peoplehood, since the newcomers to Judaism, presumably, relate more easily to religious beliefs and rituals than to ethnic folkways.[62] Some communal leaders also worry over those "conversionary households" that still maintain a dual identity and incorporate Christian traditions.[63] At least one survey found converts unusually sanguine about the prospects of their own children intermarrying. Given such attitudes, the question arises whether converts will be one-generation Jews whose parents and children are Christians.[64] It is too early to judge and certainly impossible to generalize about these matters, but sufficient evidence is available to suggest that converts bring an enthusiasm to Judaism that often encourages born Jews to take another, more positive look at their tradition.[65]

Another population that has spurred Jewish religious revival are born Jews who chose to intensify their involvements with Judaism. The most visible of these are the so-called *baalei teshuvah* (literally, "masters of return") who turn to Orthodox Judaism. In truth, there are far more *baalei teshuvah* in the liberal movements of American Judaism than in Orthodoxy, if we define the term not as a turn to Orthodoxy but as a decision to heighten one's commitment to Jewish religious practice—in any of its forms. Contemporary American Judaism *in all its permutations* relies upon a population of Jews that has consciously opted for increased participation in religious life, an increase measured by the distance traveled from the Judaism practiced by the *baal teshuvah*'s parents and from his or her earlier Jewish involvements.[66]

Orthodox *baalei teshuvah* have received the most sustained attention, perhaps because their choices often involve a rejection of modernity and an extreme break with their past lives. The story of the passage of an upper-middle-class suburbanite from the Midwest to the Lubavitch community in the Crown Heights section of Brooklyn formed the dramatic core of a series of articles in the *New Yorker*.[67] And a popular work of fiction explored the relationship between a professional woman living in Manhattan and her daughter, who joined a religious community in Jerusalem and in the process came to accept her community's traditional understanding of women's proper role and to reject her mother's feminism.[68]

Since midcentury a range of institutions have been established by Orthodox Jews to encourage such acts of "return." The Lubavitch movement of Hasidism became especially active, establishing outposts in smaller Jewish communities and on college campuses and providing services to Jews on the periphery. Since the 1960s special yeshivas have been established in the United States and Israel to create an environment for intensive Jewish study and living that can provide *baalei teshuvah* with the religious "background" they lacked. In truth, most *baalei teshuvah* who turn to Orthodoxy travel a more conventional road: they are attracted either because their spouse is Orthodox or because they have been exposed to Orthodox synagogues, day schools, and youth programs.[69]

Non-Orthodox religious institutions play a similar role. Although the phenomenon receives little attention and most writers on *baalei teshuvah* do not even consider non-Orthodox Jews, the presence of such "returnees" in synagogues, adult education centers, PTAs of Conservative and Reform day schools, and other Jewish institutions is much in evidence. Each year many if not most Conservative rabbis help several families in their congregation make their kitchens kosher; some of the same families assume an active role in synagogue life. The student bodies of *all* the liberal rabbinical seminaries consist overwhelmingly of individuals who have opted to live a more religious and observant life than the one in which they were raised. In fact, the liberal rabbinical seminaries today attract students who must first learn to live as religious Jews before they can be taught more advanced texts and religious skills; that is, they are fundamentally *baal teshuvah* yeshivas. The articulated goals of *all* the liberal movements in American Judaism are to provide outreach to Jews who must be educated to observe religion. Given the importance of this movement of return, it is not accidental that several works of nonfiction have attracted considerable attention because they trace the paths of Jews who have found their way to intensified religious involvement but not necessarily to Orthodoxy.[70] It also accounts for the popularity of how-to books for Jewish religious living.[71]

PORTALS TO RELIGIOUS COMMITMENT

Innovative educational programs created since midcentury have played a major role in providing an opportunity for unaffiliated Jews to learn about their religious civilization. Unquestionably, the most dramatic explosion of Jewish learning has taken place on American college campuses. Whereas in the 1950s there were no more than a dozen full-time positions in Judaica at American universities, the 1960s and 1970s marked a period of explosive growth, as hundreds of new positions and programs in Judaica were established. In some years of the 1970s between thirty and forty new positions were created annually. Judaica programs, offering courses in Hebrew and Yiddish, Jewish history, thought, and literature, and even rabbinics now exist at most major institutions of higher learning.[72]

Much of this growth was funded by local Jewish communities or alumni who view Jewish studies programs as a means to offer Judaic content to young Jews during their college years. Within the Jewish community, the campus experience is perceived as inherently dangerous to the identity formation of young Jews, and courses in Jewish studies are viewed as a partial remedy, providing an anchor to Jewish life. Faculty members staffing Jewish studies programs do not necessarily share the views of donors who established their positions; they argue that the nature of academic inquiry is antithetical to the kind of Jewish apologetics that may suit the needs of the Jewish community. As a result, there is much unresolved tension over how Jewish studies relates to the needs of the Jewish community.[73]

For students, however, the proliferation of Jewish studies programs has been a boon. While pursuing their undergraduate studies, they can choose from rich offerings that expose them to classical and modern Jewish texts. They have the opportunity to study Bible, rabbinics, Jewish mysticism, liturgy, Jewish thought, and Jewish history on a sophisticated level that will inform their Jewish outlook. Moreover, they are exposed to academicians who, however unconsciously, may serve as role models for engagement with Jewish texts and thought. As Michael Fishbane of the University of Chicago has argued: "Teachers, like the texts studied, disclose new possibilities and modes of being-in-the-world. . . . We . . . are complex combinations of our studies and of modern culture. As such, we are models of various possibilities of contemporary synthesis, even as we point the way to understanding older models of personal and cultural synthesis."[74] Jewish studies courses, in short, provide a new and potentially stimulating setting for college students to reflect on the nature and meaning of their Jewish identity and religion.

Israeli schools of higher learning have emerged as a vital adjunct to American Jewish educational institutions. Since 1967 thousands of American Jews have gone to Israel for a summer, a semester, or a year of study that exposes them to the Hebrew language, Israeli society, the land of Israel, and intensive textual reading. Some find their way to yeshivas that cater to *baalei teshuvah* from the Diaspora.[75] Others enroll in year-abroad programs at Israeli universities. And still others participate in work-study programs at kibbutzim. As is the case with Jewish studies programs, there has been little research assessing the exact impact of study in Israel, particularly upon the religious outlook of students. But evidence from one study of rabbinical students at the Jewish Theological Seminary of America suggests that these two types of study are major feeder programs for the Conservative rabbinate.[76] There is reason to suppose that the same pattern applies at other rabbinical schools.

The most important development in the Jewish schooling of children is the continuing growth in day-school enrollment. A census of Jewish education conducted in the early 1980s enumerated 499 day schools throughout the country, which enrolled 28 percent of students receiving a Jewish education. In a few localities, most prominently New York, slightly more than half of all children receiving a Jewish education were enrolled in a day school.[77] The growth of the Conservative movement's Solomon Schechter day-school movement, the establishment of several day schools under Reform auspices, and the extensive network of Orthodox day schools reflect the growing conviction of religious educators that such schools offer the best hope of transmitting a strong Jewish identity. By contrast, assessments of supplementary programs (Hebrew schools and Sunday schools) are almost uniformly negative, as the following report issued by the Board of Jewish Education of New York observes bleakly: supplementary "schools do a very poor job in increasing Jewish knowledge in all subject areas; they show no success in guiding children towards increased Jewish involvement; and they demonstrate an inability to influence positive growth in Jewish attitudes."[78] Researchers have found that a threshold of Jewish education must be reached in order to form a strong identity and religious commitment;[79] this cannot occur in a supplementary school with its sparse hours, but it can be accomplished in day schools.

A plethora of Jewish summer camps supplement school programs. It is estimated that some twenty-three thousand children attend sleepaway camps under religious auspices; approximately twenty-four thousand attend Jewish sleep-away camps sponsored by Zionist organizations, cultural groups, and Jewish community centers, and seventy-eight thousand children attend day camps sponsored by Jewish community centers and Y's.[80] Increasingly, camps under communal or cultural auspices offer some religious component. From the perspective of Jewish educators, summer camping offers an unparalleled opportunity to socialize young Jews into a religious community.[81]

The formal offerings on campuses and at Israeli institutions coupled with religious schools and camps, conversion and adult education programs offered by synagogues, and the courses taught at Jewish community centers, outreach centers,[82] family retreats,[83] and informal neighborhood study circles serve as portals of reentry into Jewish religious life. These programs take into account that many of their students were raised in families that did not transmit an intensive knowledge of Judaism. Much of Jewish education today is directed to a generation of "orphans in Jewish history," a designation coined by Paul Cowan[84] whose autobiographical book was emblematic of the quest for identity by a segment of American Jewry seeking to journey from rootlessness to reconnection with Jewish life—and especially religion.

RECLAIMING THE SYNAGOGUE

This discussion of educational outreach programs underscores the importance of official institutions in the efforts to revive Jewish religious life: synagogues and formal schooling constitute the most important portals to Judaism for converts and *baalei teshuvah*. Even though many of the movements we have discussed, such as feminist Judaism, the havurot, and some of the special-purpose groups, rebelled against established institutions such as the synagogue, those institutions continue to play a vital role in the religious revival.

They have done so because contrary to their reputation as rigid and hidebound institutions, synagogues and other denominational structures have borrowed freely from popular religion, albeit at a slow pace. We have already noted the creation of havurot in synagogues across the country as means to establish more intimate fellowship among members of large congregations. Other expressions of popular religion have entered synagogue programming as well—prayers and projects for the preservation of the environment,[85] soup kitchens and shelters for the homeless,[86] interfaith services to bridge social and racial differences, and special religious services for Jews with AIDS.[87] Synagogues of all denominations have been especially active in promoting outreach programs and separate religious services for single Jews, who tend to be unaffiliated. By offering an informal service led by a guitar-playing cantor, one Conservative congregation in Washington, D.C., attracted some fifteen hundred single Jews on "an ordinary Friday evening." Over 350 of these singles eventually joined the congregation, thus demonstrating the importance of such programs for congregational growth.[88]

Synagogues have been affected most ubiquitously by feminist Judaism. In just two decades, women have assumed positions of equality in many congregations, serving as rabbis, cantors, and officers; they are called to the Torah, lead Torah discussions, and participate actively in life-cycle ceremonies. Undoubtedly, feminists have chafed at the slow pace of change. But even with the very real resistance put up by some members, synagogues—even some Orthodox congregations— have changed at least some of their practices to meet women's demands for a greater role.[89]

This process has been abetted by the introduction of special adult education programs designed to prepare women for participation. Often called "adult Bat Mitzvah" classes, these intensive educational programs teach Hebrew reading and synagogue skills. For some they provide an opportunity to assume more rigorous religious obligations, much as does the Bat Mitzvah celebrated by girls.[90] The adult Bat Mitzvah thus combines aspects of Jewish popular religion with the official program of synagogues. As noted by Rabbi Avis Miller, women have become interested out of a dual motivation—"part feminism, part return to Judaism."[91]

Synagogues are also responding to the desire of members for more participatory services. Rabbis are well aware of the need to create a community within their congregations, which can only happen if they empower their congregants to rely less upon the clergy and formal services. Although systematic information has not been gathered by the major religious movements, fragmentary evidence exists of significant movement toward lay participation in many synagogues.

Item: A Conservative congregation in Minneapolis has taught cantillation skills to hundreds of its members, who then share the responsibility of reading from the Torah on a rotating basis.[92]

Item: The Reconstructionist movement insists that its rabbis view themselves as facilitators, rather than as authority figures who set religious policy.[93]

Item: Many Orthodox synagogues have no need for a cantor because members take turns leading the services; some do not have a rabbi either.

Item: A Reform rabbi exhorts his colleagues to ignore the numbers of congregants who attend services but to work instead to "create a sharing worship community."[94]

Item: A recent study of Conservative synagogues in New Jersey found that regular synagogue attenders overwhelmingly favored a less formal religious service, which features a discussion rather than a sermon, congregational singing rather than cantorial solos, children present in the synagogue rather than banished to separate services, and more participation by the congregation.[95]

All of these are symptoms of the revolution that is taking place in synagogue life, which is transforming some congregations into less formal and more participatory religious communities.

SPECIAL-PURPOSE GROUPS

Religious renewal, as our survey of the American Jewish landscape makes clear, emanates both from the more established denominational institutions and from new types of groups. Denominations and their congregations continue to serve as the major institutions of American Judaism, but they also interact with parallel groups that express new and often transdenominational needs. The nature of this interaction is most evident in the relationship between feminist Judaism and established synagogues. Feminist Judaism, for example, has multiple concerns. It looks first to meet the special needs of Jewish women—to assure that women can assume new roles in the public arena of Judaism and also give expression to the religious sensibilities of their gender; and it simultaneously promotes its program as a vehicle for the revitalization of all Jewish religious life. Similarly, other Jewish groups also share the essential qualities of the new special-purpose groups in American religion—they cut across denominational lines and appeal to a specific segment of the population, while also aiming to reinvigorate religious life in general.

The sociologist Robert Wuthnow has provided the most detailed portrait of such groups and their new role in American religion.[96] According to Wuthnow, there are over five hundred such special-purpose religious groups in America. Many offer a program that combines a political agenda with religious activism, but others look to meet different types of needs. What unites all these groups is the clearly delimited services they provide and their appeal to relatively small groups of like-minded people. They do not compete with established religious institutions but rather complement them: "Besides holding membership in denominations and attending worship services at local churches on Sunday mornings," notes Wuthnow,

> people now have the option of participating in many other kinds of groups; specialized ministries, coalitions, home fellowship groups, quasi-religious seminars, and so on. Some of these activities may be held in the same local churches in which people worship on Sunday morning; others may be held in someone else's church; still others, outside church buildings entirely. . . . Almost by definition, these groups appeal to narrower segments of the population.[97]

Most of the Jewish special-purpose groups we have encountered have modeled themselves after or have their counterparts within American society at large. The same demand for fellowship and participation that inspired the founding of havurot led to the creation of "such para-denominational movements as evangelicalism, charismatic renewal, Cursillo and Walk to Emmaus, Marriage Encounter, liturgical renewal," in Christian churches, writes the sociologist R. Stephen Warner.[98] Even in so hierarchical a tradition as Catholicism, lay participation in religious rituals has been increasing.[99] Feminist Judaism also has close ties to its Christian counterparts. And the success of the Metropolitan Community Church, a network of churches for homosexuals, undoubtedly served to encourage the creation of gay synagogues.

Most important, Jewish special-purpose groups have been inspired by the individualistic and pluralistic qualities of American religious life in the late twentieth century. "There seems little question," writes William McKinney, "that for the mainline churches, at least, individualism in religion reigns supreme. Questions of authority, discipline, community, and order seem foreign."[100] Jewish religious life has adapted to this individualism by fragmenting into subgroups that can meet the needs of many different types of Jews. American Judaism is able to spawn so many new types of religious groups because American society at large accepts the diversity of religious expression. Wuthnow's conclusions about American religious life describe the Jewish religious scene as well: "In becoming more oriented to the self, in paying more explicit attention to the symbolism, in developing a more flexible organizational style, and in nurturing specialized worship experiences, American religion has become more complex, more internally differentiated, and more adaptable to a complex, differentiated society."[101]

To be sure, some patterns within the Jewish community differ from those of the larger American scene. Denominational institutions appear far more important to Jewish special groups than to their Christian counterparts. Many such groups rely upon funds donated by the denominations. And members of the Jewish special-purpose groups rely heavily upon the religious schools, summer camps, and youth programs of the major denominations for the education of their children. The traditional Jewish emphasis upon education necessitates a different relationship with established synagogues and schools than appears evident among Christian special-purpose groups. But fundamentally, the differentiation described by Wuthnow characterizes Jewish religious life as well and contributes further to the fragmentation of those Jews most engaged in the religious revival.

PART III

The Fragmenting World of Organized Judaism

5

Reform: Change in Both Directions

Changes in patterns of observance and popular religion that swept through the American Jewish community in recent decades have profoundly remade organized religious life. All of the movements of American Judaism have responded to new social and communal challenges, and in turn each movement has been forced to react to the new directions taken by other groups along the religious spectrum. As a result, all four major movements in American Judaism have repositioned themselves in ways that have heightened religious polarization. We begin this section on denominational life with a discussion of the Reform movement, which has introduced some of the boldest changes and thereby challenged all the other movements to respond.

Since the mid-1960s the official positions of the Reform movement regarding a range of religious practices and ideological issues have been shaped by two seemingly contradictory impulses. On the one hand, Reform has sanctioned a number of radical departures from traditional practice: it was the first to ordain women as rabbis and cantors; it steadfastly refused to place sanctions on rabbis who officiated at mixed marriages; and most dramatically, it unilaterally redefined Jewish identity. On the other hand, the Reform movement has reintroduced or signaled its willingness to tolerate many customs that had been rejected in the past: in many temples men don yarmulkes and prayer shawls, kosher meals are prepared, and Hebrew usages have been reinstated. The shift is highlighted by two decisions of the movement's Responsa Committee. In 1955 the committee supported congregations which insisted that Bar Mitzvah and wedding ceremonies be consistent with the ways of Reform Judaism and therefore traditional customs were *not* to be permitted if requested by the celebrating families. In 1979 the same committee stated: "Nothing would . . . hinder us from readopting customs once omitted if a new generation finds them meaningful and useful in its practice of Judaism. . . . We are willing to change in both directions."[1] For much of its history, the Reform movement established limits and did not hesitate to prohibit traditional Jewish practices that it considered outdated. Today, Reform is open to change in both directions—toward a more radical break with traditional practices and toward an unprecedented openness to traditional teachings.

This eclecticism has been made possible by a rethinking of the Reform position. Whereas Reform was formerly a movement that on principle said no to some aspects of Jewish tradition, it is now a movement that is open to all Jewish possibilities, whether traditional or innovative. The guiding principle of Reform today is the autonomy of every individual to choose a Jewish religious expression that is personally meaningful. The result is a Judaism open to all options and therefore appealing to a broad range of Jews—including those who have long felt disenfranchised, such as Jews married to non-Jews and homosexuals. The dilemma this raises for the Reform movement is one of limits, of boundaries. If the autonomy of the individual prevails above all else, what beliefs and practices unite all Reform Jews? Is there a model Reform Jew? And is there anything a Reform Jew can do to place himself or herself beyond the pale of acceptable behavior? Thus far, Reform Judaism has been unable to answer these questions, a remarkable development in a movement that began with very firm negations and affirmations, that stated explicitly in its first platforms which Jewish traditions were to be rejected and which embraced.

THE ABANDONMENT OF IDEOLOGY

Not surprisingly, the issues that have prompted the most intense debate within the Reform movement have revolved around questions of definition and boundary. As we have already seen in chapter 1, the reintroduction of some rituals during the 1950s already engendered debate over the future direction of Reform, with some prominent rabbis expressing their concern that the movement was losing its way and becoming less distinctive. The debate became considerably more vociferous as Reform Judaism instituted several radical new changes during the 1970s. Three issues especially sparked controversy: the introduction of a new prayer book to replace the venerated *Union Prayer Book* that had done service for eighty years; the decision of growing numbers of Reform rabbis to officiate at mixed marriages; and the desire of the movement to produce an updated platform to replace earlier ideological statements. In each case, Reform was torn between respect for the autonomy of the individual and the need to define a clear-cut position. And in each case, the former principle triumphed over the latter, pluralism triumphed over definition.

Toward a New Reform Liturgy

The push to compile a new prayer book for the Reform movement to replace the *Union Prayer Book* (UPB)[2] began in earnest in the 1950s and gained momentum in 1966, when a symposium on liturgy was planned for the journal of the Reform rabbinate. Initially there was much inertial resistance to change: it was argued that the venerable UPB, the Haggadah, and the *Rabbi's Manual* were "properties" of the Central Conference of American Rabbis and ought not to be tampered with. If rabbis felt uncomfortable with parts of these works, the argument went, they could use them with greater selectively. Others, however, contended that the UPB was no longer consonant with the mood of the movement and that an entirely new prayer book, compiled with the cooperation of rabbis, writers, psychiatrists, philosophers, and educators, was needed. Proponents of a new prayer book complained that the UPB was composed in an archaic language and filled with obscure references. The UPB's theological stance, with its heavy emphasis upon the dependence of humans upon an omnipotent God, was unattuned to the contemporary mood. And its prayers were remote from the actual concerns of Reform worshipers.[3]

The movement away from the UPB took tangible form first in the summer camps and youth programs sponsored by the National Federation of Temple Youth. Rejecting the Victorian language of the UPB as well as the formal style of worship, Reform youth developed a creative liturgy movement, which adopted the style and outlook of the 1960s counterculture. As recalled by a participant:

> These services were invariably topical, dealing with the current political and social issues of the day. Guitar was *de rigueur*. Services were in the round. Participants sat on the floor. The services were often leaderless. There was an emphasis on small physical distance between worshipers. It was natural: always done in a circle; relatively short, but expandable, according to the needs of the moment; visual; aromatic; mystical. . . . [The services] expanded the acceptable liturgy. Psalms, Buber, Gibran, and Dylan often freely co-mingled on the mimeographed page.

This "cut-and-paste service" quickly found its way into congregational life; hundreds of Reform temples began in the 1960s to compile informal "creative liturgies" that were distributed in photocopied form. Clearly, pressure was building among rabbis and the laity for a new siddur (prayer book).[4]

This ferment culminated in 1975, with the publication by the Central Conference of American Rabbis (CCAR) of *The New Union Prayerbook*, entitled *Gates of Prayer* (GOP), containing services for "weekdays, Sabbaths, Festivals, and prayers for synagogue and home." Among the innovations of this prayer book were the following: a Hebrew, as well as English, title; a partial attempt to deal with the male-oriented language of earlier liturgies; longer passages in Hebrew and from the traditional liturgy; a heavy emphasis upon Israel and Zion; explicit references to the Holocaust; and—symptomatic of the new mood—the inclusion of ten distinct Friday evening services (as well as a half-dozen Sabbath morning services), which have been described as ranging from "basically Conservative to Reconstructionist, to neo-Hasidic, UPB Reform, to polydox." As a former president of the CCAR noted, within the GOP there coexist both "theistic and non-theistic services."[5] Clearly, these diverse outlooks were included because they could all be found within the Reform movement. But the unwillingness to choose from among them indicates that Reform opted for freedom of choice rather than a clearly defined belief system. Noting the criticism that "only the bookbinder's art could press together so much contradiction between the covers of a single volume," the historian Michael Meyer highlighted the critical issue in *Gates of Prayer:* "The internal dissonance was troublesome only if consistency was judged more valuable than inclusiveness."[6] The Reform movement, that is, opted for an inclusive rather than a theologically consistent prayer book.

Despite its wide, perhaps near universal acceptance by Reform temples, *Gates of Prayer* continues to stir debate within the Reform movement.[7] A symposium held to mark the tenth anniversary of its appearance revealed a range of criticisms: some found it unwieldy because it is so heavy; others viewed it as essentially a rabbi's instrument; still others found it a poor pedagogic tool, since it lacked explanatory notes; and yet others resented its continued use of sexist language in reference to God. But the central controversy revolved around the issue of Reform definition.[8] As one Reform rabbi wrote: the UPB "was torn from my hands by my trustees who insisted that our congregation adopt the new [*Gates of Prayer*]. . . . I am not in sympathy with the new wave of Reform, the *kipa-talit-kashrut-mila-tevila* school which now seems to dominate the movement. I subscribe to the mission idea and the social justice emphasis in conventional Reform."[9] *Gates of Prayer* underscores the departure of Reform from its earlier position, but it does not present a coherent vision of what Reform ideology constitutes today, other than an amalgam of contradictory ideologies within American Judaism.

The Centenary Perspective

The difficulty of defining a Reform outlook was further highlighted when the CCAR tried to draft a new ideological platform on the occasion of its centennial. This new platform was to take its place in a series of rabbinic pronouncements that included the Pittsburgh Platform of 1885 and the Columbus Platform of 1937. The committee empaneled to draft the platform was, however, unable to complete its work in time for the 1973 Centennial of the Union of American Hebrew Congregation (UAHC); indeed, the Centenary Perspective did not appear until 1976.

In his preface to a special issue of the *CCAR Journal* introducing the Centenary Perspective, Rabbi Eugene Borowitz, chairman of the special committee that eventually drafted the statement, outlined some of the ideological differences that impeded progress. He described how, in the wake of the CCAR decision in 1973 urging rabbis to refrain from officiating at mixed marriages, "internal dissension among the rabbis had risen to such a point of intensity that there seemed the possibility of the Reform movement splitting. . . . Ideologically what troubled members of the [CCAR] was the place of freedom in Reform Judaism versus that of discipline." Borowitz went on to describe candidly how the Centenary Perspective was drafted in a deliberate attempt to avoid dissension and focus on commonalities. Three issues were deemed paramount: "1. What is the nature of a Reform Jew's religious obligations? 2. What are our duties to the State of Israel and to the communities in which we live? 3. How do we balance our duties to our people and to humanity at large?" To these were added the question of living with diversity within the Reform movement, "particularly since it seemed to have come to the point of tearing us apart."[10]

The Centenary Perspective responded to the latter issue by turning diversity into a virtue: "Reform does more than tolerate diversity; it engenders it." Thus, it is not a common ideology that unites Reform Jews but rather a "spirit of Reform Jewish beliefs." These include a belief in God, albeit a deity whose role is not clearly defined; an identification with the Jewish people, the bearers of Judaism; and a belief in Torah, which "results from meetings between God and the Jewish people." The chief manner in which these beliefs are acted upon is through the fulfillment of "obligations" that include "daily religious observance." Significantly, the Centenary Perspective qualifies what is meant by obligations: "Within each area of Jewish observance, Reform Jews are called upon to confront the claims of tradition, however differently perceived, and to exercise their individual autonomy, choosing and creating on the basis of commitment and knowledge." Once again, when confronted with the tension between freedom of individual choice and guidelines for belief and practice, the Reform movement opted for the former.

Rabbinic Officiation at Mixed Marriages

The most bitter debate pitting movement discipline against the principle of individual autonomy erupted in 1973, when the Reform rabbinate debated a resolution that urged members of the CCAR to desist from officiating at mixed marriages. The proposed resolution not only reaffirmed the movement's long-standing view "that mixed marriage is contrary to the Jewish tradition and should be discouraged" but also declared its "opposition to participation by its members in any ceremony which solemnizes a mixed marriage." The resolution dictated a course of action to members of the CCAR who dissented from this view, urging them to

1. refrain from officiating at a mixed marriage unless the couple undertakes to study for conversion; 2. refrain from officiating at a mixed marriage for a member of another congregation served by a Conference member unless there has been prior consultation; 3. refrain from co-officiating or sharing with non-Jewish clergy in the solemnization of a mixed marriage; 4. refrain from officiating at a mixed marriage on *Shabbat* or *Yom Tov.*

To give yet further weight to the resolution, the president of the CCAR published an essay in the official journal of the Reform rabbinate entitled, "Enough," a plea to his members to desist from participation in "ecumenical marriages."[11]

The ensuing debate evoked a range of passionately held views. As noted by Alfred Gottschalk, president of Hebrew Union College, the debates "dealt with clerical prerogatives; . . . the principles of Jewish tradition; . . . practices of ethics and points of *Halacha.*" Speaking for rabbis who officiated at mixed marriages, Irwin Fishbein pleaded with his colleagues to recognize that rabbis do not have the power to prevent intermarriage by refusing to sanction such marriages; he urged them "not to slam a door that may be only slightly ajar" by refusing to officiate; and he called upon them to utilize their persuasive, rather than coercive, powers to encourage mixed-married couples to participate in Jewish life and to win them over by exposing them to all that is positive in Judaism. Speaking for CCAR members who supported the resolution, Rabbi Joel Zion portrayed "mixed marriage without prior conversion [as] a serious threat to the survival of the Jewish people." He then raised the issue of drawing the line, describing his decision to enter the rabbinate in order "to lead my people, not to be led by them; to set standards for Jewish survival, not to be set upon by those who seek a convenient answer to a religious problem." "We rabbis are the last bastion in the struggle for Jewish survival," Zion declared. "The time has come for us to announce that our liberalism would go no further when survival is at stake."[12]

When the debate ended, the entire section aimed at rabbis who officiated at mixed marriages was dropped. The resolution as adopted declared its opposition to officiation at mixed marriages but also recognized that members of the CCAR "have held and continue to hold divergent interpretations of Jewish tradition." The principle of individual autonomy prevented the conference from passing a resolution that did anything more than urge "voluntaristic responsiveness to the demands of Jewish law and the needs of the entire people."[13] Yet even this mild attempt at using a "collective voice to exert moral deterrence"[14] prompted over one hundred dissident rabbis to found the Association for a Progressive Reform Judaism in September 1974. Its primary concern was to uphold the right of every Reform rabbi to decide individually whether to officiate at a mixed marriage.[15] The failure to pass the original resolution of 1973 and the splintering of the CCAR in response to the revised resolution further highlight the challenge posed by the Reform movement's embrace of individual autonomy at the expense of movement discipline and coherence.

RELIGIOUS PRACTICES: CHANGE IN BOTH DIRECTIONS

Reform Judaism's commitment to individual autonomy has led to considerable revision in matters of religious policy and practice. Rituals long deemed obsolete by the movement have been reinstated, while other traditional practices that Reform had never openly rejected in the past have now been abandoned. In its attitude toward tradition, the Reform movement is indeed open to change in both directions.

The openness to tradition is striking in a series of major publications issued by the CCAR since the early 1970s. Most of these works are part of a series of volumes whose titles contain the words "Gates of." Several volumes provide liturgies and guidance for the High Holidays, festivals, home observances, and even penitential prayers (*selichot*). Additionally, there is a new Haggadah for Passover and a major new commentary on the Pentateuch. All of these volumes are handsomely produced and contain a goodly amount of Hebrew, as well as commentaries from a range of classical and contemporary Jewish sources. The "Gates of" series is unprecedented as a guide for the Reform laity, teaching in detail about Jewish living, observance, and prayer.[16]

Perhaps the most pioneering volume of all is a work entitled *Gates of Mitzvah: A Guide to the Jewish Life Cycle.* Mitzvah, the book declares, "is the key to authentic Jewish existence and to the sanctification of life. No English equivalent can adequately translate the term. Its root meaning is 'commandment' but *mitzvah* has come to have broader meanings." The book's introduction clarifies the radical departure implicit in a new Reform emphasis upon mitzvah. Formerly the movement had viewed ritual commandments, as opposed to ethical ones, as "optional or even superfluous." But this dichotomy is now rejected, for "the very act of doing a *mitzvah* may lead one to know the heart of the matter. . . . Ritual, as the vehicle for confronting God and Jewish history, can shape and stimulate one's ethical impulses." The volume then surveys a range of observances related to birth, childhood, education, marriage and the Jewish home, and death and mourning. One of the most striking passages deals with Jewish dietary laws: "The fact that *Kashrut* was an essential feature of Jewish life for so many centuries should motivate the Jewish family to study it and to consider whether or not it may enhance the sanctity of their home." Nevertheless, this openness to traditions that had once been declared obsolete is continually qualified by a nondirective approach, summed up by the following disclaimer: "Even within the realm of *mitzvah* various levels of doing and understanding might exist." *Gates of Mitzvah* reaffirms the Reform movement's twin commitments to "Jewish continuity and to personal freedom of choice."[17]

A good deal of the pressure to move toward greater traditionalism has emanated from rabbinical students and some faculty and administrators at various branches of the Hebrew Union College. Much to the displeasure of some senior faculty members, rabbinical students in the 1970s began to don yarmulkes and introduce traditional rituals into their personal observances. Matters came to a head when some students began to lobby for kosher food at the Hebrew Union College to facilitate their observance of the dietary laws. For a brief period, the cafeteria at the Cincinnati branch dispensed food on two separate lines—one for kosher food and the other for nonkosher food. (Subsequently, the alternatives became vegetarian food and non-kosher food.) Two branches of HUC also signaled their greater desire to identify with a more parochial version of Judaism when they opted to refer to their chapels as synagogues.[18] It appears that rabbis ordained in recent years, as well as new faculty members appointed since the mid-1970s with the tacit support of the president of HUC, Alfred Gottschalk, are spearheading the turn to greater traditionalism.[19] As a result, the official periodicals of the movement serve as forums for discussion about the meaning of halakhah, the pertinence of Hasidism, and the need for guidelines for Jewish religious behavior within Reform Judaism.

The renewed interest in traditionalism manifests itself in a variety of ways within Reform temples, which over the past two to three decades have introduced the following: an increased number of readings in Hebrew (which are now spoken with an Israeli, Sephardic pronunciation); an *amidah* prayer, during which congregants are asked to stand; a cantor who serves as a *shaliach tzibur*, as the emissary of the congregation, something that non-Jewish choir members may not do; tolerance of male members who wear yarmulkes; and the near universal Bar and Bat Mitzvah.[20] Moreover, the liturgies employed by many temples reflect the emphasis upon tradition that one finds in the "Gates of" series. According to the most recent survey of congregational practices conducted in 1990 by the Commission of Religious Living of the UAHC, the reappropriation of once abandoned rituals continues: 146 out of 425 responding congregations observed the second day of Rosh Hashanah and close to 60 percent held services on Saturday mornings even when there was no Bar or Bat mitzvah; the same percentage claimed to provide yarmulkes for male worshipers.[21]

Perhaps the most dramatic evidence of the penetration of new ideas into the institutional sphere was the 1985 decision by the Union of American Hebrew Congregations to support the establishment of Reform Jewish day schools. Earlier debates over this subject, beginning in 1969, had produced no such support. But despite vehement opposition and a relatively close vote of 58 percent in favor and 42 percent against, the 1985 motion carried. As of early 1986 there were ten day schools under Reform auspices in North America.[22] The creation of day schools by a movement that had long emphasized universal concerns and steadfastly supported public education as the preferred vehicle represented a significant turn toward Jewish particularism.

These steps toward greater traditionalism have been counterbalanced by several radical departures from earlier Jewish practices. The first such departure occurred in response to the feminist movement. In the late 1960s, HUC began to enroll women in its rabbinical programs, a decision that had already been sanctioned by the CCAR in 1922 but had never been acted upon until the women's movement spurred an interest in the matter. In 1972 Sally Preisand became the first woman to be ordained as a rabbi in North America.[23] Twenty years later, HUC had ordained 195 women in the United States and 1 in Israel.[24] HUC was also the first to invest women as cantors, beginning this in 1975. By the late 1980s the majority of students enrolled in the cantorial programs of the Hebrew Union College were women.[25]

The openness of the Reform movement to women's participation was reflected in synagogue life as well. A survey of "women in the synagogue today" conducted in 1975 found that virtually every Reform congregation included in the survey responded affirmatively when asked whether women participated in the following synagogue activities: being counted in a minyan (a religious quorum), reading *haftarot* (passages from the prophetic and later biblical writings), opening the ark, being called up (having *aliyot*) to the Torah, carrying a Torah on Simchat Torah (a holiday celebrating the Torah), giving a sermon, chanting the service, and chanting *kiddush* and *havdalah* prayers at the onset and conclusion of the Sabbath, respectively. Interestingly, a major variable determining the openness of a Reform temple to women's participation was its age:

> The classical Reform synagogues, which are older, allowed little non-rabbinical participation of any type. The rabbi . . . controlled the service. . . . However, the newer congregations, in moving back toward tradition, have reinstituted Sabbath morning services, including reading from the Torah, thus encouraging more participation by members in general. A by-product of these old-new forms is the availability of honors in the Torah service to women.[26]

A second area of radical departure for Reform concerns the decision to welcome homosexual congregations into the Union of American Hebrew Congregations. The issue first arose in the early 1970s, when Jewish homosexuals began to form synagogues in a number of localities across the nation. The head of the UAHC, Rabbi Alexander Schindler, turned for a responsum to his colleague Solomon Freehof, the most respected ajudicator of Reform Jewish law. Freehof ruled that

"homosexuality is deemed in Jewish law to be a sin. [But] . . . it would
be in direct contravention to Jewish law to keep sinners out of the congregation. To isolate them into a separate congregation and thus
increase their mutual availability is certainly wrong." Despite this ruling against the creation of separate congregations for homosexuals, a
number of Reform rabbis encouraged the formation of homosexual
congregations, by offering their facilities for religious services.[27] In
1977 the UAHC resolved to support and welcome homosexual congregations as affiliates. And in subsequent resolutions it urged the
inclusion of homosexuals in all aspects of congregational life.[28]

The next logical step in this direction was approval of homosexual
rabbis, which occurred in June 1990. The Ad Hoc Committee on
Homosexuality and the Rabbinate of the CCAR urged that "all rabbis,
regardless of sexual orientation, be accorded the opportunity to fulfill
the sacred vocation which they have chosen." It therefore called for
new initiatives to educate congregations because "the unique position
of the rabbi as spiritual leader and Judaic role model makes acceptance
of gay and lesbian rabbis an intensely emotional and potentially divisive issue." The committee also supported the admission of homosexual students to the Hebrew Union College and then to the CCAR
upon ordination. The statement however did include an uncharacter-
istically prescriptive pronouncement that evoked criticism:

> In Jewish tradition heterosexual, monogamous, procreative marriage is
> the ideal human relationship for the perpetuation of the species,
> covenantal fulfillment and the preservation of the Jewish people. While
> acknowledging that there are other human relationships which possess
> ethical and spiritual value and that there are some people for whom
> heterosexual, monogamous, procreative marriage is not a viable option
> or possibility, the majority of the committee reaffirms unequivocally
> the centrality of this ideal and its special status in kiddushin. To the
> extent that sexual orientation is a matter of choice, the majority of the
> committee affirms that heterosexuality is the only appropriate Jewish
> choice for fulfilling one's covenantal obligations.[29]

Not surprisingly, this statement prompted dissent from both ends of
the spectrum. A minority of the committee affirmed "the equal possibility of covenantal fulfillment in homosexual and heterosexual relationships. The relationship, not the gender, should determine its Jewish value—Kiddushin."[30] Lesbian and gay Reform rabbis felt the

resolution did not go far enough in characterizing homosexual and heterosexual relationships as equally sacred.[31] On the other side were Reform rabbis who could not square their movement's position with Jewish tradition. Rabbi Ronald Millstein argued that ordination as a rabbi is not "a civil right, but a title of Jewish honor, which obligates the holder to be an exemplar of Jewish ideals. . . . It takes some exegesis to affirm that a homosexual relationship is reflective of a normative Jewish ideal." Rabbi Philip Bergman opposed the decision on the grounds that "if an individual has a lifestyle that does not reflect the Jewish concept of *mishpacha* [family], that individual cannot be a role model for our people." But proponents of the move agreed with Rabbi Roland Gittelsohn, who argued that "it is a gross injustice, not only to them but to our congregations, to make it difficult for [gay and lesbian Jews] to serve in their professions." Furthermore, it suited the self-image of some Reform leaders to have their movement in the vanguard. Rabbi Peter Knobel noted with pride that "aside from the Unitarians and the Reconstructionists, we are the first religious movement to make this declaration."[32] The decision on homosexual rabbis further enabled the Reform movement to project itself as "the most liberal single religious body in all of American life."[33] It was made possible by the movement's willingness to break with traditional Judaism in a radical fashion as contemporary needs warranted.

Perhaps the most radical departures of the Reform movement in the realm of practice have come in response to the issue of mixed marriage. Reform's preoccupation with this problem stems largely from the high rate of intermarriage among congregants. In response, the movement has deliberately decided to recruit new members from mixed-married couples within the Jewish community. Reform leaders openly acknowledge that as a result of these two trends, within the next few decades over half the families in Reform temples will be intermarried couples and their children.[34] The pages of Reform journals are replete with articles about the unprecedented challenges posed by this vast population. To illustrate their predicament, two Reform rabbis compiled a typical list of challenges posed by their congregants:

1. "You mean that I can remain a member of the congregation but my new wife cannot be a member?";
2. "I was born in this community and I want my children to have the same religious experiences that I had";

3. "My husband is not interested in becoming Jewish but I want him to know and participate in the Temple";

4. "Rabbi, can my wife (not Jewish) bless the candles the night we sponsor the Oneg Shabbat?"[35]

Notwithstanding its openness to mixed-married couples, the Reform movement remains committed to converting the non-Jewish spouse in intermarriages. When the rate of intermarriage began to rise in the 1960s Reform institutions established conversion programs that enrolled thousands of students.[36] And by the early 1980s the movement announced an active outreach program aimed at all non-Jewish spouses married to Jews. Reform has committed itself to a program of winning over mixed-married couples by making the Reform temple hospitable and welcoming, rather than rejecting and coercive.[37]

It was in the context of mixed marriage that the CCAR voted at its annual convention in 1983 to redefine Jewish identity. Rabbinic law has traditionally defined a Jew as someone born to a Jewish mother or someone who has undergone conversion. In its 1983 ruling, the CCAR created new criteria to define Jewishness: that a child has at least one Jewish parent; and that the child's acceptance of Jewish identity must be "established through appropriate and timely public and formal acts of identification with the Jewish faith and people."[38] Interestingly, Jewish identity is no longer automatic for one born to a Jewish mother but now involves some unspecified test of creed as well. In the debate over the resolution, key proponents of the change, such as Rabbi Alexander Schindler, argued that the resolution merely affirmed explicitly practices that had existed on a de facto basis in the Reform movement; that it ameliorated the condition of Jewish fathers who wished to raise their children as Jewish; and that it continued the process of equalizing the status of males and females, since it avoided giving preferential treatment either to Jewish mothers or to Jewish fathers. Opponents of the resolution feared the new definition would turn the Reform movement into a sect, with offspring who would not be acceptable as marriage partners for other Jews. Moreover, they argued, it was a mistake to break so radically with the definitions of identity accepted by the Jewish people; and they feared further attacks upon the status of Reform in Israel. The resolution was adopted on March 15, 1983, and immediately set off protests in the Orthodox and

Conservative communities because of its far-reaching impact on all sectors of the Jewish community.[39]

THE QUESTION OF LIMITS

As it charts its new course in the last decades of the twentieth century, the Reform movement has increasingly been forced to confront the question of limits. One of the leading advocates of the turn to spirituality and of openness to tradition, Rabbi Lawrence Kushner, defines the tradition "as a great banquet table" to which Reform Jews are obligated "to go back again and again." But the Reform movement has steadfastly refused to distinguish the main course from the side dishes. By encouraging each individual Jew to pick and choose from the tradition as he or she sees fit, has the movement abandoned all hope of defining normative behavior? Moreover, the radical departures from Jewish tradition on questions such as homosexuality and patrilineality have prompted some opponents to ask, Is everything under the sun acceptable? Hence, the question of limits has become the most pressing issue confronting movement leaders in the waning years of the twentieth century.[40]

A flash point was reached in the early 1990s, when a congregation espousing Humanistic Judaism applied for membership in the Union of American Hebrew Congregations. Consisting of some two hundred Jewish members, including some quite prominent individuals in the Cincinnati Jewish community, the congregation employed a liturgy that had excised all references to a supernatural power. The challenge posed by this applicant was whether a congregation needed to worship God in order to join the UAHC. In response, Rabbi Alexander Schindler was prompted to wonder aloud at a national convention: "Is there *any* ideology that is beyond the pale of Reform? Just what *is* essential to a Reform outlook, what is optional—and what, if anything, is forbidden?"[41]

The CCAR Committee on Responsa decided that "there are limits, *yesh gevul*. Reform Judaism cannot be everything or it will be nothing." Accordingly, it ruled against admitting the Congregation for Humanistic Judaism into the UAHC. (Despite this ruling, the application was still pending in 1992.) Dissenters, however, fought the decision. Professor Eugene Mihaly of the Hebrew Union College warned that denying membership to the congregation "would undermine the cherished legacy of freedom—the hallmark of Reform Judaism." Rabbi A. Stanley Dreyfus argued for toleration, noting that the movement had always been reluctant to demand adherence to a creed. Arguing in defense of the responsum, Professor Michael A. Meyer noted that "if the presence or absence of God does not qualify as a limit, then faith in God or its absence would be irrelevant to Reform Judaism."[42] Rabbi Gunther Plaut put it succinctly: "Admitting Beth Adam congregation would mean that atheism is a legitimate Reform option."[43]

The question of limits has been raised on a more practical level in congregational life as a result of the Reform policy to reach out to mixed-married couples. Congregations have interpretated this policy in a variety of ways. Some severely restrict any participation of the non-Jewish spouse in the sphere of worship even as they welcome that spouse into the temple. But most Reform temples are far more open. A survey conducted by the Commission on Reform Jewish Outreach found the following: 88 percent of Reform congregations accept the membership of non-Jews as part of a family membership; 62 percent of those congregations permit non-Jews to vote on synagogue matters and 87 percent permit non-Jews to serve on synagogue committees; 27 percent permit non-Jews to serve as officers. In the ritual life of congregations, more than 90 percent permit non-Jews to participate in life-cycle events in some way; 41 percent allow non-Jews to light Sabbath candles in the synagogue. Remarkably, 22 percent allow a non-Jew to have an *aliyah* to the Torah. Most of these decisions were, however, taken in the absence of a written policy on the role of non-Jews in the ritual life of the synagogue.[44] The need to define a clear-cut policy came to a head in the early 1990s, as the extent of non-Jewish participation became public knowledge. When it was revealed, for example, that the copresident of a Reform sisterhood was a church-going Catholic, the National Federation of Temple Sisterhoods restated its long-standing policy that every sisterhood officer must be Jewish. Questions about limits persist as it becomes known that some temples invite non-Jews to play a role in religious services and some Reform congregations permit the performance of mixed marriages in the sanctuary.[45]

As it has repositioned itself, the Reform movement has become more cacophonous, even as it has gained significantly in adherents. Reform

Jews advocate contradictory approaches to Judaism; proponents of Classical Reform vie with champions of spirituality and traditionalism. An advertisement in the *Chicago Tribune* proudly associates Sinai Congregation with Classical Reform and rejects charges that Sabbath services on Sunday constitute assimilation, for it is "assimilation no greater than that practiced by those of our people who worship today as their Eastern European ancestors worshipped." The ad proudly embraces "Classical Reform . . . as the historical, liberal interpretation of our Jewish faith and tradition. . . . We believe in emancipating Judaism from dogma, from superstition, from irrelevant customs; we affirm the very heart of progress and evolution has been a dynamic force in our faith."[46]

On the other end of the spectrum, the late professor Jakob Petuchowski of Hebrew Union College devoted perhaps his last public pronouncement to a scathing critique of the Reform movement for its capitulation to secularism and the political Left. Lamenting the triumph of secularists in Reform temples, he bitterly pronounced as "half-hearted [the] attempts to retrieve a few traditional ceremonies that had been jettisoned in an earlier stage of Reform Judaism's development." Petuchowski saw the new openness to homosexual rabbis and atheistic congregations, as well as the agenda promoted by the Religious Action Center, as "a Jewish form of institutionalized secularism," which had "captured" the Reform movement.[47]

If Petuchowski lamented the absence of true religiosity, his colleague at the Hebrew Union College, Alvin Reines, ridiculed the new Reform flirtation with spirituality, a "Madison Avenue fad word." "I think this kind of attempt to increase supernaturalism among modernist Jews is doomed to failure," Reines wrote. "When someone goes into a deep depression, you do not send them to talk to God. You get them a psychiatrist."[48]

Rabbi Sanford Seltzer announced the virtual demise of Classical Reform, "which in its pristine form no longer exists, although there are variations still practiced in some synagogues throughout the country."[49] And his colleague Rabbi Martin Beifield, representing Classical Reform, castigates the new turn to ritual: "We were never a religion that said, 'If it feels good, run with it.' The purpose of Judaism is to transform the world and its people. It's much easier to light candles and be done with it."[50] Even the decisions on mixed marriages and patrilineality continue to evoke protest and second thoughts: one hundred rabbis, including the heads of HUC-JIR, the UAHC, and the CCAR, issued a statement in December 1985 declaring that there cannot be a Jewish marriage between a Jew and non-Jew, thus rebuking some two hundred colleagues who officiated at mixed marriages.[51] And Alfred Gottschalk, president of Hebrew Union College, offered to reconsider the decision on patrilineality were the Orthodox to accept the legitimacy of Reform rabbis.[52]

Even as it has lost ideological coherence, Reform has surmounted the loss of self-confidence it experienced in the middle decades of the century and has transformed itself into a self-assured movement convinced that it "represents for most Jews the authentically American expression of Judaism."[53] Under a new generation of leaders who assumed executive office since the late 1960s (including Alexander Schindler of the UAHC, Joseph Glaser of the CCAR, and Alfred Gottschalk of HUC), the movement has charted a new course.[54] It has revamped its ideological program and religious practices to broaden its appeal to sectors of the Jewish community that had often felt alienated—feminist women, mixed-married couples, homosexuals, and also Jews within other movements who wished to exercise free choice in defining their Jewish commitments. Reform today is inclusive, reintroducing once abandoned practices while also instituting new ones. Based on such an appealing program, the movement is confident that it will "harvest the demographic trends [within American Jewry] to its own benefit."[55] In their more expansive moods, some leaders express in public their belief that Reform will one day become *the* Judaism of all non-Orthodox Jews in America, encompassing liberal Jews ranging from Classical Reformers to Reconstructionists to Conservative Jews. Rabbi Alexander Schindler expressed the new triumphalism of Reform—and its disdain for other movements—in an address to the CCAR: "Orthodoxy's mass strength was easily confined to the first generation of American Jews, and Conservative Judaism gives evidence of being essentially a second generation phenomenon. The future belongs to us."[56]

Demographic studies suggest that the new direction charted by Reform has already begun to yield results. The movement is growing more rapidly than any other and partially at the expense of its competitors. But within the Reform camp there are some who question whether triumphalism is appropriate at a time when Reform synagogues are "increasingly understood as a place and not a community . . . [as] a religious service station rather than a Jewish center."[57] Others are concerned about the manner in which the movement has sacrificed coherence for pluralism, making Reform unity "institutional and fraternal, rather than theological or ideological."[58] It is too early to assess the long-term consequences of present trends within Reform, but no one can gainsay that it has reformed itself considerably in recent decades.

6

Orthodoxy: Triumphalism on the Right

During the past quarter century two major trends have marked the development of Orthodox Judaism in America. First, Orthodoxy has achieved an unprecedented degree of respectability in the eyes of both non-Orthodox Jews and non-Jews. Where once Orthodoxy had been written off as a movement of immigrants and poor Jews, it is now regarded as a movement with staying power and appeal to Jews from across the religious spectrum. As the sociologist Charles Liebman has noted, "This is the first generation in over 200 years—that is, since its formulation as the effort by traditional Judaism to confront modernity—in which Orthodoxy is not in decline."[1] Even though Orthodoxy is not growing numerically, its comparative stability, particularly as measured by the ability to inculcate a strong sense of allegiance among its young, has given the movement significant credibility and dynamism. Indeed, the movement's programs, particularly with regard to youth, are being increasingly imitated by other denominations.

The second trend that characterizes Orthodoxy is the shift to the right in the thinking and behavior of Orthodox Jews. Orthodox Jews today observe ritual commandments more punctiliously than they did at midcentury; they regard rabbinic authorities who adjudicate Jewish law conservatively as more authoritative than their more liberal counterparts; and in their attitudes toward non-Orthodox Jews, they tend to be more exclusive than before. Both the emergence of a stronger Orthodoxy and the movement's shift to the right have reshaped relations between Orthodox and non-Orthodox Jews.

It is not accidental that both of these patterns have developed in an American environment that has witnessed the reemergence of conservative Christian groups as powerful social and political blocs. American society since the 1960s has become considerably more hospitable to religious groups that offer a firm anchor during times of social upheaval: the certitudes offered by religiously conservative groups draw admiration in a society buffeted by change and cultural relativism. Moreover, as American society has become more diversified and increasingly respectful of expressive individualism, it paradoxically has more tolerance for groups that separate themselves religiously— including those groups that reject the value of pluralism. As we discuss the remarkable achievements of Orthodoxy in recent decades, we need to bear in mind these larger social and religious transformations without which Orthodox advances would have been far more difficult.

PROBLEMS OF DEFINITION

Considerable difficulties inhere in any discussion of the Orthodox world.[2] Like their counterparts in other religious movements, Orthodox Jews do not share a single clearly articulated theology, let alone movement ideology. All movements in American Judaism contain within them a broad range of views that are granted legitimacy and a fair hearing. Where Orthodoxy differs as a movement is in the degree of intolerance displayed by different sectors of the same movement toward each other. This is evident in the expressions of dismay that modern Orthodox Jews voice about "the black hats"—more right-wing Orthodox types—moving into their neighborhoods.[3] Even within the Orthodox right, there have been pitched battles between adherents of different Hasidic sects.[4] And when it comes to matters of ideology, more right-wing Orthodox groups consistently delegitimate the authority of more moderate Orthodox rabbis. Thus, ultra-Orthodox Jews may accept Modern Orthodox Jews as observers of the commandments—and therefore as superior to non-Orthodox Jews—but they do not accord Modern Orthodox rabbis the right to interpret religious law.[5] And the right-wing Orthodox press, while contemptuous of almost all Jews, reserves its greatest scorn for the policies of moderate Orthodox groups.[6] Despite the far-reaching disagreements within each of the other branches of Judaism, similar delegitimization does not exist. The student of Orthodoxy is thus faced with the question of whether Orthodoxy can be viewed as a coherent and united movement at all.

Further, Orthodoxy is institutionally fragmented in a manner not paralleled within the other movements. Whereas Reform, Reconstructionist, and Conservative Judaism have within them a single organization of congregations, a single rabbinic organization, and a single institution for the training of rabbis, Orthodoxy has a multiplicity of organizations for each purpose.[7] Such institutional diffusion has apparently not hindered Orthodoxy, but this has created difficulties for the students of Orthodox life—particularly in determining who speaks for it. There are many conflicting voices.

The issue of authority is more complicated in Orthodoxy than in any other denomination. In some ways, Orthodox Jews are the most likely to accept the opinion of a rabbi as authoritative on questions of Jewish living. Indeed, some Orthodox Jews surrender a considerable amount of their autonomy to rabbis, to the point of trusting their sages to make decisions for them on sensitive financial and professional matters, and even on personal family questions, such as whom to marry and how many children to bring into the world. At the same time, Orthodox Jews are less dependent on a rabbinic elite to guide their fortunes than are those in other denominations. Pulpit rabbis have less status in the Orthodox world than in any other segment of the Jewish community, and most Orthodox institutions rely heavily on lay rather than rabbinic leadership. For this reason, many of the most important developments within Orthodoxy that we will discuss are not traceable to any elite institution or to the pronouncements of any particular rabbi.

A useful way to categorize Orthodox Jews was put forward by Charles Liebman. In his pioneering study, he differentiated between the "uncommitted Orthodox," the "modern Orthodox," and the "sectarian Orthodox." The first were East European immigrants who, out of inertia rather than religious choice, identified as Orthodox, or they were individuals who had no particular commitment to Jewish law but preferred to pray in an Orthodox synagogue. The modern Orthodox "seek to demonstrate the viability of the *halakha* for contemporary life . . . [and also] emphasize what they have in common with all other Jews rather than what separates them." The sectarians are disciples of either *roshei yeshiva* (heads of yeshivas) or Hasidic rebbes, whose strategy it is to isolate their followers from non-Orthodox influences.[8] Liebman underscored the deep divisions among Orthodox Jews regarding the proper way to respond to non-Orthodox coreligionists.

Since Liebman developed this scheme, the fortunes of these groupings have shifted and the sectarians have gained ground, particularly because they have fought against accommodation to modern culture. The sociologist Lynn Davidman captures an essential difference in the approaches of modern and traditional types of Orthodox Jews when she describes their approach to modernity:

In order to convince the urban, professional newcomers to the [modern Orthodox] synagogue of the validity of a religious world view requiring obedience to received tradition and strong allegiance to community, the rabbis emphasize its compatibility with the dominant individualism of the secular culture. They blend the need for adherence to religious law with an affirmation of modern subjectivism by asserting that Orthodoxy enhances people's individuality.

By contrast, in the more traditional setting, such as a Lubavitch yeshiva for women,

the Lubavitch actually attempt to reverse the prevailing rationality of modern Western culture. They reassert the primacy of traditional religious world views, and their teachings emphasize the importance of God in the religious system of belief. . . . The teachers here are not interested in providing rationales because they do not want to communicate that they are selling a product to a consumer who is free to accept on the basis of an evaluation of its benefits.

The critical fissure, then, is between Orthodox Jews who accommodate to modernity and those who resist it. The former "negotiate a means of existence . . . to incorporate modern conceptions of pluralism, rationalism, and feminism," whereas the latter "represent an attempt to *resist* the dominant culture and offer a radical alternative to it."[9] The lines between these two groupings sometimes blur and the resisters choose their issues carefully rather than condemn modern culture in a blanket fashion. But the broad categories utilized by

Davidman help define what Orthodox Jews themselves refer to as the "right" and "left" of their grouping.[10]

Since most academic observers of Orthodoxy come from the centrist or left wings, it is instructive to conclude our discussion of definitional issues with the analysis of a defender of the right. Rabbi Aryeh Z. Ginzberg "identified the basic areas of outlook in which the 'right' differs from the 'left'" as follows:

> Whether taking secular ideas into one's formulation of Jewish thought will corrupt or contribute to a correct understanding of Judaism; whether Zionism as conceived in today's Jewish world should be deemed as a secular national-political aspiration or as a major aspect of one's religious *Weltanschauung;* whether coming to an accommodation with Reform and Conservative religious movements constitutes a compromise of Orthodox principles. Another question—whether adopting aspects of the feminist movement distorts the true Jewish outlook.[11]

From the perspective of the right, these ideological differences are paramount—and nonnegotiable.

ORTHODOXY'S NEWFOUND SELF-CONFIDENCE

All of the major groups within the Orthodox camp have participated in an unprecedented revival during the past two decades. This revival may be measured by numerous changes.

Orthodox Jews have entered the public arena confident that their display of distinctive religious behaviors will not hinder their economic and social mobility. Whereas at midcentury Orthodox Jews who wished to advance in non-Jewish environments believed it necessary to blend in, by the 1970s and 1980s male Orthodox students and professionals had taken to wearing a yarmulke on university campuses, in law offices, on hospital wards, and in some cases even in state and municipal legislatures. (Their female counterparts may also be identified by distinctive, though less obtrusive, items of dress, such as the modest garb of some Orthodox women and special hair coverings.) Orthodox Jews in recent decades have also demanded of their employers the right to leave their jobs early on Friday afternoons when the Sabbath begins early, as well as the right to absent themselves on religious holidays. In fact, a legal defense agency, the Commission on Law and Public Action (COLPA), was founded by Orthodox attorneys precisely to pressure employers to comply with the needs of Orthodox employees. It is now assumed by Orthodox Jews that observance of Jewish traditions ought not to limit one's professional opportunities.[12]

Orthodox Jews actively engage in the American political process to further their own aims. In this regard, the most right-wing sects have been especially adept at exploiting political opportunities. It has now become routine in New York politics for local and even national politicians to pay court to Hasidic rebbes. What is less well known is the sophisticated lobbying effort that won for Hasidic groups the status of a "disadvantaged group," with the attendant entitlement to special federal funds.[13] It is symptomatic of Orthodoxy's political activism and self-assertion that eight Orthodox groups banded together in 1988 to form the Orthodox Jewish Political Coalition to lobby in Washington, D.C.[14]

Orthodox groups have taken advantage of new technologies to facilitate religious observance. The revolution in food manufacturing and the proliferation of processed foods made it possible for Orthodox Jews to arrange for kosher certification, a stamp of approval that many manufacturers regard as a means of increasing their market share among observant Jews and even among non-Jews who deem such certification as evidence of a product's high quality. According to one report, there were sixteen thousand products with kosher certification in the late 1980s, compared with only one thousand a decade earlier.[15] Advances in food technology have also made it possible to produce new kinds of kosher products, such as frozen challah dough (for the Sabbath bread), ersatz crab meat, *pareve* (nondairy) icecream and cheesecake, and high-quality kosher wines. Technology has also been harnessed to create a new institution in American Jewish life—the "*eruv* community." Beginning in the 1970s dozens of Orthodox synagogues negotiated the rights to string wire on existing telephone poles in order to delimit their geographic enclaves, a legal fiction that created private domains in which carrying items and pushing strollers are permissible on the Sabbath.[16] There is no doubt that by making religious observance easier, the *eruv* community and the broad array of kosher products have rendered Orthodoxy that much more attractive.

Orthodox Jews have also employed new media technologies to disseminate their versions of Judaism. Interestingly, one of the first Jewish groups to utilize cable television technology was the Lubavitch movement, which televises the speeches of its rebbe, Rabbi Menachem

M. Schneerson, from Lubavitch headquarters in Crown Heights, Brooklyn, throughout the world. The Lubavitch movement publishes the *Moshiach Times: The Magazine for Children* in comic-book format.[17] And in areas of dense Orthodox concentration, Jewish organizations and private entrepreneurs have created Torah Tape Libraries, audio-cassettes on "subjects ranging from the study of traditional texts to sermons and expositions of the Orthodox *hashkafa* [worldview] on contemporary issues."[18] More significantly, Orthodox publishing houses have produced a vast array of religious literature. Mesorah Publications, with its Artscroll series, is arguably the largest publisher of Jewish books today. Beginning with its first volume, *The Megillah: The Book of Esther* and continuing with the *Complete Siddur* and High Holiday prayer book, many of the books published by this private firm have sold over one hundred thousand copies. Its hagiographic biography of Rabbi Moshe Feinstein was an immediate best-seller.[19] Significantly, this publishing house is identified with right-wing Orthodoxy. Its Bible commentaries and volumes on Jewish history give no credence to modern, critical scholarship.[20] Nonetheless, Artscroll books, according to the firm's publisher, are purchased by readers spanning the spectrum from "Kollel families" to "Conservodox."[21]

Orthodox Jews have established a wide range of vibrant institutions for the socialization of their youth and the maintenance of identity among adults. We shall yet discuss the profound impact of the day-school movement and Orthodox synagogues. But in this context, less formal institutions are worth noting. In a few large cities where Orthodox Jews are most densely concentrated, such as New York, Miami, and Los Angeles, they have opened pizza parlors, Chinese and Italian restaurants, vegetarian emporia, and fast-food chains serving burgers and frankfurters—all kosher. Entrepreneurs in New York even launched a kosher cruise ship, dubbed the "Glatt Yacht," which circled Manhattan on summer nights; elsewhere in Manhattan one can find entertainment at a "Kosher Komedy Klub."[22] These establishments further attest to the efforts of Orthodox Jews across the spectrum to harness food technology and adapt to American food tastes while remaining observant. Equally important, these establishments are important social institutions: kosher pizza parlors serve as hangouts, particularly for Orthodox adolescents, much as do their nonkosher counterparts; and fancier restaurants cater to adult Orthodox Jews. These institutions not only enable Orthodox Jews to partake of the good life, eat the types of foods favored by their American neighbors, and participate in the trend among the upwardly mobile to "eat out" rather than at home, but they also help reinforce the cohesion and solidarity of the Orthodox group. Orthodox Jews maintain a wide range of institutions aside from the synagogue to keep the individual within a tight-knit community.

Even as some Orthodox Jews have made their way into key institutions of American industry, politics, and culture, others have moved to cut themselves off from the surrounding society. While some Orthodox Jews have insisted that American society accept them within its elite institutions as Orthodox Jews, others have insisted on their right to segregate themselves. Beginning in the 1960s a few Hasidic groups embarked on land-purchase programs in areas of rural New York State, with the avowed intention of incorporating themselves as separate villages designed solely for adherents of their own group.[23] It is possible to view such communities as attempts to escape from America, but they may also be seen as a further indication that Orthodox Jews insist on living in America on their own terms: the separatists are secure enough about their acceptance to turn their backs on the larger society.

Orthodox Jews have become so certain that their version of Judaism is the only correct interpretation and the only avenue of Jewish survival that they have launched programs to help other Jews "return" to Judaism, that is, become Orthodox Jews. The pioneers in this endeavor have been Lubavitch Hasidim, who amidst much ballyhoo in the general media launched their "mitzvah mobiles" in the early 1970s.[24] Stationing themselves in public areas and on university campuses in boldly marked trucks, disciples of Rabbi Schneerson met with non-Orthodox Jews for the avowed purpose of convincing them to increase their levels of observance. As the Lubavitch movement and other Orthodox groups succeeded in wooing Jews from non-Orthodox backgrounds to their way of life, the organized Jewish community took note, particularly the non-Orthodox movements that had sustained "defections." It is hard to gauge exactly how many non-Orthodox Jews turned to Orthodoxy as so-called *baalei teshuvah* (literally, "masters of return"). According to Herbert Danzger, an authority on the phenomenon, nearly one-quarter of all Orthodox Jews in New York are more observant than their parents and hence may be considered *baalei teshuvah;* several hundred males from non-Orthodox backgrounds currently study in outreach programs sponsored by Yeshiva University, the Lubavitch movement, and yeshivas in the United States and Israel. Danzger sees the *baalei teshuvah* transforming Orthodoxy into a movement of choice, rather than of birth.[25] Still, it is too early to assess the long-term impact of *baalei teshuvah* on the Orthodox world. In the short term, however, the very phenomenon of nonobservant Jews turning to Orthodoxy has raised the movement's self-esteem and increased its prestige in the broader American Jewish community.

To a greater extent than any other movement, Orthodoxy has been able to project itself as a movement that attracts young people. On an average Sabbath, many Orthodox synagogues are teeming with young parents and their children. At parades and other public displays, Orthodox groups marshal vast numbers of young people. And through their network of day schools, youth programs, and summer camps, Orthodox organizations have created social environments for their children to interact with like-minded young Jews. The success of these programs is enhanced by the perception of many in other Jewish religious movements that their own youth are not sufficiently integrated into Jewish communal activities.

Orthodox Jews have assumed unprecedented positions of power and influence within the organized Jewish community. Since the mid-1970s individual Orthodox Jews have risen to leading administrative posts in the Council of Jewish Federations, the American Jewish Committee, the American Jewish Congress, the Conference of Presidents of Major Jewish Organizations, the World Jewish Congress, and a range of local federations and other Jewish agencies. Their presence is symptomatic of a shift in priorities of these organizations to what have been deemed "survivalist issues" and away from the traditional "integrationist" agendas. In turn, these officials have spurred organizations to a further rethinking of their priorities. By insisting on assuming their rightful place within organized Jewish life, Orthodox Jews as individuals have also moved organizations to meet the minimal religious needs of observant Jews: providing kosher food at Jewish communal events; not conducting business on the Sabbath or religious holidays; and providing the opportunity for public prayer.[26]

Orthodoxy has been the beneficiary of much media coverage and has learned to exploit such coverage. Unlike earlier coverage of some Hasidic sects in the general American press, which focused on their exoticism, more recent reports have emphasized the warm communal spirit and decent values promoted by the Orthodox world. Non-Orthodox Jewish writers, themselves often searching for rootedness and meaning, have rhapsodized over the world of Orthodoxy. And the Orthodox, in turn, have cooperated in such ventures. It was a telling sign of the new perspective that a non-Orthodox Jewish woman on the staff of the *New Yorker* was given entrée to the Lubavitch community of Crown Heights to carry out research for a series of articles. Not only could her positive portrait not have been published in such a periodical earlier in the century, but it is doubtful that an Orthodox group would have been receptive to such an inquiry, let alone to a woman reporter, in a previous period.[27] Positive media coverage of this sort provides further evidence of Orthodoxy's new respectability and in turn increases the movement's self-confidence.

WHY THE REVIVAL?

How do we account for Orthodoxy's impressive rebound in recent decades? Perhaps the key to Orthodox success has been its educational institutions. As noted above, Orthodoxy began to invest heavily in all-day religious schools at midcentury. In 1940 there were only thirty-five Jewish day schools in the United States, scattered in seven different communities, but principally located in the metropolitan New York area. Within the next five years the number doubled, and day schools could be found in thirty-one communities. The postwar era witnessed an even more impressive surge: by 1975 there were a total of 425 day schools, including 138 high schools, with a total enrollment of 82,200 scattered in 160 different communities. It is estimated that approximately 80 percent of all Orthodox children were enrolled in day schools by the 1980s, a percentage that is still growing.[28]

Day schools serve as the Orthodox community's key instrument of formal education and socialization. With at least half of each day devoted to Jewish studies, these schools have the time to teach students both the skills necessary for praying and for studying Jewish texts in their original Hebrew or Aramaic, and also the proper observance of rituals. Equally important, day schools are an environment that fosters a strong attachment to the Orthodox group: they prescribe proper religious behavior and impart strong ideological indoctrination; and they create an all-encompassing social environment where lifelong friendships are made. According to one study of a leading Orthodox day school, even students from non-Orthodox homes developed a strong allegiance to Orthodoxy due to their ongoing exposure to the school's programs. Moreover, the majority of students were as religiously observant or even more so than their parents.[29] The day-school movement has transformed American Orthodoxy by providing a generation of baby-boom children with an intense educational and social experience that has won them over to Orthodoxy and rendered them more observant and Jewishly more knowledgeable than their parents' generation.[30] At midcentury the proliferation of day schools was effecting a quiet revolution that few contemporaries noticed; by the 1970s and 1980s Orthodoxy began to reap the benefits of its educational investments.

Complementing the day-school movement is a series of other institutions designed to socialize the younger generation of Orthodox Jews. Orthodox synagogues of various stripes have introduced separate religious services led by young people for their peers, as well as a range of social, educational, and recreational programs to provide an Orthodox environment outside of school. In addition, Orthodox groups have invested heavily in summer camps that provide an all-embracing Orthodox experience. Beyond that, Orthodox teenagers typically spend some time in Israel, again in an Orthodox ambience. According to one estimate, two-thirds of Orthodox versus only 15 percent of non-Orthodox adolescents had been to Israel.[31] Orthodox Jews thus provided a range of supplements to the day school that involved youths in interconnected programs. Each reinforced the other's educational goals and embraced young people in ongoing Jewish living.

A second factor in the revitalization of Orthodoxy was the participation of Orthodox Jews in the postwar economic boom, which brought unparalleled affluence to Americans. By the mid-1960s Orthodox Jews were no longer necessarily the poorest sector of American Jewry, as they had been for the most part in earlier decades. Like their counterparts in other movements, increasing numbers of Orthodox Jews earned college and graduate degrees and entered the professions. These occupations freed Jews from the need to work on the Sabbath, thereby eliminating a conflict between economic necessity and religious commandments that had bedeviled tradition-minded Jews in earlier periods. Moreover, with their higher incomes, Orthodox Jews were able to join the general exodus to new neighborhoods and became avid consumers of Orthodox goods and services. Thanks to their newfound affluence, Orthodox Jews could afford to send their offspring to day schools from kindergarten through high school and also provide them with summer camps and trips to Israel. In general, Orthodox Jews were able to partake fully of American life even while adhering to traditional observance. The link between religious traditionalism and poverty and the backward ways of the Old World had been broken.[32]

An important consequence of this new affluence was that it enabled Orthodox Jews to insulate themselves more effectively from the rest of the Jewish community. With their host of synagogues, day schools, recreational programs, journals, restaurants, summer camps, and so forth, Orthodox Jews, in their largest centers of concentration, can live in separate communities that rarely interact with the larger Jewish populace. Even within the structures of existing communities, Orthodox Jews have managed to obtain the right to separate programs geared to their own needs. Jewish communal organizations set aside special resources that are tacitly understood to be for the exclusive use of Orthodox Jews.[33] Living in separate countercommunities that insulate them from the larger Jewish community helps foster an élan among Orthodox Jews and a belief, particularly among the youth, that they are the saving remnant of American Judaism.

Third, a series of developments within the broader American environment has given an important boost to Orthodoxy. Particularly during the 1960s and 1970s, when experimentation and rebellion were given free rein within American society, those who were repelled by the new social mores found solace in the stability of Orthodoxy. More recently, the comparatively lower rate of divorce and substance abuse within Orthodox families has led adherents, as well as outsiders, to perceive Orthodox Judaism as a bulwark of family stability.[34] In short, the chaotic course charted by American society has made the relative serenity of Orthodoxy appealing. At the same time, the neutrality of American culture has made it possible for Jews to identify with Orthodoxy without having to defend their distinctive ways. As Charles Liebman has noted, "The very absence of rigid ideational and cultural structures which characterizes modernity, the undermining of overarching moral visions and the celebration of plural beliefs and styles of life, invite culturally deviant movements."[35]

Finally, Orthodoxy has achieved increased stability in recent decades because it has policed its own community more rigorously and has defined its boundaries more sharply. Where once a great range of religious behaviors was tolerated and the movement contained a vast population of nominal adherents, Orthodox Jews today are far less tolerant of deviance. Far more than any other movement in American Judaism, Orthodoxy in its various permutations has set limits and defined acceptable and nonacceptable behavior. And more often than in any other Jewish environment, individuals in an Orthodox setting are likely to be asked to leave a synagogue or suffer ostracism for dressing inappropriately or transgressing a religious prohibition. This has a twofold psychological impact: first, it attracts individuals who prefer explicit guidelines for proper behavior to the burden of autonomy that is the lot of modern individuals; and second, it sharpens the group's boundaries, thereby providing adherents with a strong feeling of community and belonging.[36]

THE SHIFT TO THE RIGHT

More rigorous self-policing is but one manifestation of Orthodoxy's shift to the right, a shift expressed in changed behavioral norms, political judgments, educational preferences, choice of leaders, and attitudes toward Western culture and non-Orthodox coreligionists. The move to the right has transformed the nature of such formerly Modern Orthodox institutions as the Young Israel movement, once the vanguard of American Orthodoxy, and pushed them quite close to the strictly Orthodox Agudath Israel.[37] It has led to the veneration of right-wing yeshiva heads who seek to insulate their disciples from Western modes of thought and torpedo efforts at cooperation between Orthodox and non-Orthodox groups. And it has demoralized rabbis who formerly spoke for Modern Orthodoxy. According to one of the intellectuals fighting to create a "truly Modern Orthodoxy," there are optimists and pessimists concerning the viability of such an effort: "The latter think that the modern Orthodox have already lost the battle of determining the future of the American Orthodox community to the traditionalists; the optimists, while acutely aware of the stark reality that the modern Orthodox may be losing the battle, nevertheless maintain . . . that the battle is not yet irretrievably lost." [38]

One telling piece of evidence attesting to the ascendancy of the

Orthodox right is the virtual disappearance of the term "Modern Orthodoxy." As Rabbi Walter Wurzburger, its champion, observed, "The mere fact that the term 'Modern Orthodoxy' is no longer in vogue and has been replaced by an expression ['Centrist Orthodoxy'] that deliberately avoids any reference to modernity speaks volumes."[39] This is not to suggest that Orthodox Jews do not live in the modern world. They most emphatically do, but their attitude toward that world has changed. Few Orthodox spokesmen any longer articulate the undergirding assumption of Modern Orthodoxy, namely, that a synthesis of traditional Judaism and modern Western culture is not only feasible but desirable. The thought of the leading ideologue of modern Orthodoxy in the nineteenth century, Rabbi Samson Raphael Hirsch, is now reinterpreted by his disciples as having urged *Torah im Derekh Eretz*, a synthesis of traditional Judaism and Western culture, as merely a *temporary* solution to the pressing needs of the day; now, it is argued, such a goal is no longer desirable.[40]

The retreat from an ideology of synthesis is evident at Yeshiva University, formerly the fountainhead of Modern Orthodoxy. The altered spirit was evident already by 1980, when the registrar of Yeshiva's Rabbi Isaac Elchanan Theological Seminary compared the present cohort of rabbinical students with their predecessors of the mid-1960s: "Things are entirely different. . . . [T]heir whole outlook, sexual, religious, anti-college except in the narrowest, most utilitarian sense, is completely different from what it used to be. We have moved way to the right."[41] The shift is also apparent at Yeshiva College. In the mid-1980s the undergraduate student newspaper published a symposium entitled "Why Do [Yeshiva Men] Attend College?" As noted by the editor, this question should never have been raised at a college that had functioned for decades with the motto *Tora U'Mada* (Torah and Science), but "Yeshiva's motto does not offer a simple solution to this complex issue." In fact, one of the symposiasts, an American-trained Talmudist, argued that "secular pursuits . . . for their own sake are dangerous on many grounds," particularly because they may not aid in "developing one's self Jewishly." Exposure to non-Jewish art, literature, and thought is deemed either a threat to Jewish belief or a frivolous departure from what is ultimately important—knowledge of the Torah.[42] Thus, even within the walls of Yeshiva University, the insular views of the Orthodox right have made significant inroads.

The shift is also evident in the declining authority of Yeshiva University's rabbinic alumni. *Tradition*, the journal established to represent the point of view of the Modern—now centrist—Orthodox rabbis, gives voice to a rabbinic establishment under siege from elements on the Orthodox right.[43] Writers frequently lament their lack of recognition by their own flock, let alone by Orthodox Jews further to the right. Virtually all contemporary *gedolim* (recognized rabbinic authorities within the Orthodox world) identify with right-wing Orthodoxy, and their views are rarely challenged.[44] Some insiders see this state of affairs as stemming from a failure to produce adjudicators of rabbinic law who have a Modern Orthodox outlook.[45] Others believe that modern Orthodox leaders simply cannot compete with the charisma of traditionalist leaders, who, as products of European yeshivas, are deemed more authentic than American-trained rabbis and seem uncompromised by any accommodation to modernity.[46] Yet others focus less on individuals than on ideology, noting the inability of Modern Orthodox rabbis to confront the right and counter its message with a coherent program for Modern Orthodox living.[47]

The weakness of the Modern Orthodox rabbinate is underscored by its reliance on the Orthodox right for its official prayer book. Rather than commission one of its own members to prepare an authorized prayer book, as it had done in the past, the Rabbinical Council of America (RCA) has utilized *The Complete Artscroll Siddur*, a product of the rightist yeshiva world. For its edition of this siddur the RCA added only one substantive modification—the Prayer for the State of Israel, which the Artscroll editors understandably had omitted given their non-Zionist, pro-Agudath Israel ideology. There is no small irony in the fact that the RCA thus commissioned its opponents in the Orthodox world—traditionalists who do not accept the legitimacy of centrist Orthodox rabbis—to provide its official prayer book.[48] The pulpit rabbis of centrist Orthodoxy face not only delegitimation but also a growing rate of attrition within their congregations. Younger members are increasingly attracted to small, informal synagogues (*shtieblach*) or early (*hashkomah*) services within established synagogues. In either event they separate themselves from the larger congregation. Writing in the mid-1970s, Rabbi Steven Riskin, arguably the most charismatic figure within the Modern Orthodox rabbinate, noted that inroads by Lubavitch and right-wing yeshivas resulted in "the draw[ing] off from the Modern Orthodox shul of many of the young yeshiva graduates, much to the chagrin of the local *Rav* [pulpit rabbi] who has tailored his sermons and rabbinic style to the tastes of the 'young people.'"[49]

Even within centrist Orthodox institutions, one sees a palpable shift to the right. One of the harbingers of change was the elimination of mixed social dancing at synagogue functions. Whereas in the mid-1950s it was commonplace for Modern Orthodox synagogues, especially Young Israel congregations, to hold square dances for their youth and social dancing at banquets, such activities are now banned by Orthodox synagogues.[50] The question of mixed dancing received national prominence in 1990, when the agency certifying *kashrut* on the Glatt Yacht, a ship that circumnavigated Manhattan while patrons dined on strictly kosher meals, withdrew its certification—not for any dietary improprieties but because the ship permitted couples to dance together. As the head of the certifying company conceded, many Orthodox synagogues in the past had allowed social dancing, but now "when we certify an establishment as kosher, it must meet all regulations of Jewish law, including the entertainment."[51] Centrist Orthodox synagogues are also far more apt today to demand punctilious observance as a prerequisite for leadership within the congregation, let alone for service as a *shaliach tzibur* (prayer leader). There is less tolerance today for members who are only nominally Orthodox. Not surprisingly, formerly Modern Orthodox day schools are also moving to the right, as evidenced by curricular revisions that downgrade the study of Hebrew language and literature, as well as the erosion of coeducation. Whereas Modern Orthodox day schools formerly separated the sexes around the age of puberty, they now tend to separate boys and girls in the third grade or even earlier. The new tenor is summed up in the somewhat self-mocking, somewhat bitter jokes about Orthodoxy's "*Chumrah*-of-the-Month Club," as growing numbers of Orthodox Jews accept the need for more and greater stringencies.[52]

WHY IS THE RIGHT GAINING STRENGTH?

In light of the increased acculturation, upward mobility, and Americanization of Orthodox Jews, how is the move to the right to be explained? One would have expected to the contrary, that as more Orthodox Jews attained a high level of secular education and entered the professions, they would move in the direction of "synthesis" rather than insularity. Why, then, has the right made such deep inroads in the larger Orthodox community?

The answer lies with the day-school movement. Just as it is the most significant factor in the revival of Orthodoxy, it also is the key to understanding the rightward shift of Orthodoxy. Put simply, many of the personnel that serve as teachers and even principals of Judaic studies in the day-school network are products of the yeshiva world, a conglomeration of academies for higher rabbinic studies established by East European refugees from Nazism who attempted to re-create Lithuanian-style yeshivas on American soil. Graduates of these institutions, as well as followers of the Lubavitcher Rebbe, another exemplar of right-wing Orthodoxy, constitute the main pool of educators for Orthodox Jewish day schools. By contrast, few graduates of Yeshiva University's rabbinical program enter the relatively poorly paying field of Jewish education. (Indeed, most do not even enter the practicing rabbinate.) As teachers of Jewish subjects in day schools, the products of the yeshiva world have imposed their worldview upon the schools and their youthful charges. It is hence not surprising that they have conveyed a reverence for their mentors, the *roshei yeshiva* (the heads of the yeshiva world), and a corresponding contempt for the pulpit rabbis who are in the main products of Yeshiva University.[53] It is also not surprising that these educators have imparted their understanding of Jewish learning to their students—an approach based on the insularity of the yeshiva world, which rejects modern critical scholarship and does not expect its graduates to have a university education. Products of the Orthodox right also disseminate the yeshiva world's pro-Agudah, non-Zionist attitudes to their young charges, a factor that has led to the eclipse of the B'nai Akiva youth movement.[54] And finally, these teachers have taught their disciples how to study rabbinic texts rigorously and observe Jewish law punctiliously. The right has triumphed because during the quiet revolution in Orthodox education that marked the middle decades of the century, it controlled the education of youngsters from Modern Orthodox homes and made sure that they were better educated and more rigorously observant than their parents.

In creating this quiet revolution, the yeshiva world transformed itself from a formerly elite coterie into a movement designed to win the allegiance of the Orthodox masses. Put differently, the elite religion of the yeshiva world has triumphed over the folk religion of American Orthodoxy: to be part of the Orthodox community today increasingly requires a sophisticated knowledge of rabbinic texts and the acceptance of the ideology of the right.[55] This has been achieved by elevating the yeshiva world and its leaders to a position of authority and by downgrading the role of the local pulpit rabbis. Moreover, the elite religion of Orthodoxy is now defined by rabbis who inhabit the insular world of the yeshiva, rather than by communal rabbis who are in touch with "Jews in the street."[56]

A number of other factors have also facilitated Orthodoxy's move to the right. Within some sectors of the more acculturated Orthodox community, a kind of "discount theory of Judaism" prevails. This theory has been described by Lawrence Kaplan as follows: since " 'more is better'—for the children, that is (they'll lose some of it later, or so the theory goes)—and since their conception of Judaism is the traditional Orthodox one, for them it is the traditional Orthodox yeshivot that represent the 'more.'" Many highly acculturated Orthodox parents fear that their children will join the slide to assimilation that characterizes so much of American Jewish life. They therefore expose their children in school to a Judaism that is far to the right of their own thinking in the hopes that even if their children move away from religious observance, they will at least end up near Modern Orthodoxy.[57]

Beyond these calculations, certain environmental factors have also favored the Orthodox right. One is the prosperity of Orthodox Jews, which makes it possible for them to send their children to religious schools well into their college years. After their children finish high school, Orthodox families can afford to send them to Israeli yeshivas for further study, as a kind of finishing-school experience in an environment shaped by the attitudes of the Orthodox right. Then again, the waning decades of the century have been a time of declining confidence throughout the West concerning the viability of modern cultural norms. This mood has strengthened the hand of fundamentalists throughout the world, including traditionalists in the yeshiva world who reject the values of secular America. Finally, none of the communal circumstances that formerly put a brake on religious extremism in the European Jewish context play a role in American Jewish life. Orthodox halakhic authorities do not have to accommodate to the broader needs of the Jewish community; on the contrary, they wish to segregate their followers from the non-Orthodox world. Thus, adherence to the stringencies of more right-wing rabbis in itself becomes a test of allegiance, regardless of the merits of the rabbinic decisions. As one observer notes: "The Orthodox minority will accept whatever halachic [rabbinic] authorities dictate."[58]

THUNDER ON THE RIGHT

The consequences of this shift to the right may be observed in the responses of centrist Orthodox rabbis to new challenges. One challenge was mounted from within, by some Orthodox women who were members of centrist Orthodox synagogues. They sought to reconcile their commitment to Orthodoxy with the new feminist consciousness of the 1970s and 1980s. Blu Greenberg, perhaps the most articulate representative of this group, related the following anecdote to describe her own growing discomfort with the role assigned to women in Orthodox synagogues. At one Simchat Torah celebration in the late 1970s the rabbi of her congregation pleaded for quiet, adding that "we won't complete the service until every single person here has had a *hakafah*" (has carried a Torah scroll around the synagogue).[59] Since within Orthodox synagogues women do not participate in the *hakafot*, the rabbi had unthinkingly relegated his female congregants to the status of nonperson. Because they accepted the separation of men and women in their own synagogues and the impossibility of women participating actively in the religious services, Orthodox women who wished to assume an active role in religious services founded a network of *tefillah* (prayer) groups in the 1970s.[60] These prayer circles took steps to avoid conflict with the larger Orthodox community: they scheduled services only once a month, so that members could continue to attend their own synagogues on three Sabbaths out of every four; they also omitted those sections of the service that may only be recited by a quorum of men; and they eschewed the term "minyan," denoting an official prayer quorum, to avoid any suggestion that they were engaged in an activity reserved solely for men.[61]

With only a few exceptions, rabbis of centrist Orthodox synagogues responded negatively to these activities by their own female congregants.[62] As a consequence, the *tefillah* groups met in private homes for the most part, because only a handful of synagogues offered them space. Moreover, when prayer groups did turn to rabbis for halakhic guidelines, they were rebuffed. As one of the leaders of the movement observed, this was one of the few times in Jewish history "that Jews turned to rabbis for *halachic* advice and were refused."[63]

Several years after these groups first appeared, the president of the Rabbinical Council of America brought the issue before a group of five Talmudists at Yeshiva University, asking them for a formal *teshuvah* (legal responsum) concerning the standing of such groups in Jewish law. The resulting one-page statement prohibited women's prayer groups, ruling them a "total and apparent deviation from tradition." The statement added that "all these customs are coming from a movement for the emancipation of women, which in this area is only for licentiousness." The RCA, centrist Orthodoxy's rabbinic body, then approved publication of the responsum as a "guideline" for Orthodox rabbis.[64]

There is no way to judge how such an issue would have been resolved in an earlier era in the history of American Orthodoxy. Women's prayer groups, after all, were responses to two new developments: the influence of the feminist movement of the late 1960s and the 1970s and the coming of age of Orthodox women who had acquired a high level of literacy in Hebraica and Judaica in Orthodox day schools. What is noteworthy, however, is the uncompromising stance adopted by rabbis toward their own congregants. Rather than seeking a means to accommodate Orthodox feminists or channel their energies productively, most rabbis in what was formerly the Modern Orthodox rabbinate treated women's *tefillah* groups as deviant and undeserving of support, let alone a home in the Orthodox synagogue.

A similar hard-line stance has been taken toward Orthodox rabbis who do not tow the party line. In 1990 a move was underfoot in the centrist Rabbinical Council of America to expel several prominent colleagues identified with "liberal" views, among them Rabbis Irving Greenberg and Avi Weiss. In part, this was an institutional struggle to oust members who had joined the Fellowship of Traditional Rabbis, a group founded in 1988 by rabbis on the left of the Orthodox spectrum who felt overwhelmed by the rightward tilt of Orthodoxy.[65] But the move against dissenters was also designed to stifle prominent Orthodox rabbis who advocated warmer relations with non-Orthodox Jews and sought ways to accommodate Orthodox women's *tefillah* groups. The matter was eventually dropped, when the targets of the RCA investigation launched a barrage of negative publicity in Jewish newspapers to defend themselves in public and castigate their opponents as "McCarthyists."[66]

The intolerance within the centrist Orthodox camp is exceeded by the vituperative attacks of the right wing on the centrists. An advertisement for an evening of denunciation and exposé captures the tone of the right-wing attacks: "Hear how centrism and many of its proponents are breaking with masora [Jewish tradition]. . . . Hear about their latest proposals which will encourage intermarriage through improper conversions, and how to stop them."[67] New groups such as the Council for Authentic Judaism, seek to "expose" prominent Orthodox leaders identified with the left as pagans and teachers of Christianity; they are convinced that centrism "is no longer Judaism, but another religion."[68] When Rabbi Steven Riskin, the founder of one of the largest Modern Orthodox synagogues in America, embarks on a speaking tour, flyers branding him a "heretic" are posted in synagogues.[69] And when a member of the centrist Rabbinical Council of America wrote an Op-Ed piece in the *New York Times* challenging the propriety of the Lubavitcher Rebbe's intrusion into Israeli politics, he was castigated in print as an "enemy, destroyer, and devastator of Israel," harassed with anonymous telephone calls, and warned that Lubavitchers were "watching and following" him.[70] These and many other incidents make abundantly clear that the triumph of the Right has been achieved in part by coercion and intimidation.

The new religious militancy of Orthodoxy has translated into a hardening of positions regarding the non-Orthodox world. From the perspective of Orthodox rabbis, recent decisions taken by non-Orthodox movements represent acts of aggression against Orthodoxy, let alone "Torah true" Judaism. The president of the RCA, Rabbi Milton Polin, observed in 1987:

> We are in a war, not one that we started, but one from which we shall not withdraw, over such issues as patrilineal descent, the American military chaplaincy [that is, whether women rabbis will serve], funding for Israeli institutions by the Jewish Agency, and over the establishment and recognition of Reform and Conservative Judaism in Israel.[71]

Orthodox groups have responded to these developments by limiting their participation in organizations that include non-Orthodox leaders. In recent years increasing numbers of centrist rabbis have supported the 1956 ruling by yeshiva heads banning cooperation with non-Orthodox rabbis. Within the Rabbinical Council of America pressures have mounted to desist from involvement with non-Orthodox rabbis.[72]

There is also a greater willingness on the part of Orthodox rabbis to express in public their disdain for the religious activities of Jews outside of their camp. Already in the 1950s Orthodox decisors ruled that synagogues lacking a *mechitsa*, a barrier between men and women, are illegitimate[73] and that marriages performed by Conservative and Reform rabbis are not religiously valid and therefore do not require a Jewish bill of divorce (*get*).[74] But in the 1980s these decisions were openly proclaimed. Thus, the rightist rabbinic organization, Agudas Harabbonim, began to place newspaper advertisements urging Jews to stay home on the High Holidays rather than attend a non-Orthodox synagogue.[75] Moreover, in September 1988 the same organization announced a new campaign to educate Jews that Reform Judaism "leads to mixed marriage" and that Conservative Judaism is "even more harmful because it acts as a 'steppingstone' to Reform."[76]

This hardening of positions and shift to the right may be interpreted in two ways. In the first instance it may be viewed as a triumph of the elite within the yeshiva world over the folk-religion that had been Americanized Orthodoxy, or as the conquest of "life tradition" by "book tradition," to use the words of the sociologist Menachem Friedman.[77] The new elite religion of Orthodoxy not only writes off the folkways of traditional Jews, as well as the practices of non-Orthodox Jews who are unprepared to become *baalei teshuva*,[78] but it also insists that any compromise with modern culture is to be rejected as un-Jewish and inferior.

The shift to the right may also be interpreted as a symptom of deep insecurity and retreat into insularity, of fear that the corrosiveness of modern American culture will eat away at the Orthodox population just as it has sapped non-Orthodox movements. Thus, even as it revels in its success in retaining the allegiance of its youth, the *Young Israel Viewpoint* publishes such articles as "Why Are Young Israel Children Going Astray?"[79] And even as what was formerly Modern Orthodoxy moves to the right, a symposium is held at a Young Israel convention that poses the question: "The Lifestyles of the Modern American Orthodox Jew—Halachic Hedonism?"[80]

The point was driven home by a leading spokesman for centrist Orthodoxy:

While we have created many observant Jews, we have not created many religious Jews. Mitzvah is clearly the *sine qua non* of Jewish living, but it is only the first step towards becoming a religious Jew. For many however, it has become both the first and last step. When it is possible for a Jew to don tefillin, be rigorous in kashrut observance, live a life marked by many *humrot* [stringencies], and yet be lax in his *ben adam la'havero* [dealings with fellow human beings], something is clearly not right (or left, or centrist). . . . If Orthodoxy is not to harden into a wall of self-congratulation, we must mount a serious assault on the most difficult barricade of all: the character of our people and the nature of our piety, and—if I may be innovative—our awareness of God. Otherwise we will become secular Jews with yarmulkes, de-religionized observant Jews.[81]

Even as Orthodoxy has emerged in the last quarter of the twentieth century as an outspoken and triumphant force, it continues to struggle with self-doubt about its ability to cope with modernity and endures an internal *Kulturkampf* between its modern and antimodern wings.

7

Conservative Judaism and the Challenge of Centrism

Far more than the other denominations, Conservative Judaism experienced severe turbulence and initially even demoralization between the mid-1960s and the mid-1980s. This resulted in part from a letdown following the end of the movement's period of heady growth immediately after World War II. Since the Conservative movement had been the greatest beneficiary of the post–World War II boom in synagogue expansion, it not surprisingly was hardest hit when growth halted. As observed by Mordecai Waxman, one of Conservative Judaism's most articulate rabbinic spokesmen, the movement "grew by leaps and bounds, without much effort or forethought" immediately after the Second World War because "Conservative Judaism was the most obvious answer to the needs and desires" of Jews who sought an "American Judaism." "The result was that Conservative Judaism mistook a historical hiccup for a historical inevitability."[1] When the underlying reasons for the massive postwar expansion disappeared, the movement had to compete more aggressively for members and was forced to confront its own limitations.

Equally important, Conservative Judaism experienced turmoil because forces both within and outside the movement confronted it with provocative new challenges. The movement had long managed to paper over serious ideological differences within its ranks during the boom years. But by the late 1960s and the early 1970s internal dissent had intensified and new alliances were forged to press for change. With each step toward ideological and programmatic clarification, one faction or another of the Conservative coalition felt betrayed.

In addition, Conservative Judaism's once enviable position at the center of the religious spectrum turned to a liability as American Judaism moved from an era of relative harmony to intense polarization. As the conflict between Reform on the left and Orthodoxy on the right intensified, the Conservative movement, as the party of the center, found itself caught in a cross fire between two increasingly antagonistic foes, and hard-pressed to justify its centrism. As Ismar Schorsch, chancellor of the Jewish Theological Seminary, has observed, the center "must produce an arsenal of arguments for use against both the left and right which, of necessity, often include ideas that are barely compatible."[2] Buffeted by severe jolts from outside, when Reform and Orthodoxy became more extreme in their postures, and under attack from members of their own coalition, the leaders of Conservative Judaism were forced to confront the possibility that the center could not hold. In response to these challenges, Conservative Judaism has charted a new course, albeit one that continues to occupy the center.

STRAINS IN THE CONSERVATIVE COALITION

The Conservative movement has long been based on a divided coalition. Writing at midcentury, Marshall Sklare noted the gap between the masses of Conservative synagogue members and the rabbinic and lay elites of the movement. Whereas the elites shared similar standards of religious practice and a common ideological commitment, even if they were not in complete agreement on all theological nuances, the masses of synagogue members were unaware of Conservative ideology and often were only minimally observant. According to Sklare's analysis, "Conservativism represents a common pattern of acculturation—a kind of social adjustment—which has been arrived at by lay people. It is seen by them as a 'halfway house' between Reform and Orthodoxy."[3] For the elite, by contrast, Conservative Judaism encompassed a spectrum of views regarding theology, revelation, the question of religious authority, and the peoplehood of Israel that distinguished it from its Reform and Orthodox counterparts. Conservative Judaism offered the elite a distinct program for Jewish living in the modern world.[4]

Even within the elite there was a considerable distance between the Seminary "schoolmen" and the rabbis in the field. As one of the rabbis bitterly put it: "Certain members of our faculty, our parents [sic], have put us in shackles and in bonds, and in irons, so that we cannot move. . . . [This] is humiliating to us. . . . [They] laugh at us as ignoramuses . . . [and imply] that we have been graduated as social workers and not as rabbis for humanity."[5] This rabbi's brutally honest statement draws attention to one aspect of the gap—the failure of the Seminary's faculty to accord empowerment and legitimacy to their students during the first half of this century. But the gap within the Conservative elite also consisted of a tacit understanding concerning the division of labor within the movement. As observed by Neil Gillman, a professor of Jewish theology at the Seminary:

> All of the groundbreaking Conservative responsa on synagogue practice [and] Sabbath observance . . . came out of the Rabbinical Assembly. . . . For its part, the Seminary Faculty remained within the walls of scholarship. It issued no responsa. If anything, it maintained a stance of almost explicit disdain toward all of this halakhic activity. . . . This relationship was actually a marriage of convenience. The Faculty could cling to its traditionalism, secure in the knowledge that the real problems were being handled elsewhere. The Rabbinical Assembly looked at its teachers as the hallmark of authenticity, holding the reins lest it go too far.[6]

The gap between Seminary and rabbinate was symbolized by the maintenance of separate seating in the Seminary's own (and only) synagogue until the 1980s, even as virtually every rabbi ordained by the institution served in a congregation that had instituted mixed seating of men and women—the hallmark of a congregation's movement from Orthodoxy to Conservatism.

By the late 1960s and the 1970s the long-standing "discontinuities and conflicts" within the Conservative movement, to use Sklare's formulation, grew more aggravated. First, there was the gap between rabbis and their congregants. The issue was directly confronted by Hershel Matt in the mid-1970s in a letter to his congregants explaining why, after twenty-eight years in the rabbinate, he had decided to leave the pulpit: "The present reality is that affiliation with a congregation or even election to the Board or to committees does not require any commitment" to the primary purpose of a synagogue—"seeking to live in the holy dimension of Jewish life . . . trying to accept the obligation and joy of worshipping God, . . . trying to learn Torah from the rabbi."[7] For Matt, the contradiction between the rabbi's vision of a synagogue community and the reality of that synagogue community was too great. A decade later a younger colleague of Matt's, Shalom Lewis, published an essay describing the loneliness of the Conservative rabbi:

> The loneliness we suffer is not necessarily social but spiritual. We might bowl, swim, and *kibbitz* with the best of them, but we are still in another world entirely. We quote Heschel and no one understands. We perform *netilat yadayim* and our friends think we're rude when we are momentarily silent. . . . We walk home, alone, on Shabbos. I am blessed with a wonderful social community, but I have no spiritual community in which I have companions.[8]

When a few well known pulpit rabbis left their congregations either to take communal positions or to settle in Israel during the post-1967 spurt of *aliyah* (settlement in Israel), there was much talk of demoralization within the Conservative rabbinate—albeit very little tangible evidence of attrition.[9]

To some rabbis, the gap between them and their congregants was not only a source of frustration but also a sign that the movement was in danger. To be sure, Conservative rabbis have for decades bemoaned their inability to convince the masses of their congregants to live as observant Jews. In 1960, at the time of most rapid growth within the Conservative movement, Rabbi Max Routtenberg spoke of the "mood and feeling among many of us that our achievements touch only the periphery of Jewish life and that our failures center around the issues that concern us most as rabbis and as Jews."[10] Almost two decades later Stephen C. Lerner characterized the problem even more bluntly: "The major problem is that we have been or are becoming a clerical movement. We have no observant laity and even our lay leadership is becoming removed from the world of the traditional family."[11] In the intervening years, as we noted in our discussion of the 1960s, Conservative rabbis repeatedly ventilated their frustrations and disappointments in movement journals and at national conventions.[12]

The observations of leading sociologists further added to the pessimistic mood. Marshall Sklare, the author of the definitive sociological study of the Conservative movement in its heyday, turned bearish about the future of the Conservative movement. In addition to the movement's internal problems, Sklare also highlighted the resurgence of Orthodoxy, which despite earlier prognostication to the contrary was generating commitment among its youth. This proved particularly galling to many Conservative rabbis who had parted ways with their own Orthodox upbringing, convinced that Orthodoxy was doomed because it could not address the needs of Americanized Jews.[13]

The findings of Charles Liebman and Saul Shapiro in a survey conducted at the end of the same decade and released at the 1979 biennial convention of the United Synagogue offered evidence to substantiate the thesis that the Conservative movement was in decline.[14] Liebman and Shapiro contended that almost as many young people reared within Conservative synagogues were opting for no congregational affiliation as were joining Conservative synagogues. Further, they contended that among the most observant younger families, particularly as defined by *kashrut* observance, there was a tendency to "defect" to Orthodoxy. Here was evidence of a double failing: a movement that had invested heavily in Jewish education in the synagogue setting seemingly did not imbue its youth with a strong allegiance to the Conservative synagogue; and rabbis who themselves had rejected their Orthodox origins now found their "best" young people—including their own children—rejecting Conservatism for Orthodoxy.

In truth, many of the "best" of Conservative youths were choosing a path other than Orthodoxy, one that was to have a far more profound effect upon the movement than denominational "defections." Beginning in the early 1970s, products of Conservative synagogues, youth movements, summer camps (known as Ramah camps), and the Seminary were instrumental in the creation of the countercultural Havurah movement.[15] Although Conservative Jews did not monopolize Havurah Judaism, they played key roles as founders, theoreticians, and members. The first to suggest the applicability of early rabbinic fellowships as a model for the present age was Jacob Neusner, who had been ordained at the Seminary.[16] The first and perhaps most influential of all havurot was founded in Somerville, Massachusetts, in 1968 by a group of Ramah and Seminary products under the leadership of Arthur Green, a rabbi ordained at the Seminary. The guiding force in the founding of the New York Havurah, as well as the journal *Response*, was Alan Mintz, who had earlier served as the national president of

United Synagogue Youth, the Conservative youth movement. The books that served as primers of Havurah Judaism, the *Jewish Catalogues*, were compiled by products of Conservative youth programs. And the most important and enduring journal to emerge from the Jewish counterculture, *Response*, according to Bill Novak, an early editor, "grew out of a particularly intense summer at Ramah (the Mador Program in the Poconos, 1965)."[17]

To some observers, such ferment might serve as evidence of a movement capable of inspiring creativity and intense Judaic involvement among its youth. The various volumes of the *Jewish Catalogue* became best-sellers; *Response* served as an important vehicle of communication for the "sixties generation"; and the Havurah movement inspired Reform, Reconstructionist, and Conservative synagogues to rethink their programs and adapt the fellowship model to their own purposes. And yet, symptomatic of the Conservative mood in the 1970s, these phenomena were taken as evidence of failure. The rebellious attacks upon the Conservative synagogue and establishment were taken at face value. Leaders of Conservative Judaism concluded that they had failed because young products of the movement felt alienated from Conservative synagogues and other movement institutions.[18]

What were the causes of this alienation? Richard Siegel, one of the editors of *The Jewish Catalogue*, offered the following analysis of the link between Havurah Judaism and the Conservative movement in an address to the national convention of the Rabbinical Assembly:

> Ramah created a new Jewish lifestyle. . . . A group of discontents was created [due to experimentation at Ramah], a group of people who had a vision of something different from what went on in synagogues. . . . In essence, it was an internal development within the Conservative movement which had within it the seeds of internal contradiction, and its own destruction, in a way. The Conservative movement was unable to absorb . . . to meet the religious needs of a group of young people.[19]

For Siegel, then, it was the intense experience of participating in a Jewish religious community at Camp Ramah that prompted the emergence of the Havurah movement as a substitute for what young people regarded as the formal and sterile atmosphere of the large Conservative synagogue. As Susannah Heschel put it to another group of Conservative rabbis: "The movement has succeeded too well in educating its children, because these children feel they have no proper place in

Conservative life." Precisely because they had been taught well by the Conservative movement, Havurah members felt discomfort in Conservative synagogues, whereas most other members were unable to participate in a religious service conducted entirely in Hebrew. Products of Ramah and other Conservative educational ventures could lead their own services rather than depend upon a rabbi and cantor to guide them through the liturgy.[20]

In the short term Heschel was correct in noting the alienation of some of these youths from Conservative synagogues. But there is substantial evidence that many of the formerly disaffected, including those who continued to worship within the Havurah setting, increasingly participated in Conservative institutions: they sent their children to Solomon Schechter schools and Ramah camps; they identified with the liturgy and ideology of Conservatism; and most importantly, they moved from the periphery to the center of Conservatism's institutional life.[21]

It is this later development, rather than the loss of its youth, that accounts in large measure for the turbulence within Conservative Judaism during the past two decades. Put simply, leadership in the movement—its national institutions, synagogues, rabbinate, and various organizational arms—passed into the hands of men and women who were reared in the pews of Conservative synagogues and socialized in its Ramah camps and United Synagogue Youth programs. And that transition brought dislocation and turmoil to the movement for over a decade.

The biographies of movement leaders tell much of the story. When Gerson D. Cohen assumed the chancellorship of the Jewish Theological Seminary of America in 1972, he brought with him years of experience as an early participant in the Ramah experiment. His successor, Ismar Schorsch, shared such experiences and is himself the son of a Conservative rabbi. Equally important, the Conservative rabbinate has been recruiting growing percentages of its members from Conservative homes. During the first half of the century the majority of rabbinical students at JTS came from Orthodox families and educational institutions. The percentage of such students has since dwindled, so that hardly any current rabbinical students are drawn from the Orthodox community. Instead, close to one-third are either from Reform backgrounds or from unaffiliated families or are converts to Judaism, while the other two-thirds are products of the Conservative movement.[22] And the Seminary faculty too has been replenished with American-born Jews, who for the most part were educated within Conservative institutions.

The new elite of the Conservative movement differs from its predecessors of earlier generations in two significant ways. First, leaders are far less tied to the world of Orthodoxy. Earlier leaders of the movement, whether out of nostalgia or resentment, were emotionally engaged with the Orthodox world of their youth. Today's leaders regard Orthodoxy as alien and accordingly feel fewer constraints in setting their own course. Second, and even more important, the new elite of the Conservative movement is far more prepared to put into practice the logical consequences of Conservative ideology. It is particularly significant that many of the new elite had experience in Ramah camps, because Ramah, as one observer noted,

> is the battleground par excellence for Conservative Judaism, where theory and practice must and do meet. . . . [Only Camp Ramah] constantly turn[ed] to the central educational institution, the JTS, to ask what are the permissible limits of experimentation in Jewish prayer? What are the permissible limits of Shabbat observance? What precisely is the role of women in Conservative Jewish life?[23]

Precisely because it created a total Jewish environment, Ramah provided a setting to explore what it means to live as a Conservative Jew on a day-to-day basis. Products of Ramah were therefore prepared to put Conservative ideology into action once they assumed roles of leadership within the movement.

As the Conservative movement's elite changed in character, the structure of alliances within the Conservative coalition shifted dramatically. The "schoolmen" described by Sklare in the mid-1950s now included some women, but even more important, the group included homegrown products with strong ties to the Conservative movement and no allegiances to Orthodoxy. The same was true in the rabbinate and organizational leadership. Thus, coalitions for change cut across the movement, rather than remaining solely within one segment of the rabbinate, as had long been the case. The issue of women's ordination that agitated the Conservative movement for a decade would serve as the symbol of change and also the catalyst for further realignment within the movement.

WOMEN'S ORDINATION AS SYMBOL AND CATALYST

Although Conservative Judaism had long accepted mixed seating of men and women in synagogues and since the 1950s had increasingly celebrated the coming of age of girls in Bat Mitzvah ceremonies, it was only in the early 1970s that the movement addressed more far-reaching questions concerning the status of women in religious life. Pressures for such reconsideration arose from several quarters. Most generally, there was the American feminist movement, which since the mid-1960s had sought to "raise the consciousness" of society to discrimination suffered by women. Gradually, in the early 1970s small groups of women began to take up the banner of this cause within the Jewish community. One such group that received particular attention due to its proximity to the JTS and its adept self-advertisement in the media called itself Ezrat Nashim—a Hebrew pun that referred to the separate women's gallery in traditional synagogues, which symbolized Jewish women's segregation, but also implied a pledge to provide "help for women." Ezrat Nashim pressed its agenda at the convention of the Rabbinical Assembly in March 1972 and demanded the following: that women be granted membership in synagogues, be counted in a minyan, be allowed to participate fully in religious observances, be recognized as witnesses before Jewish law, be allowed to initiate divorce, be permitted and encouraged to attend rabbinical and cantorial school and perform as rabbis and cantors in synagogues, be encouraged to assume positions of leadership in the community, and be considered bound to fulfill all mitzvot (commandments) equally with men. These demands drew special attention because they were put forward by self-proclaimed "products of Conservative congregations, religious schools, the Ramah Camp, LTF, USY, and the Seminary"—in short, by insiders.

Until a detailed history of Jewish feminism is written, it will not be possible to determine how many Conservative women supported these demands, how quickly the movement spread, and whether there was significant grass-roots support for change in the status of women. What is clear, however, is that the issue evoked a sympathetic response from the Conservative rabbinate. This can be seen in the growing attention to women's issues in both the journal and the convention proceedings of the Conservative rabbinate, beginning shortly after the aforementioned convention. In terms of action, in 1973 the Rabbinical

Assembly's Committee on Law and Standards adopted a *takkanah* (legislative enactment) permitting local rabbis to decide whether to count women as part of the prayer quorum (*minyan*). The next year the same committee heard papers on whether women could serve as rabbis and as cantors and whether they could serve as witnesses and sign legal documents such as *ketubot* (wedding contracts). Supporters of women's equality concluded that existing legal opinions of the Conservative movement's Law Committee provided sufficient basis for change in the status of women, while opponents of egalitarianism remained unconvinced.[24]

When news about the decision on counting women in a minyan became public knowledge through articles in the general press, Conservative opponents of "egalitarianism"—the term that came to be applied to the equal treatment of women—began to organize. The decision had placed such rabbis on the defensive with their own congregants. How could individual rabbis committed to the traditional role differences of men and women in the synagogue continue to justify their practices if a *takkanah* permitting the counting of women in the *minyan* (prayer quorum) had been passed by the legal body of the Conservative rabbinate? And once a small minority of the Law Committee had sanctioned other changes in the status of women, how could a rabbi opposed to these changes resist the pressures of congregants? The actions of the Law Committee, it was argued, undermined the authority of the individual rabbi. Furthermore, opponents contended, the committee had assumed an unprecedented role as an advocate of change. According to surveys taken at the time, only 6 percent of the Conservative rabbinate allowed women to be counted in the minyan. The committee, and particularly its chairman, Seymour Siegel, a professor at the Seminary, were accused of taking a new activist role within the movement.[25] In short order, rabbis opposed to the decisions of the Law Committee organized a body initially known as the Ad Hoc Committee for Tradition and Diversity in the Conservative Movement and subsequently renamed the Committee for Preservation of Tradition within the Rabbinical Assembly of America. Thus, even before the issue of women's ordination was formally raised, the battle lines were drawn within the Conservative rabbinate.[26]

In response to prodding by the leaders of the Rabbinical Assembly,[27] the chancellor of the Seminary, Gerson D. Cohen, convened a special national commission in the late 1970s to explore the feasibility of ordaining women.[28] After a year of work, the commission's majority voted affirmatively. Since the role of the contemporary rabbi "is not one which is established in classical Jewish texts," they contended, there is "no specifiable halakhic category which can be identified with the modern rabbinate." Traditional halakhic (rabbinic) laws preventing women from serving as legal witnesses, members of a *minyan*, and as prayer leaders (*sheliheitsibur*) had already been addressed by the Committee on Law and Standards. Furthermore, "the halakhic objections to the ordination of women center around disapproval of the performance by a woman of certain functions. Those functions, however, are not essentially rabbinic, nor are they universally disapproved, by the accepted rules governing the discussion of halakha in the Conservative Movement." Second, the majority contended that "ethical considerations," principally the belief that "each person should have at least a legally equal opportunity to pursue a chosen career," should be followed, "especially when no halakhic violation is involved." Yet a third consideration concerned the seeming contradiction between (1) the movement's long-standing commitment to equal education for boys and girls, (2) its celebration of Bar and Bat Mitzvah ceremonies, and (3) of late, the equal participation of girls and women in the religious services of many synagogues, on the one hand, and movement opposition to women's pursuit of a career in the rabbinate. Finally, the majority was also moved by evidence suggesting popular support within the movement for women's ordination.[29]

Once the commission reported its findings to the Rabbinical Assembly, attention turned to the faculty of the Seminary. During the course of the commission's hearings, Chancellor Gerson Cohen had shifted his position from a desire to maintain the status quo to enthusiastic support of women's ordination. He took it upon himself to bring the matter before the faculty of the Seminary within one year, an undertaking that itself precipitated further controversy, for there was no procedural precedent for such a decision. In December 1979 the matter was brought before the faculty and tabled in order to soothe the divisiveness it engendered.[30]

The issue came to a head again in 1983 due to pressure from the Rabbinical Assembly. The RA decided to consider for membership Beverly Magidson, a rabbi ordained at the Hebrew Union College. Like all candidates for admission not ordained by the JTS, Magidson needed the support of three-quarters of the rabbis present at the convention in order to gain admission. Magidson failed to receive the necessary votes, though she did receive the support of the majority of the convention delegates.[31] But it was clear from the vote of 206 in favor of Magidson's admission to 72 opposed that it was only a matter of time before a woman rabbi would be admitted to the RA and that the Seminary could no longer defer a decision.[32]

In the fall of 1983 Chancellor Cohen once again brought the issue of women's ordination to the faculty. In the interval, several of the staunchest opponents of women's ordination had left the faculty, and Professor Saul Lieberman, the Seminary's leading Talmudist and an intimidating figure even after his retirement from the faculty, had passed away. Clearly outnumbered, most opponents of women's ordination, principally senior members of the rabbinics department, refused to attend the meeting. By a vote of thirty-four to eight, with one abstention, and over a half dozen faculty members absent in protest, the faculty voted to admit women to the rabbinical school on October 24, 1983. By the following fall nineteen women were enrolled in the rabbinical school; one of them, Amy Eilberg, was ordained in May 1985 on the basis of her academic attainments during years of graduate studies.[33]

The protracted and bitterly divisive debate over women's ordination went beyond the issue of women's status in Judaism to the broader questions of movement definition. Both sides in this debate perceived the debate as a struggle for the soul of the movement. Predictably, given the centrism of the movement, advocates of opposing positions branded their opponents as either reform radicals or Orthodox obstructionists. This was particularly evident during the debate over Magidson's application for admission to the RA in 1983. Opponents explicitly stated that if the RA votes affirmatively, "we are going to be publicly identified with the Reform movement";[34] supporters feared that by rejecting Magidson, "we will be subjecting ourselves to ridicule. . . . Our own communities and our congregants will lump us with Orthodox intransigents."[35] And in a blistering critique, Harold Schulweis asked:

> If we had a *teshuva* [responsum] from Moshe Feinstein or from Yossef Ber Soloveitchik [leading Orthodox decisors], using precisely the same arguments that we have heard, permitting the ordination of women . . . who would object to it? . . . I put it to you that nobody would oppose it, not because there has been any substantive, argumentative

hidush [new interpretation] involved, but because of who would have said it. . . . I put it to you that this is a form of de-legitimation, the self-delegitimation of our movement.[36]

Schulweis's sarcastic analysis highlighted the uncertainty within the movement over how to introduce change and who had the authority to innovate. Indeed, the issue of women's ordination forced the Conservative movement to confront its deep divisions over the question of religious authority.

The issue of women's ordination heightened these divisions and also exposed the movement's indecision. As Benjamin Kreitman noted in an address to his colleagues: The tensions in Conservative Judaism

> have made us ideologically neurotic and religiously timid. . . . We are part neo-Orthodox and in part right-wing Reform. We have learned to live with some egregious contradictions, not the least being the protest against *aliyot* [Torah honors] for girls in United Synagogue Youth while a Seminary commission is taking testimony on whether to admit women into the Rabbinical School for ordination. . . . We must find the way to a distinctive, normative teaching which is neither neo-Orthodox nor neo-Reform.[37]

The long stalemate over women's ordination was symptomatic of the movement's paralysis.

Eventually, however, the movement was forced to take a stance. Unlike other provocative issues, women's ordination impinged on many sectors of the Conservative movement and therefore could not be ignored. Whereas earlier controversial decisions, such as the Law Committee's stance on the permissibility of driving to synagogue on the Sabbath, had affected only individual Jews, the ordination of women as rabbis directly affected all segments of Conservative Jewry. Congregations would eventually have to decide whether to hire a woman as a rabbi; members of the Rabbinical Assembly would have to decide whether to accept women as colleagues, particularly as witnesses in legal actions; and members of the Seminary faculty would have to decide whether to train women as rabbis. Once ordained as rabbis, women would assume a central role that could not be ignored.

The way in which this issue impinged on all aspects of the movement was especially dramatized by the need of the Seminary faculty to take a stand. For the first time, the faculty of the Seminary, particularly the Talmud faculty, which had rarely participated in debates over practical halakhah, was forced to take a stand on a matter that emanated from within the movement: in a stunning reversal of the usual process by which Seminary faculty members participated in religious decisions only if they chose to do so, forces within the movement now pressed the Seminary to alter its admissions policies for the rabbinical school. The Seminary was challenged to confront its ambivalent relationship with the Conservative movement.[38]

Finally, the ordination question was symbolically crucial because the new constellation of forces within the movement was openly arrayed. The opposing forces were not necessarily traditionalists versus disciples of Mordecai Kaplan, as had been the case for decades within the Conservative movement. The coalition supporting women's ordination drew its strength from Seminary faculty members—including junior faculty in the Talmud department—and from Conservative rabbis who denied they were challenging halakhah (the structure of rabbinic law). Rather, they demanded that the movement permit women rights that were not forbidden them by halakhah or that could be justified on the basis of proper halakhic process, utilizing accepted rabbinic legal categories. In short, the issue was not Kaplan's formulation of giving halakhah a vote but not a veto; instead, supporters of women's ordination argued for the implementation of policies that were halakhically feasible, even if such actions departed from traditional practices. The issue of women's ordination thus solidified the new alignment within the movement and also prompted further rethinking, as supporters of religious innovation not only won their battle but also seized control of the movement's institutions and redefined its agenda.

REDEFINING THE MOVEMENT

The crisis of Conservative morale during the late 1960s and the 1970s and the subsequent internal struggle over women's ordination pressured the leaders of Conservative Judaism to define the movement's program. The result was an outpouring of programmatic statements, halakhic works, and liturgical compositions unprecedented in the history of Conservative Judaism. Even the decades-old pleas of rabbis and lay people for explicit statements of Conservative belief and practice were heeded. The result was the publication for the first time—more than a century after the founding of the Jewish Theological Seminary—of a statement of Conservative principles issued jointly by all major agencies of the movement. The Conservative movement was now determined to stake out a clear position in the Jewish community and to maintain it aggressively.

Beginning slowly in the early 1970s and then intensifying in the 1980s, the movement published a series of volumes defining the Conservative position. First came the *Mahzor for Rosh Hashanah and Yom Kippur,* the High Holiday prayer book (1972);[39] the end of the decade saw the publication of Isaac Klein's *Guide to Jewish Religious Practice* (1979), the first codification of the movement's halakhic rulings, albeit one written from the perspective of a highly traditional Conservative rabbi.[40] In the 1980s came a Passover Haggadah, the service for the Passover meal (1982),[41] a new prayer book (1985),[42] works on the Conservative approach to Jewish law, such as Joel Roth's *Halakhic Process: A Systemic Analysis*[43] and the collected responsa of the Committee on Jewish Law and Standards (1988).[44] Most notably, in 1988 a joint ideological committee chaired by Robert Gordis and encompassing all organizations of the movement issued *Emet Ve-Emunah,* a statement of beliefs and principles.[45] The leadership of Conservative Judaism, so long berated by critics for avoiding issues of ideological and halakhic definition, finally put forth its views on a whole range of issues.

Although the new publications do not speak with one voice or suggest anything resembling unanimity, several trends are evident. First and foremost, Conservative Judaism reiterated its desire to occupy the center of the religious spectrum: the statement of principles speaks of "the indispensability of Halakhah" and "the norms taught by the Jewish traditions." By emphasizing a normative approach to Jewish religious behavior, the Conservative movement rejected the Reform and Reconstructionist positions. Simultaneously, the statement distances itself from Orthodoxy by taking note of "development in Halakhah," and though cautioning that "the burden of proof is on the one who wants to alter" Jewish laws, it affirms the right of Conservative religious authorities to interpret and adjust Jewish law as understood by the halakhic process of Conservative Judaism.[46]

The Conservative position espoused in *Emet Ve-Emunah* is consciously centrist in seeking a path between extreme positions. As analyzed by Chancellor Ismar Schorsch, the statement of principles treats halakhah as "a disciplinary way of life which is dynamic and evolving." It expresses a "deep commitment to the survival and flourishing of Israel but . . . [does] *not* . . . accept that Judaism cannot thrive outside of a Jewish homeland." It rejects Mordecai Kaplan's views on chosenness by reasserting "the meaningfulness of the concept of chosenness, and at the same time, claims that we are open to the wisdom of Gentiles." It "depicts Jewish prayer as something firm and fixed . . . and yet [the] liturgical form is open to development, to the refraction of contemporary tastes and anxieties."[47]

A second element of the reshaped Conservative Judaism of the 1980s is an open embrace of pluralism in Jewish religious life. Within the movement itself an effort is made to embrace all Jews who identify themselves as Conservative. Even the newly published statement of principles need not be accepted "as a whole or in detail . . . [as] obligatory upon every Conservative Jew, lay or rabbinic." With regard to other Jewish groups, the statement of principles urges Jewish unity and seeks a common Jewish approach to conversion and religious divorces, vexing sources of friction between the various denominations.[48]

A third feature of the new Conservative position is strong support for gender equality. The statement of principles explicitly affirms the equality of the sexes. Though the movement strives for pluralism and the statement of principles recognizes that "there is a wide spectrum of opinion within our movement with regard to the role of women in Jewish ritual," it has clearly shifted to support of egalitarianism. The new *Siddur Sim Shalom* takes cognizance in the Hebrew liturgy of the possibility that women will don a *tallit* (prayer shawl) and *tefillin* (phylacteries), and includes a blessing (*mi she-berakh*) for a woman called to the Torah. While stopping short of making equality of the sexes an absolute norm of Conservative Judaism, movement leaders have indicated clearly where their sympathies reside.[49]

As enunciated by Kassel Abelson in his presidential address to the Rabbinical Assembly in 1987, Conservative Judaism is a "traditional *egalitarian* movement."[50] Traditionalism has been affirmed in the maintenance of Hebrew as the essential language of the liturgy; in the continuing assertion of the need for *keva*, an established structure "for the times, content, and order of prayer";[51] for the reaffirmation that Judaism is a normative and binding legal system; and for the reiteration of the role of rabbis as decisors of Jewish law. As a gesture of support for the traditional stance of Jewish law, the Rabbinical Assembly even went to the unusual length of affirming as a "standard" the belief that Jewish descent is conveyed only through the mother, thereby subjecting any rabbi who acts upon the patrilineal redefinition of Jewish identity to expulsion from the Rabbinical Assembly.[52] By affirming the need for conversion to Judaism as the only acceptable way for a non-Jew to enter the covenant and by rejecting the redefinition of Jewish identity introduced by Reform and Reconstructionist colleagues, the Conservative rabbinate sought to reiterate its fidelity to tradition on the most controversial and divisive issue on the Jewish religious agenda. But on the status of women, there is little doubt of the commitment to egalitarianism.

Within synagogues, a wide range of new practices has been introduced regarding the status of women. Surveys conducted during the 1970s suggested that growing numbers of Conservative congregations were electing women as officers and including them as equal participants in religious services by counting women in a minyan, calling them to the Torah, and permitting them to chant portions of the services. In a study issued in 1988, it is evident that this process has continued apace. According to a survey of every North American affiliate of the Women's League for Conservative Judaism compiled by Edya Arzt (Arzt counts 705 affiliates at approximately 850 Conservative synagogues), the following statistics emerge: "Better than half the congregations do count women in the *minyan* (446) and do give them *aliyot* on all occasions (456). An additional 61 congregations give women *aliyot* on special occasions, such as an anniversary or a *Bat Mitzvah* or jointly with their husbands." In addition, another 100 congregations were actively engaged in or planning to study the question of women's participation. Arzt found distinct patterns based on geographic location; opposition to women's participation was greatest in Brooklyn and Long Island, began to wane west of the Hudson, and was least evident on the West Coast, where the majority of congregations were egalitarian.[53]

The movement took steps to reassure traditionalists who are not egalitarian of their proper place within Conservative Judaism. At virtually every official function of the movement such as conventions, two simultaneous prayer services were conducted, one identified as "traditional" and the other as "egalitarian." Similarly, the Jewish Theological Seminary has sponsored two concurrent prayer services since the mid-1980s.[54] Pluralism is thus not only a watchword in relations with other movements in Judaism but a pragmatic tool for maintaining peace within the movement.

CONTINUING POLARIZATION

The Right Secedes

Efforts to promote pluralism, however, have not dampened controversy in the era since the ordination question was settled. Sectors of the Conservative movement opposed to egalitarianism continue to nurse their grievances and flirt with secession. And there are groups on the left of the spectrum that agitate for new reforms.

As soon as the decision on the ordination of women was taken in the fall of 1983, opponents of egalitarianism organized the Union for Traditional Conservative Judaism (UTCJ) as a lobby within the movement. Emerging from earlier pressure groups that had fought against changes in the status of women within religious law, the UTCJ in time broadened its mandate to represent the interests of those within the Conservative coalition who felt that the movement had strayed away from tradition. The complaint of this group was enunciated by an outspoken lay member in an essay entitled "Relief for Beleaguered Traditionalists": "Your rabbi is touting *Sim Shalom* [the new prayer book] as the greatest liturgical innovation since the Sh'ma [the biblical credo]. Your synagogue's ritual committee is again considering women's participation and seems to go along with whichever side seems the loudest. You've seen some food in the synagogue kitchen that makes you wonder whether you can eat there."[55] Rabbis who founded the traditionalist lobby pronounced "Conservative *halacha* dead" and mourned "the demise of Conservative Judaism."[56]

Claiming in the late 1980s to represent "500 rabbis (including some 150 Orthodox rabbis who identify with our philosophy) and over 5,000 lay families,"[57] the UTCJ kept pressure on the Conservative movement through the adroit use of the media. Whenever the Conservative movement took a decision that did not conform to its views, the UTCJ managed to get equal time in the Jewish press, even though its leaders represented only a small population of Conservative Jews.

The Union's boldest challenge to the Conservative leadership came through the establishment of a separate Panel of Halakhic Inquiry, which, among other things, restated the objection to women as rabbis and counting women in a prayer quorum. A responsum dealing with the new Conservative prayer book ruled that "although *Siddur Sim Shalom* may be used as a resource work, it should not be used for the purpose of fulfilling one's prayer obligations," because it introduces "gratuitous changes," eliminates gender distinctions, "extirpates or modifies almost all positive references to . . . sacrificial ritual," and through its alternative readings, undermines the obligatory nature of Jewish prayer.[58] (Significantly, another responsum fully supported the rights of women to create their own prayer groups and rejected the halakhic stand adopted by the "Yeshiva Five," thereby declaring the Union's independence from Orthodoxy.)[59]

In 1990 the UTCJ took steps to break with the Conservative movement. It founded the Institute for Traditional Judaism (or *Metivta l'Limudei Hayahadut*) as a new nondenominational rabbinical seminary. Its faculty is headed by Professor David Weiss Halivni who resigned from the Jewish Theological Seminary after the ordination vote; and it is staffed by teachers ordained at both JTS and Yeshiva University. The Institute's motto is "Genuine Faith in Intellectual Honesty"—an indirect criticism of the two institutions between which the *Metivta* positions itself: JTS presumably lacks the former and YU the latter.[60]

In May 1990 the UTCJ changed its name to the Union for Traditional Judaism,[61] a further step away from the Conservative movement. The new body strives to serve as a bridge between the right wing of the Conservative movement and the Modern wing of Orthodoxy and in fact has made overtures to the latter.[62] As distinct from its most outspoken leaders, who have broken with the Conservative movement, the Union remains primarily an enclave of Conservative Jews dissatisfied with recent trends in their movement. The rabbis who constitute the core of the Union are bound to the Conservative movement through institutional loyalty and congregational affiliation. More problematic for the Conservative movement are the lay people who may switch their allegiances to Orthodox synagogues. Much to their regret, most Conservative leaders concur with Stephen Lerner's assessment that many of "the Orthodox leaning in U.S.Y. [the youth movement] and the community at large are increasingly finding *mechitsa* shuls in which to *daven* [synagogues with men and women seated separately], and nothing we do will bring these people back"—from Orthodoxy.[63]

Ironically, the rabbinic core of the Union for Traditional Judaism today plays much the same role within the Conservative movement as the Reconstructionist wing had played during the middle decades of the century. As analyzed by Gilbert Rosenthal, "The left wing believed itself the odd-man out. The Reconstructionist wing complained that our movement was too bound to *tradition*, too obsessed with *nostalgia*, too submissive to the rule of the Seminary faculty." Since the secession of Reconstructionism from the Conservative movement, "there is virtually no articulate left wing in our movement. Instead the odd-man out is the right-wing, which ... has considered itself increasingly trampled upon and isolated. Today's critics decry our movement for being too obsessed with *change*, with *radicalism*, with departures from Halakhic norms."[64] Members of the Union, by contrast, are convinced that the Conservative movement no longer has an articulate left wing because Reconstructionism has triumphed. As one member of this group has put it: "The Reconstructionist majority [of the Conservative movement] has coopted Traditional language and has not made its very non-Traditional meaning clear."[65] Given such a perspective, it is understandable that the Union's newsletter is entitled *Hagahelet*, the "burning ember," to underscore the views of the late Professor Saul Lieberman that the Union represented the "last burning ember of Jewish law in our movement."

Pressure from the Left

After several years of relative quiescence, the left wing of the Conservative movement was galvanized by a new issue—the religious status of homosexuals. The issue arose when several groups questioned the Conservative movement's Committee on Law and Standards on the halakhic position regarding the employment of homosexuals in positions of religious leadership. One Conservative congregation wished to know whether it was permissible to employ a lesbian as executive director. And the Gay and Lesbian congregation Beth Simchat Torah in New York City sought the services of the Rabbinical Assembly in its search for a rabbi. In 1990 the Conservative rabbinate had passed a resolution opposing civil discrimination, violence, threats, and prejudice directed at homosexuals, and reiterated its welcome of "all Jews, gay men and lesbians ... as members in our congregations."[66] One year later the Law Committee took up the question of whether openly avowed homosexuals may be employed in positions of religious influence.

The Law Committee received a responsum from Rabbi Bradley Artson advocating the acceptance of homosexuality and heterosexuality as equally valid expressions of love. "Homosexuality can be (like much of heterosexuality) healthy, natural, supportive of family values, and stability," Artson wrote. Arguing that biblical prohibitions were written at a time when "only homosexual acts between heterosexual people" were known, Artson urged "that homosexuality is to be considered a *halakhically*-acceptable sexual orientation, provided that this sexuality is expressed within the context of a mutually-exclusive, committed, adult relationship." Practically this meant "the desirability of developing ceremonies for sanctifying such a homosexual relationship as well as for formally terminating it. Sexual orientation per se would no longer provide halakhic grounds for the denial of synagogue office or honors, for exclusion or expulsion from the rabbinate, the cantorate, or from Jewish education."[67]

The opposing position was argued at great length by the chairman of the committee, Rabbi Joel Roth. Reviewing biblical and rabbinic literature, he found unequivocal opposition to homosexual behavior, noting that the halakhic prohibition against homosexuality

> is not open to any real doubt, nor does modern knowledge offer any compelling reason to seek to overturn the normative precedents. It must follow, therefore, that the halakhically committed Jewish community cannot ... take any act or espouse any action which could reasonably be understood to imply the co-equality, validation or acceptability of a homosexual lifestyle.

Practically, according to Roth, this meant that the Conservative movement may count homosexuals in the prayer quorum and call them to the Torah, but that homosexuals should not hold any positions of influence in the organizations and educational institutions of the Conservative movement and there should be no public celebration of homosexual commitment.[68]

After months of debate the committee agreed on a set of principles conforming mainly to the position espoused by Roth. It reaffirmed the biblical condemnation of homosexuality but allowed local rabbis discretion in hiring homosexuals as teachers and youth leaders. As understood by Rabbi Joel Myers, executive vice president of the Rabbinical Assembly, "The decision affirmed the status quo by making clear that homosexuals 'are not equal in status' with heterosexual Jews."[69]

Barely six weeks later at the convention of the Rabbinical Assembly, Conservative rabbis overruled the conclusions of their own law committee. The RA voted to create a commission to study the complex question of homosexuality and permitted member rabbis to serve homosexual congregations. Although the Jewish Theological Seminary and the United Synagogue quickly announced their refusal to participate in any process of reevaluation,[70] forces on the left of the Conservative movement have decided to press their agenda, once again raising the question of whether the Conservative movement can hold together its fragmented coalition.

Although the Conservative movement continues to struggle with internal disunity, it succeeded in relieving its institutional paralysis through the resolution of the women's ordination issue. Both the break with Orthodoxy implicit in the decision to ordain women as rabbis and the break with Reform and Reconstructionism over patrilineal descent have given the Conservative movement "boundary issues" to differentiate itself from other denominations and put into action its ideology of "tradition and change." For many in the movement, that ideology is concretized in the "egalitarian traditional" religious service, one in which women, as well as men, don *tallit* and *tefillin* (prayer shawl and phylacteries) and chant the prayers according to the traditional *nuschaot* (melodies) and read from the Torah portion according to the accustomed cantillation.[71]

With the successful, though not unanimously accepted, resolution of many of their most bruising internal struggles, movement leaders are displaying a new feistiness in asserting the Conservative agenda on the American Jewish scene. Thus, Robert Gordis challenged Reform to abandon patrilineality as a misguided departure from the unified approach of the Jewish people.[72] Similar challenges have been issued by movement leaders to the position of Orthodoxy vis-à-vis other matters. Chancellor Ismar Schorsch publicly declared his determination to become more denominational, to "bring a Conservative interpretation of Judaism to Europe as well as South America" and Israel, and to challenge opponents of the movement in the United States.[73] Concluding that American Judaism has entered a "virulently denominational age"[74] of religious polarization, Conservative leaders have clearly resolved to assert in the public arena the correctness of Conservative Judaism's recently modified, yet still centrist position.

8

The Reconstruction of Kaplanian Reconstructionism

The most significant development in Reconstructionism during the past quarter century is its reconstitution as a fourth religious movement that claims parity with the Orthodox, Conservative, and Reform branches of Judaism.[1] Whereas, Reconstructionists had long identified themselves as the left wing of the Conservative movement,[2] by the early 1960s followers of Mordecai Kaplan embarked on an independent course. Not surprisingly, once that decision was taken and the process of building a movement began in earnest, many of Kaplan's ideas came under fire from within. Ironically, the institutional growth of the movement has gone hand in hand with a reassessment of the teachings of the founder, Mordecai Kaplan. In fact, Reconstructionism has been reconstructed.

BUILDING A FOURTH MOVEMENT

Reconstructionism has existed as an ideological program since the publication of *Judaism as a Civilization* in 1934. Mordecai Kaplan, the primary ideological spokesman for Reconstructionism, promoted the vital necessity for reconstructing Jewish life as a means of coping with modernity, and particularly with the challenges posed by the American environment. Priding himself on his rational approach to issues and his quest for intellectual consistency, Kaplan had little patience for many traditional aspects of Judaism, such as belief in a supernatural God or the concept of the chosen people, let alone for its more mystical concepts. For much of his life Kaplan was convinced that his program would become American Judaism, rather than merely another Jewish denomination.

The emergence of Reconstructionism as a distinctive movement began when Kaplan's disciples founded a seminary designed to produce a cadre of rabbis to carry the Reconstructionist message. Ira Eisenstein, one of the key promoters of an institutional break with Conservative Judaism, noted that Reconstructionism had thus far relied upon rabbis ordained within the Conservative Seminary and, to a lesser extent, those in the Reform movement who had been persuaded by Kaplan's ideas. If the movement was to chart an independent course, it "would have to develop leaders who were not defectors from other groups." Moreover, the growth of Reconstructionist congregations depended upon the ability to provide them with rabbinic leaders.[3]

In the fall of 1968 the Reconstructionist Rabbinical College opened its doors in Philadelphia. The site had been chosen largely because of a special arrangement between the new college and the Department of Religion at Temple University in Philadelphia.[4] RRC, as it became known, was to train rabbis who combined a knowledge of the Jewish tradition with an understanding of other religious faiths. Accordingly, students pursuing rabbinical studies were required to enroll simultaneously as doctoral students in the Department of Religion of Temple University.[5] The goal was "to produce a rabbi capable of confronting the secular world, acquainted with Christianity and other religions, committed to the application of Judaism to the social problems of our day."[6]

Not surprisingly, the first years of the college were marked by considerable instability: a succession of deans and presidents oversaw operations; the requirement that students earn a doctorate in religion was first modified and then dropped entirely; and faculty members came and went. But the basic conception of the curriculum remained intact. Guided by Kaplan's view of Judaism as "an evolving religious civilization," the curriculum each year introduces students to a different era of Jewish civilization: students are first exposed to biblical civilization; in each succeeding year a different period of Jewish history—rabbinic, medieval, modern, and contemporary, respectively, forms the core of required courses. This curricular structure sets RRC apart from all other rabbinical seminaries.[7]

The 120 men and women ordained by RRC in its first two decades[8] have provided the Reconstructionist movement with a cadre of rabbis not beholden to any other movement and imbued with a shared allegiance to Reconstructionist institutions and ideology. Most of these alumni do not occupy pulpits in Reconstructionist congregations. Rather, they hold positions in Reform and especially Conservative synagogues, where some serve as emissaries for Reconstructionism, and others adopt the ideology of the congregation. These rabbis, far more than the relatively few congregations and havurot within the movement, provide Reconstructionism with a presence within the American Jewish community.

By contrast, the Reconstructionist movement itself remains minuscule, even as it aspires to become a fourth branch of American Judaism and expects to be treated with parity by the larger branches of Judaism. According to the National Jewish Population Survey of 1990, just over 1 percent of adult Jews in the core population of American Jews identify as Reconstructionists, which translates into some forty-six thousand individuals.[9] The Federation of Reconstructionist Congregations and Havurot (FRCH) consisted of some seventy affiliates by the early 1990s. Although this represents a trebling of affiliates since 1980, it must be borne in mind that most of these institutions have relatively few members: some fellowships number as few as fifteen families, and congregations generally number between thirty-five and two hundred families. In the New York area, where close to half of America's Jews live, some two thousand families are affiliated. These numbers, therefore, suggest that as a movement, Reconstructionism lags far behind its counterparts numerically—indeed, it is even dwarfed by some Hasidic sects.[10]

RETHINKING KAPLAN'S SYSTEM

In the process of becoming a fourth movement, Reconstructionism has moved boldly in several areas. Much to the dismay of many older disciples of Mordecai Kaplan, RRC and its rabbinic graduates have introduced far-reaching revisions of Reconstructionist thought. They have justified these revisions as being true to Kaplan's principles for reconstruction, even though they depart from his actual positions. Certainly, the Reconstructionist circle today offers some of the most radical and experimental approaches to contemporary Jewish living.

The innovative dimension of Reconstructionism is evident from several positions taken by the movement in recent decades. One involved the thorny issue of mixed marriage. Whereas the Reform rabbinate drew widespread attention—and opprobrium—for its decision on patrilineal descent in 1983, the Reconstructionist movement had already passed a similar resolution at its annual convention fifteen years earlier. In May 1968 Reconstructionism recognized as "Jewish the children of mixed marriage—when the mother is not Jewish—if the parents rear the child as a Jew (providing the boy with circumcision), matriculating the child in a religious school so that the child may fulfill requirements of bar or bat mitzvah or confirmation. No other formal conversion rites for the child will be required."[11] On a related matter, the Reconstructionist Rabbinical Association drafted "Guidelines on Intermarriage" that outlined the proper role of rabbis at mixed marriages: the guidelines urged rabbis to reserve the use of the "traditional wedding ceremony (*kiddushin*) for the marriage of a Jew to a Jew," because Jewish sancta and traditions do not belong at a mixed wedding ceremony; however, the guidelines affirmed that attendance at and/or participation in a civil marriage ceremony between a Jew and a non-Jew" should be at the rabbi's discretion if the couple has expressed a "determination to pursue, in the course of an on-going Jewish identification, ties with the Jewish community and the establishment of a Jewish home."[12] The Reconstructionist rabbinate, in short, does not impose sanctions upon rabbis who participate in mixed-marriage ceremonies.

A second area of far-reaching innovation concerns the role of women in Jewish life. Kaplan's pioneering efforts in regard to women's participation in synagogue life are well known. In 1922 his daughter Judith was the first to celebrate a Bat Mitzvah ceremony; in 1951 his synagogue, the Society for the Advancement of Judaism, began to call women to the Torah and count them in a minyan.[13] When RRC was established, women were quickly admitted. Still, as Rabbi Arthur

Green, president of the college noted, it was only in the 1980s that gender equality became a "bedrock principle" of Reconstructionism. This means that

> in no move toward Jewish unity and interdenominational rapproachment will we compromise the following: the full participation of women on all levels of Jewish leadership, including the rabbinic; the welcome offered to women to participate and be counted as full equals in all areas of Jewish ritual life; the acceptance of women as partners with men in legal decision making, witnessing, and participation in a *bet din* (rabbinic court); or the right of a woman, in the absence of other good alternatives, to end a marriage with a Jewish divorce obtained in a non-degrading manner.[14]

The latter issue is particularly telling. Whereas the Conservative movement and to a lesser extent the Orthodox movement have sought ways to remedy the plight of *agunot* ("anchored" women, chained to marriage because they did not receive a bill of divorce from their husbands) and the Reform movement for the most part did away entirely with a Jewish divorce, the Reconstructionists introduced an egalitarian *get* (bill of divorce), "in which the wife responds to her husband's bill of divorce by issuing a similar document in return [and] when the husband is not willing to act, Reconstructionist rabbis have also allowed for a female-initiated Jewish divorce."[15] For Reconstructionists, this innovation exemplifies their commitment to egalitarianism, as well as their desire "to bring Jewish observance into line with contemporary views of marriage."[16]

In recent years Reconstructionists have acted upon their commitment to egalitarianism not only in ritual matters and policy decisions but also in the liturgical sphere. During the 1980s a committee of rabbinic and lay members of the movement prepared a new prayer book that aimed for complete egalitarianism between men and women and planned to eliminate the male-dominated imagery of the traditional liturgy.[17] The fruit of their labor, *Kol Haneshamah*, a prayer book for the Friday evening service, offers gender-neutral "translations," while retaining much of the traditional text with its male-dominated imagery. As Rabbi Mordechai Liebling, executive director of FRCH, explained, "We're committed to complete gender neutrality in our English. Hebrew isn't a gender-neutral language, so there's not much we can do, except add the *imahot* [matriarchs]."[18] In its translations, *Kol*

Haneshamah offers worshipers the options of referring to "God" or the tetragrammaton (the four-consonant Hebrew name for God) or *Yah* (a more gender-neutral name for God), and it strives to translate references to the attributes of God into gender-neutral language; for example, *malkeinu* (our king) becomes "sovereign."[19] Reconstructionsts are proud of their sensitivity to gender-neutral liturgy, another example of their pioneering efforts to equalize the status of women in Judaism— efforts that go back to the Bat Mitzvah of Judith Kaplan.

Congregational life has been a third arena for innovation. In recent years Reconstructionists—especially rabbinic leaders—have rethought the relationship between rabbis and their congregants. Whereas the "Platform on Reconstructionism" refers rather vaguely to the importance of democracy in Jewish communal life, other movement guidelines define matters more clearly.[20] In the "Guidelines on Intermarriage," for example, the movement spells out its explicit commitment to "the rabbi as a teacher and guide, the participation of laity in the formulation of religious standards, and the setting of policy through democratic and communal procedures."[21] The role of the rabbi is thus significantly redefined—some would say diminished. The Reconstructionist rabbi "serves not as a judicial authority but rather as a learned teacher— someone who by virtue of his/her greater knowledge of Jewish civilization, can assist other Jews in studying the tradition and reaching their own decisions."[22] Rejecting the traditional role assigned to rabbis by virtue of their expertise in Jewish law, Reconstructionists "seek to empower all Jews who are willing to assume the responsibility through serious study and authentic experimentation."[23] The ultimate arbiter, then, is the congregation, which is vested with the authority to make "all decisions, including decisions about ritual, . . . in a democratic fashion."[24] To ensure democratization, Reconstructionists have developed clear-cut procedures for participatory decision making within smaller havurot, larger congregations, and the Federation of Reconstructionist Congregations and Havurot. Process, then, and not only ideology, is now an identifying characteristic of Reconstructionism.[25]

Though Mordecai Kaplan had written about the desirability of creating a Jewish community governed according to democratic principles, he had not emphasized the need to democratize synagogue life. Indeed, there is nothing in his long association with synagogues or with organized Jewish life, including the Reconstructionist movement, to suggest that he was prepared to relinquish control over decision making. The new emphasis on democratization is therefore one of many departures from Kaplanian thinking instituted by contemporary Reconstructionists.[26]

Matters even more central to Kaplan's thinking have also been reevaluated. In recent years some prominent Reconstructionists have advocated a return to the belief in a supernatural God, a belief emphatically rejected by Kaplan. While the "Platform on Reconstructionism" draws a distinction between traditional Judaism's "conception of a supernatural God who possesses such attributes as goodness, justice, righteousness, and mercy" and the Reconstructionist affirmation of "a conception of God as the Power or Process that makes for salvation, or human fulfillment," it also affirms "that *belief in God* is more central to Jewish religion than a specific *conception* of God."[27] This cautious approach is necessary to accommodate the growing numbers of Reconstructionists who reject the Kaplanian view of God. As one recent alumna and faculty member at RRC put it, "Claims about hope and goodness are quite implausible in anything *but* a supernatural context"; accordingly, she affirmed her belief in a supernatural and personal God.[28]

The emergence at RRC of neo-Hasidism, with its emphasis upon experiencing God through song and body movement during the course of prayer, further threatens to undermine the traditional Reconstructionist conception of God. Stalwart Kaplanians regard neo-Hasidism as incompatible with Reconstructionism, because it introduces mystical conceptions of God rejected by Kaplan and draws upon Hasidic teachings in which Kaplan had little interest. Writing in the journal of the Reconstructionist Rabbinical Association, Sidney Schwarz has thrown down the gauntlet over this issue:

> The many people in the movement, both teachers and students, . . . [could] point out all of the aspects of the Jewish world views which are Reconstructionist—they are politically liberal; they want peace in the Middle East; they want social justice; they want to have Jewish lifestyles and yet not be chained to *halacha*; they seek intimacy in religious fellowship; they are egalitarian; they want to strengthen Jewish life and community.

But a nonsupernatural theology is the "non-negotiable element for Reconstructionism."[29] With the influence of neo-Hasidism and concerns with spirituality on the rise, it is likely that the Kaplanian conception of God will continue to be questioned and modified.[30]

A similar challenge has been mounted to yet one other cherished principle of Reconstructionism: Kaplan's rejection of the concept of the chosen people. In a 1982 symposium on the future of Reconstructionism, several participants "indicated that the Kaplanian position on the chosen people might be *passé*."[31] There is yet further evidence of rethinking on the matter in the following statement issued by the movement's prayer book commission in 1982: "There is a historical link between chosenness and the idea of holiness and covenant. Our sense of destiny has been necessary for Jewish survival. Thus, we should affirm that we consider ourselves to be chosen *for* rather than emphasize what we are chosen *from*. This principle can be implemented by emphasizing vocation."[32] The new Friday evening siddur, *Kol Haneshamah*, takes a middle course between Kaplan's rejection of chosenness and the traditional formula in the *kiddush* (the sanctification of the Sabbath) proclaiming the election of Israel: instead of "you have chosen us" in the latter or "you have drawn us near to your service" in Kaplan's version, *Kol Haneshamah* substitutes "for you have called to us," thus "imagin[ing] a God who calls all humanity and makes holy those who, like Israel, heed the call and engage in God's service."[33] These modifications of Kaplan's language suggest that the concept of the chosen people, albeit somewhat redefined, is gradually being reinstated.

How do we understand this retreat from basic Kaplanian concepts and the introduction of new principles? At least three factors are reshaping Reconstructionist ideology. First, there is the changing constituency of the movement; it draws today from a totally different population than it did at its inception. Writing at midcentury, Rabbi Harold Schulweis, a leading disciple of Kaplan, characterized the original followers of Reconstructionism as the "struggling 'twice-born': Those who at one time experienced Orthodoxy and rejected it . . . and who later feel the need to return but to a tradition nourished by a thoroughgoing intellectual modernity."[34] By contrast, an editorial in the *Reconstructionist* described a very different constituency in the 1980s: "There are many members of FRCH affiliates who have joined because of the atmosphere and spirit of these groups. These people are unaware of the movement's philosophy in all its details."[35] Unlike the adherents cited by Schulweis, who were renegades from Orthodox homes, today's Reconstructionists are newcomers to Judaism. When

Kaplan spoke of the right of tradition to cast a vote but not a veto, he appealed to a constituency that knew how tradition voted. Today, Reconstructionism must appeal to a generation that has first to be educated about the nature of Jewish tradition before it can decide on its limits.

A second factor promoting ideological ferment is the presence on the RRC faculty of figures associated with countercultural tendencies in the religious and social spheres. Reconstructionism today prides itself on "being on the cutting edge of Jewish ritual and practice."[36] It consciously reaches out to Jews who are eager to experiment, but such individuals are unlikely to accept Kaplan's views or other forms of accepted wisdom. Moreover, they are eager to incorporate the politics of the counterculture into the Reconstructionist agenda. Thus, faculty members and alumni of the RRC have recently raised issues such as the following:

1. The creation of "an ethical kashrut." Food produced through the oppression of workers, or in factories owned by the Mafia, or where kosher certification was obtained unethically would be deemed unacceptable by a newly constituted Commission on Ethical Kashrut;[37]

2. The formation of a special havurah within a Reconstructionist congregation to provide "sanctuary for the stranger." Spurred by its rabbi, a FRCH congregation established a safe house to provide refuge for victims of political persecution who had immigrated to the United States illegally;[38]

3. Radical experimentation in feminist liturgy. A rabbinical student at the RRC introduced "ancient israelite feminine God-images . . . in an experimental liturgical context." Advocating a radical feminist position that "Liberal Judaism integrate women not only into its organization structure as rabbis, cantors and lay leaders, but that it also accept women's visions and experience into its historiography and theology," the student urged an "effort to dig up women's spiritual practices from the past and see what resonates";[39]

4. Institutional affirmation of the religious equality of homosexual Jews. Most notably, a report by the Reconstructionist Commission on Homosexuality that was adopted by FRCH affirmed "that homosexuality and heterosexuality are both normal expressions of human diversity . . . [and] that both are ways of being which offer fulfillment." No other religious movement in American Judaism has expressed such a

blanket acceptance of the equal status of homosexual and heterosexual behavior.[40] Reconstructionism's openness to these experimental approaches has won it a place on the far left of the Jewish religious spectrum, a position that accords well with the countercultural roots of some of its leaders.

Finally, the movement of Reconstructionism away from Kaplanian views results from the decision to create a separate movement. As long as Kaplan was content to play the role of gadfly in the Jewish community, the success of Reconstructionism was measured by the extent to which his views were adopted by the other movements. Judged in those terms, Reconstructionism was enormously influential. But once Reconstructionism became a separate movement, its success came to depend largely upon its *distinctiveness*. Why else join a new movement? Reconstructionism has therefore been under great pressure to define its unique approach to Jewish life in a community that has already accepted much of Kaplan's program. This pressure has done much to propel Reconstructionism toward new and in some cases radical positions that are far removed from the principles of Mordecai Kaplan. Thus, a movement that began as the most sharply defined ideological group within American Judaism now serves as an umbrella for Jews with varying perspectives. When it was led by Kaplan and did not need to market itself as a movement, it was able to maintain a high degree of ideological purity. Once it decided to compete with the other movements of Judaism, however, it lost many of its sharp edges: Kaplan's finely etched convictions are now blurred by his followers. Today Reconstructionism defines itself more by its process than by its united ideological commitments.

9

Religious Movements in Collision: A Jewish Culture War?

The foregoing analysis of shifts in the policies and practices of each Jewish denomination provides a necessary context in which to assess why relations between the religious groups have deteriorated in recent years. All of the movements have responded to a series of new challenges faced by the American Jewish community: the rising rate of intermarriage and the resulting question of how to integrate the children of such marriages into the Jewish community; the feminist revolution and the demands of Jewish women for equality in religious life; and the declining levels of synagogue affiliation and involvement of third- and fourth-generation American Jews, which has forced all Jewish institutions to compete for members. The policies of Jewish denominations have been shaped as well by the aggressive tenor of religious disputation that characterizes relations between segments of American Christianity—and indeed religious antagonists throughout the world.

HEIGHTENED RELIGIOUS TENSIONS

Each Jewish movement has responded differently to the new challenges and has embraced policies unilaterally, with little or no consultation with its counterparts in American Judaism. The resulting policies are shaped by profoundly different conceptions of Jewish identity, religious reform, and the future of American Judaism. The Reform and Reconstructionist position on patrilineality is incompatible with Conservative and Orthodox definitions of who is a Jew. The ordination of women as rabbis is viewed by some as a logical extension of Jewish ethical values and by others as an unacceptable deviation from Judaism's differentiation between gender roles. And the self-segregation of Orthodox Jews, many of whose leaders refuse to participate in communal organizations that include non-Orthodox rabbis lest such participation confer legitimacy on inauthentic leaders, raises the question of whether Jews can act in concert. As Irving Greenberg has suggested, both extremes on the religious spectrum seem to have written each other off; both extremes assume that other Jews can be ignored because those others will become increasingly irrelevant to the Jewish future. Specifically, the majority of Orthodox rabbis act as if they expect the non-Orthodox world to assimilate; and the unilateralism of Reform and Reconstructionism on the issue of patrilineality suggests a belief that adherents of halakhah are a dying or fossilized breed. Only those on the Conservative right and the Orthodox left seem overly concerned about religious polarization, perhaps because they have ties to all segments of the Jewish community.[1]

Although much of this disagreement has been confined to the journals of various rabbinic organizations, a few widely reported incidents have focused public attention on the heightened religious divisiveness. One episode that came to symbolize the possibilities as well as lost opportunities for greater religious unity has become known as the Denver experiment.[2] Beginning in 1978, Reform, Conservative, and Traditional[3] rabbis formed a joint *Beit Din* (rabbinic court) to oversee conversions. (Orthodox rabbis refused to participate and there was no Reconstructionist rabbi in Denver at the time.) The purpose of this program was to avoid a situation in which rabbis in Denver did not recognize each other's converts to Judaism. Under the Denver program, each rabbi still retained autonomy to perform his own conversions, but a very significant number—approximately 750 individuals—underwent conversion in Denver through the communal rabbinic court.

In order to function in concert, all participating rabbis compromised some of their views: the Traditional rabbis "were prepared to say that even though we knew that all of the students coming out of the general conversion process would not be authentic Orthodox Jews, we were prepared to say as long as they were beginning an effort to learn Judaism and aspire to be committed Jews, we were prepared to offer our signatures." Or as another Traditional rabbi put it: "Our compromise was simply that we did not make the thorough investigation that we might have made of our own converts—whether the person, in practice, was prepared to embrace a larger measure of traditional Judaism." The Reform rabbis, in turn, compromised by agreeing to teach about traditional observances, such as Jewish dietary laws and special Passover regulations. In addition, the Reform rabbis compromised by acceding to the Traditional and Conservative rabbis' insistence that converts must go to a ritual bath (*mikveh*) and undergo a symbolic circumcision (*hatafat dam brit*).[4] Not coincidentally, the lone Conservative rabbi in Denver, whose conception of conversion represented a centrist position, served as the chairman of the board for most of its history. But the actual conversion ceremony was supervised by three Traditional rabbis.

In 1983, after six years of relatively smooth functioning, the Denver *Beit Din* was dissolved. The move was precipitated by the resolution on patrilineality adopted that year by the Central Conference of American Rabbis. This decision to redefine Jewish identity, as well as the designation of Denver as a pilot community for a new Reform outreach effort to recruit converts, convinced the Traditional and Conservative rabbis that they could no longer participate in the joint board. Although the Reform rabbis of Denver held varying views on the question of patrilineality, the national decision of the Reform rabbinate placed the Traditional and Conservative rabbis in an untenable position. They could not cooperate in a conversion program with rabbis who held so different a conception of Jewish identity. And furthermore, they could not supervise conversions that would occur with increasing frequency due to a Reform outreach effort that was inconsistent with their own understanding of how to relate to potential proselytes. Thus, the Denver program, a model for other local Jewish communities, foundered because of decisions taken far away from that community at the national convention of Reform rabbis.

The possibility of future cross-denominational cooperation in other Jewish communities was further undermined by the response of Orthodox groups to the Denver program. When the existence of that program became public knowledge (ironically, through the announcement of its demise), Orthodox groups raised a hue and cry over the folly of Traditional rabbis for even participating in a joint conversion effort. As the *Jewish Observer,* an English-language periodical of the Orthodox right, crowed:

> While compromise for the sake of unity can often make good sense, when dealing with basic principles of faith, "compromise" is actually a sell-out. . . . It is time that all Orthodox rabbis recognize that Reform and Conservative Judaism are far, far removed from Torah, and that *Klal Yisroel* [the totality of the Jewish people] is betrayed—not served— when Orthodoxy enters in religious association with them.

In the judgment of the *Jewish Observer,* "the Traditional rabbis of Denver have been party to an outrageous fraud." And lest anyone fail to grasp the implications of this fraud, the periodical's editor went on to warn "other communities contemplating this type of inter-denominational cooperation . . . [to] take note of the awesome pitfalls involved and step back from the abyss."[5]

Since the collapse of the Denver program, denominational relations have continued to deteriorate. Among the key flash points have been the veto exercised by Orthodox rabbis of the Rabbinical Council of America to prevent the newly independent Reconstructionist movement from joining the Synagogue Council of America, an umbrella agency linking the rabbinic and congregational bodies of all the other Jewish religious movements;[6] the reconstitution of the Jewish Welfare Bureau's Chaplaincy Board, which provided chaplains and other support to Jews in the military since World War I, in response to the application of a woman rabbi seeking to serve as a Jewish military chaplain;[7] and the placement of advertisements by rabbinic groups of the Orthodox right urging Jews to stay home on the High Holidays rather than worship in a non-Orthodox synagogue.[8] When the *New York Times* published a front-page article with the headline, "Split Widens on a Basic Issue: What Is a Jew?" the divisions among rabbis began to attract wider attention in the Jewish community.[9] One orga-

nization in particular, the National Jewish Center for Learning and
Leadership (CLAL), headed by Rabbi Irving Greenberg, sought to
focus communal attention on the growing rift by inviting the leaders
of all four Jewish religious movements to a conference that posed the
provocative question, "Will There Be One Jewish People by the Year
2000?"[10]

The wider Jewish community was most actively drawn into the fray
during the "who is a Jew" controversy in late 1988. As we discussed in
the introductory chapter of this book, an international debate erupted
when it appeared that the Israeli government would grant the Orthodox rabbinate the exclusive right to determine the Jewish status of converts, thereby guaranteeing the delegitimation of all conversions not
performed under Orthodox auspices.

Long after Israeli leaders had finished with the matter, the bitterness engendered by the controversy continued to fester within the
American Jewish community. Opponents of the amendment faulted
Orthodox leaders in the United States, particularly the Lubavitcher
Rebbe, who resides in Brooklyn, N.Y., for pressuring Israeli groups to
pass the amendment. Orthodox groups were castigated as divisive and
mean spirited. It was frequently argued that Orthodox Jews in America
were taking their battle against other Jewish denominations to Israel
because as a small minority they could not win such a struggle in the
United States. Moreover, non-Orthodox spokespeople claimed that
their identity as Jews was under attack. Shoshana Cardin, then the
chairperson of the Council of Jewish Federations' Committee on Religious Pluralism put it as follows: "What we're dealing with here is perceived disenfranchisement of millions of Jews. And in this case, perception is reality."[11]

Orthodox groups counterattacked. Though some Orthodox organizations supported the campaign to remove the issue of "who is a Jew"
from the Israeli political agenda (principally, the Rabbinical Council of
America), other Orthodox groups banded together to blame Reform
Judaism for causing a religious schism. In an "Open Letter to American Jews" signed by several Orthodox organizations, the Halakhic definition of Jewish identity was described as "universally accepted among
all Jews for thousands of years. Reform, however, has done away with
halacha; and the Conservative movement is forever tampering with
it."[12] In a similar vein, Rabbi Marc Angel, one of the most moderate

members of the centrist Orthodox rabbinate, lashed out at those who criticized Orthodoxy for its stand on "who is a Jew":

> Those leaders who speak so passionately for Jewish unity ought to have launched a major attack on the decision of Reform Judaism to consider "patrilineal Jews" as Jews. There has probably been nothing more divisive in modern Jewish history than this decision to unilaterally change the definition of Jewishness to include the child of a Jewish father.[13]

The recrimination and bitterness over this issue brought religious hostility between Orthodox and non-Orthodox groups to a fever pitch.

THE GREAT RIFT

The "who is a Jew" controversy set into sharp relief the central features of recent religious warfare between Jews. First, it demonstrated the inextricable connection between Israeli religious and political developments and religious divisions that characterize American Jewry. Remarkably, actions taken by rabbis in Israel who have virtually no constituency other than Orthodox Jews can spark religious conflict in the United States, where the non-Orthodox groups represent the vast majority of Jews. The hostility of Jewish religious leaders in Israel toward non-Orthodox Jews strengthens the hands of militant Orthodox groups in the U.S. and antagonizes non-Orthodox groups. It is disturbing enough to some that the chief rabbis of Israel do not set foot in non-Orthodox synagogues when they visit the United States. But when leading Orthodox rabbinic decisors of *both* the right-wing *Haredi* sector and the more moderate faction rule that "in principle it is forbidden to save the life of a Reform or Conservative Jew on Shabbat on the same basis that one is not allowed to desecrate the Sabbath to save a gentile's life,"[14] there is a serious likelihood that the religious mind-set developing within the official Israeli rabbinate will further poison relations between Orthodox and non-Orthodox Jews in the United States. In turn, the attitudes of the latter toward Israel have been affected adversely because of the perceived link between the Israeli government and the Orthodox religious establishment. According to a recent survey, the attitudes of Reform Jews toward Israel are strongly correlated with the extent to which they link Israel with its

Orthodox rabbinate; the greater the perceived link, the more alienated from Israel Reform Jews felt.[15]

Second, the intensity of the recriminations indicates that issues of personal status are now at the heart of the struggle between religious factions. The explosion, after all, came over the question of "who is a Jew." Religious polarization became more intense when Jews could no longer agree on questions of boundaries: Who is part of the group and who is outside? Whom may their children marry? Will their grand-children be considered Jewish and permitted to celebrate a Bar or Bat Mitzvah if those grandchildren have a Christian mother and a Jewish father? If their rabbi was born to a Jewish father and Christian mother, is that ordained rabbi considered to be a Jew? In the past Jewish reli-gious movements held diverse theological views and observed religious rituals differently; but the observances of one group of Jews had only a limited impact on those of another group; they could be ignored if deemed offensive. Issues of personal status, by contrast, have far wider repercussions: at stake is the community's recognition or rejection of an individual as a Jew. Soaring rates of intermarriage coupled with dis-putes over patrilineal descent will only worsen the situation: Rabbi Irv-ing Greenberg has warned that by the end of the century, there will be perhaps as many as half a million children, born to mothers converted by Reform rabbis or accepted as Jewish under the patrilineal defini-tion, whose Jewishness will not be accepted by other Jews.[16] Thus, regardless of whether the matter is ever raised again in the State of Israel, American Jews do not agree on the question of "who is a Jew."

Third, there is even no agreement as to the number of American Jews who care about these matters. One survey found that on the issue of patrilineality, the vast majority of Orthodox Jews would be "upset" if their children married someone of patrilineal descent, but only one-third of Conservative Jews and one-tenth of Reform Jews would be "upset." Thus, perhaps no more than one-quarter of American Jewry rejects the new definition of Jewish identity put forward by Reform and Reconstructionism.[17] This has led to speculation that the rejection of patrilineality by Orthodoxy and by segments of the Conservative movement will give way in time to sociological realities, namely, mass support for patrilineality by American Jewry. Other observers are not so certain, especially as evidence mounts about the minimal Jewish identity of children raised in mixed-married homes and as fears of intermarriage intensify. Orthodox Jews are not about to alter their opposition, and Conservative rabbis who overwhelmingly voted to expel from their association any colleague who accepted patrilineality may yet convince their congregants to reject patrilineality.

Finally, and most important, the "who is a Jew" controversy made evident that the critical fault line running through the Jewish community separates Orthodox from non-Orthodox Jews. Reform and Reconstructionist Jews explicitly reject Halakhah (rabbinic law) as normative; accordingly, they do not define Jewish identity on the basis of those laws. By contrast, the Conservative movement does regard rabbinic law as normative and agrees with some Orthodox positions on questions of personal status. But in the debate over "who is a Jew" and other controversies in Israel, the Conservative movement has linked arms with the Reform and Reconstructionist movements, thereby blurring its own more nuanced stance: it agrees with Orthodoxy that Jewish identity must conform to rabbinic law, but it sides with Reform on the need to break the Orthodox monopoly on interpreting Jewish law. In order to wage that political battle, Conservative Judaism has allied itself with nonhalakhic movements. The critical divide thus runs between non-Orthodox movements on one side and the Orthodox on the other.

Since the "who is a Jew" controversy, relations between these camps have continued to worsen.

Item: Rabbi Aaron Soloveitchik, the heir apparent to his brother Joseph as the spiritual leader of centrist Orthodoxy, declared that any unified effort to resolve the chaotic issues of personal status through a Jewish court that included a non-Orthodox Jew would be invalid. Moreover, he likened the very act of cooperation with non-Orthodox groups to the biblical sin of the golden calf because it would "mislead ignorant Jewish masses to worship the idol of Reform and Reconstructionist Judaism."[18]

Item: Rabbi J. D. Bleich, his colleague at Yeshiva University, the preeminent institution of centrist Orthodoxy, "proposed to resolve the problem of 'who is a Jew?' by recognizing Reform converts in Israel the same way the law recognizes Moslem and Christian converts, that is, as members of a separate religion."[19]

Item: A planned meeting between American rabbis and Pope John Paul II was almost torpedoed by denominational bickering. The Synagogue Council of America, an umbrella agency that coordinates the national policies of Jewish rabbinical and congregational organizations, was paralyzed by the insistence of the Union of Orthodox Jewish Congregations upon its right to veto the composition of the delegation. The matter became moot after the pope postponed his visit to the United States. But it is unlikely that the umbrella organization will be able to avert conflict in the future. The head of the Orthodox rabbinic group insisted on the right to veto the appointment of a homosexual or patrilinear rabbi to a position of leadership on the Synagogue Council of America.[20]

Item: The Conservative movement has embarked on a program to free itself from reliance on Orthodox functionaries. Since the late 1980s the Jewish Theological Seminary of America has sponsored programs to train Jewish physicians to perform ritual circumcision (*brit milah*) and has taught rabbis how to supervise *kashrut* (Jewish dietary requirements) in their communities.[21] Conservative institutions are also building their own ritual baths as a response to Orthodox efforts to obstruct the performance of Conservative conversion ceremonies at communal *mikvaot*.[22]

Not surprisingly, these policy decisions are accompanied by increasingly uncivil outbursts by leaders of the various factions. Name-calling and invective are now routinely injected into Jewish public discourse. In an address to the Reform rabbinate, Rabbi Alexander Schindler of the Union of American Hebrew Congregations opined: "Where Orthodoxy alone prevails—stale repression, fossilized tradition, and ethical corruption hold sway."[23] Orthodox writers, in turn, label Reform Judaism a "sect" or an expression of "deviance."[24] The upcoming generation of rabbis is likely to be even more polarized. According to a recent study, large majorities of rabbinical students at the Conservative, Reform, and Reconstructionist seminaries viewed Orthodoxy as intolerant, lacking in compassion, and dominated by their isolationist wing. Almost all Orthodox rabbinical students surveyed and two-thirds of Conservative rabbinical students regarded Reform Judaism as "assimilationist."[25]

Although some observers dismiss these rifts as minor rabbinic squabbling over turf, fragmentary evidence is surfacing of a more widespread social consequence to the religious polarization. There is some evidence of a withdrawal on the part of broader segments of the Orthodox community away from social interaction, let alone friendship, with non-Orthodox Jews.[26] Though it is not widely publicized, the implicit, if not explicit, stance of the more right-wing Orthodox groups is to avoid such social contacts.[27] One writer who examined audio tapes prepared for Orthodox children found "a universe of discourse . . . [that] is exclusively Orthodox. . . . Jews who are other than Orthodox rarely appear, and then only . . . as negative foils," as Jews who are not very smart or as potential converts.[28] Moreover, as the overwhelming majority of Orthodox youngsters now attend their own denomination's day schools, summer camps, and youth programs through their high school years, they increasingly inhabit an exclusive social world that does not even allow for contact with non-Orthodox peers. These moves toward separatism, in turn, have antagonized non-Orthodox Jews: a survey of American Jews conducted in the late 1980s found that the majority claimed to be "very offended" "by Orthodox Jews who show no respect for the way you choose to be Jewish."[29] Social barriers between the Orthodox and non-Orthodox worlds are growing higher as the religious conflict intensifies.

Recognizing the dangers to Jewish unity inherent in religious polarization, some groups have tried to bridge the divide. This is a central item on the agenda of CLAL, the National Jewish Center for Learning and Leadership, which has a specific department called Am Echad—One People. The American Jewish Committee has also acted through its Department of Communal Affairs to bring leaders of opposing groups together.[30] In local communities rabbis from across the spectrum have initiated programs to keep the lines of communication open and to cooperate on issues of pan-Jewish concern.[31] Even some of the antagonists are edging away from conflict: the increasingly right-wing Young Israel movement within the Orthodox camp saw fit at the time of the "who is a Jew" controversy to publish an advertisement in the Jewish press to express its understanding "of the pain of those who mistakenly believe that Orthodoxy has denied their authenticity as Jews." "A Jew is a Jew," the ad declared, "regardless of his affiliation—Orthodox, Conservative, Reform, or non-believer—all are, and ever will remain Jews, to be loved and cherished."[32] Rabbis across the spectrum overwhelmingly assert that Jewish leaders should display unity in public and not delegitimize other Jews. It is those very same rabbis who carry on the disputes, however.[33]

Nevertheless, despite the many laudable efforts to bridge divisions, disputes over Jewish personal status remain unresolved; profound disagreements over religious definition, legitimacy, and change fester; social interactions between different types of Jews continue to be strained or nonexistent. And in the background, Israeli political groups, which do not concern themselves with questions of religious diversity, periodically hurl incendiary challenges into the volatile brew that is American Judaism.

A JEWISH CULTURE WAR?

The informed observer of Jewish religious conflict cannot fail to note the significant parallels between developments within American Judaism and the religious upheaval within Christian denominations. "On all sides," writes Robert Wuthnow about the general pattern, "American religion seems to be embroiled in controversy. . . . Scarcely a statement is uttered by one religious group on the issues without another faction of the religious community taking umbrage. The issues themselves shift almost continuously, but the underlying sense of polarization and acrimony continues."[34] Certainly, the tone of discussion and the polarized mood within American Judaism parallel those in American Christianity. But what about the substance of the dispute? To what extent does the great rift between non-Orthodox and Orthodox Jews mirror the great divide in American Protestantism between conservatives and liberals? How apt are comparisons between Protestant fundamentalists and Orthodox Jews? And is the religious struggle gripping the Jewish community the same as the culture war waged in some sectors of American society at large?

The broad brush strokes show many similarities in both the causes and the consequences of religious conflict in American Judaism and in American Christianity. To begin with, the antagonists—religious conservatives and liberals—share a common worldview with their counterparts in other religions. As defined by James Davison Hunter, the worldview of orthodoxy in its various permutations "is the commitment on the part of adherents to an external, definable, and transcendent authority," whereas progressivists[35] share in common "the tendency to resymbolize historical faiths according to the prevailing assumptions of contemporary life."[36] This distinction applies to Jewish religious movements, which are separated by their willingness to accept a normative religious structure that is commanded by divine (transcendent) authority: Orthodoxy in all its shadings affirms such a structure; the Conservative movement officially offers a nuanced acceptance of such religious norms; and the Reform and Reconstructionist movements explicitly advocate the need to resymbolize Judaism according to contemporary assumptions and to reject a binding religious structure. Clearly, the acceptance or rejection of a normative, divinely mandated Judaism with a legal structure based on commandments is central to Jewish religious divisions.

Moreover, as Hunter notes, these worldviews then shape social assumptions, especially regarding matters of public policy. Until the 1960s conservative groups believed that their views of marriage and sexual morality were widely shared. But since the revolutions of the 1960s those comfortable assumptions have been shattered by new social patterns—increasing rates of divorce, permissive sexual mores, divergent life-styles, changing gender roles, the perceived collapse of the family, more openly expressed homosexuality, and the availability of abortion on demand.[37] Some segments of the Orthodox Jewish community have sympathized with like-minded Christians over these symptoms of declining "family values." For their part, conservative activists have worked to build alliances with Orthodox Jews, as is attested by Jerry Falwell's (founder of the Moral Majority) proud declarations of his kinship with Orthodox Jews and the publication of approving reports about the warm family life of Lubavitch Hasidim by a conservative "think tank."[38]

In truth, however, only a small segment of the Jewish population is comfortable with these alliances. To some extent Jews are held back by political considerations: there is an ingrained fear of right-wing groups, because they have traditionally harbored anti-Semites and advocated the Christianization of America. Furthermore, most Jews, including many in the Orthodox camp, cannot subscribe to the total conservative social agenda. To take the most controversial issue, most Jews of all shades support present public policy on abortion, and even the most right-wing Orthodox Jews, who reject abortion on demand, cannot support a ban on abortion, because under certain circumstances they too rule that abortion is permissible. Even Agudath Israel, an ultra-Orthodox, explicitly pro-life organization which opposes *Roe v. Wade*, stops short of supporting a ban on public funding and facilities for abortions.[39] Similarly, all religious groupings in Judaism maintain that divorce is a legitimate option. Thus, while religious liberals, the vast majority of American Jewry, actively support liberal social policies and sometimes take a high-profile stance at pro-choice rallies,[40] more religiously conservative Jews are not generally active in the American culture war over social policies—even when they sympathize with part of the conservative agenda.

This is true even of those Orthodox Jews conventionally lumped together with fundamentalists, the right-wing Orthodox, or *Haredim*, as they are now more commonly known in Jewish circles. To understand why, we first need to clarify where these Orthodox Jews converge with Christian fundamentalists. If we ignore the original defining feature of fundamentalism, the belief in biblical inerrancy,[41] it is possible to discern some important areas of convergence between the most ultra-Orthodox Jews and the right-wing of evangelical Protestantism and Catholicism. Both ultra-Orthodoxy and fundamentalism are responses to the challenges posed by modernity to traditional religion and therefore both are most likely to exist "where tradition is meeting modernity rather than where modernity is most remote." Both also engage in a struggle with their own coreligionists who are perceived as "agents of assault on all that is held dear."[42]

Haredim conform to many of the characteristics listed in a recent attempt by Martin Marty and A. Scott Appelby to classify the commonalities shared by all fundamentalists.[43]

1. They are militant. "Fundamentalists begin as traditionalists who perceive some challenge or threat to their core identity, both social and personal. . . . They react, they fight back with great innovative power."

2. They share a "certain understanding of gender, sex roles, the nurturing and education of children."

3. They fight with a chosen repertoire of resources, including "real or presumed pasts, to actual or imagined ideal original conditions and concepts, and select what they regard as fundamental."

4. They "fight under God."

5. "They will fight for a changed civil polity."

With the exception of the last point, all of these traits characterize the outlook of ultra-Orthodox Jews in the United States.

This is not to suggest, however, that ultra-Orthodoxy derives its strategies and programs from American fundamentalism. Ultra-Orthodoxy was born in Europe and its most important techniques were imported to America at the time of the Holocaust. These include a reliance on separatism in Jewish communal matters—secession from official communal functions and refusal to recognize the legitimacy of non-Orthodox rabbis, even non-ultra-Orthodox rabbis; and the elevation of the Jewish school over the synagogue as the central institution of Jewish life, thereby granting most power to rabbinic authorities in the yeshiva world, rather than to pulpit rabbis. The recent resurgence of ultra-Orthodoxy has been reinforced by the successful application of these transplanted approaches rather than by the model of American fundamentalism.

In matters of American politics, as well, ultra-Orthodox Jews pursue an approach that differs from that of Christian fundamentalists. Undoubtedly, some Orthodox Jews support conservative policy stances, indeed, certain segments of Orthodox Jews tend to vote for political conservatives.[44] But ultimately, these Jews invest little energy and money in conservative social causes—however much they may sympathize. The critical battles for Orthodox Jews are with non-Orthodox Jews and revolve around entirely different matters.

To take up the first distinction, Orthodox Jews for the most part are not invested in the struggle over public policy, the key battleground in the American religious and culture war.[45] To be sure, Orthodox Jews sometimes become activists on behalf of specific candidates, but they are drawn into politics in order to protect their communal interests, to get their fair share of government funding and protection—not in order to change American society. The conventional right-wing Orthodox perspective was colorfully expressed by Rabbi Yehuda Levin: "I had very little contact with the Gentile world. I was living in a ghetto without walls. . . . It is inbred in our community that what goes on in the outside world is *meshugah* (crazy). . . . So if it is *meshugah*, why should we bother with it."[46] Levin nevertheless became a militant anti-abortion and anti–gay rights activist, but he is the exception that proves the rule. Most Orthodox Jews do not see American public policy as their domain. They fight for their narrow political interests, not to remake American society.[47]

The only society ultra-Orthodox Jews wish to remake is Israel—for both ideological and pragmatic reasons. Orthodox groups in the United States and Israel have invested in the issue of "who is a Jew" and other questions of Israeli public policy because it offends them that Israel is not governed by traditional Jewish law. They have no such expectations of American society. Moreover, ultra-Orthodox Jews, the so-called *Haredim*, have a powerful vested interest in Israeli political life since they are supported by massive government subsidies. As Samuel Heilman and Menachem Friedman put it: "The [international Jewish] fundamentalism train is pulled by the Israeli [Haredi] locomotive; that locomotive is traveling very fast on rails maintained" by the Israeli government.[48]

By contrast, the Orthodox/non-Orthodox rift in the United States focuses not on governmental policy but on communal conflict, particularly regarding the definition of Jewish personal status. True, the various Jewish religious movements differ in their evaluations of modern culture and American mores; and they also assess gender and sexual matters differently. But the critical divide between Jewish religious groups concerns questions of personal status—marriageability and Jewish identity—which have no counterpart in Christian religious disputes. Put differently, the culture war engulfing some sectors of Christianity concerns the proper ordering of American society; at stake in Judaism are issues of group survival and cohesion. As Christians clash over theology and public policy, religious Jews battle over the boundaries of their own society—indeed, they cannot even agree on whether some of their coreligionists are actually Jewish.

CONCLUSION

Judaism within the Landscape of American Religion

PREDICTING THE FUTURE

In the closing years of the twentieth century, after decades of rapid and massive change, we have come to expect every analysis of current affairs to conclude with a prediction of the future. Eager pundits fuel such expectations by offering snap judgments not only about contemporary events but also about the likely unfolding of future events. Never mind that none of them anticipated the truly momentous changes that swept away the existing world order—not the collapse of the Iron Curtain or the phoenix-like emergence of strong freedom movements in tightly controlled totalitarian states like the Soviet Union, East Germany, and Hungary. The temperament of the time is nonetheless to expect sweeping, unequivocal predictions.

Jews are especially prone to these impulses. As witnesses to the cataclysmic events of midcentury—the decimation of one-third of world Jewry followed immediately by the reemergence of Jewish political autonomy after two thousand years—many Jews continue to think in apocalyptic terms. Jews, noted Simon Rawidowicz, are an "ever-dying people," convinced of their fragility and uncertain of their future.[1] Given the tumultuous nature of Jewish history, particularly in this century, it is no wonder that Jews fret about survival. What does the future hold? Is American Jewry doomed by intermarriage? Does the drift to religious minimalism suggest that Judaism will disappear from America within a century, within decades? Or do the pockets of religious revival offer an opportunity to resurrect American Judaism? And will religious fragmentation destroy the unity of the Jewish people?

Many writers have given in to the temptation to predict the Jewish future. In the mid-1980s, an optimistic reading of "American Jews and their lives today," received much attention: the author of this study confidently denied that "Judaism is seriously threatened by the new openness of American society." "We are," he predicted, "in the early stages of a major revitalization of Jewish religious, intellectual, and cultural life—one that is likely to transform as well as strengthen American Judaism."[2] Within just a few years, the same writer had tempered his views; new survey research, he felt, demonstrated that Jewish renewal "has played itself out."[3] A history of American Jewry written in the late 1980s concluded with the sweeping assertion that "after nearly four centuries, the momentum of Jewish experience in America is essentially spent."[4] Such exercises in prophecy are not new: forty years ago the leading American Jewish sociologist depicted Orthodox Judaism in a state of institutional decay, only to revise his gloomy assessment a few decades later.[5] Ironically, today there are Orthodox prophets who confidently predict the doom of every Jewish movement except their own.[6]

These prophets are joined by advocates of simplistic solutions for all the problems that beset American Judaism. An organization promoting Orthodox day schools proclaims its product as "a guarantee for Jewish survival," asserting that the "intermarriage rate drops to 7% for students who complete a Jewish day school education." These claims are then deemed an exaggeration by sociologists who have correlated levels of Jewish education with rates of intermarriage.[7] Other groups present their own solutions to Jewish religious crises, including acceptance of Gentiles as equal participants in synagogues, aggressive conversion programs, massive investment in Jewish day schools, and fully subsidized trips to Israel for every Jewish high school graduate. All of these solutions will yield some fruits. For one of the clear lessons to be learned from our survey of American Jewish religious life is that religious involvement of all types is chosen or rejected on a highly personal basis; and the more ways Jews can be reached, the greater the number who may choose to participate. Given the heterogeneity of American Jewry, it is unlikely that there is a single panacea for all that ails American Judaism.

We should realize as well that such discussions are not confined to the Jewish community. Since the publication in the early 1970s of Dean Kelley's *Why the Conservative Churches Are Growing*, there has appeared a spate of other books on the decline of mainline Protestantism, each book seeking to understand why some forms of religion thrive and others fail. According to Kelley, the only churches that grow in contemporary America are those that maintain a distance from American culture and help individuals solve problems of personal meaning. Other researchers wonder whether such conservative churches can appeal to a wide population; and still others question whether the spirit of American individualism will erode all denominational structures.[8]

Catholics also debate solutions to religious disaffiliation. Hardliners in the Catholic church, as in the Jewish community, have insisted on strict enforcement of traditional practices and doctrines. Some Catholics follow the hard line of the pope on divorce, birth control, abortion, the ordination of women, married clergy, and homosexuality. But others within the Church argue the need for reform in light of the large percentages of Catholics who disagree with papal teachings on all of these issues. Finally, there are those who feel the hardline stance of the Church coupled with the actual permissiveness of most Catholics is the ideal solution—Catholics want their Church to stand rock solid, even as they go about their own business.[9]

There is even no agreement as to the overall health of religion in America. For the past fifteen years, in the face of mounting evidence of religious resurgence, if not revival, the so-called secularization thesis, which predicts the inevitable decline of religion in modern societies, has come under attack: as religious groups have assumed a greater role in American politics and produced political leaders, as cults and "new-age" forms of religion have attracted the young, and as baby boomers have returned to churches and synagogues, observers have wondered about the staying power of religion. Arthur Parsons has argued that "the proliferation of religious movements in highly modern circumstances actually lends support to the . . . view that secularization is a self-limiting process whose very success unleashes regenerative religious forces."[10] But others such as Thomas Luckmann question whether all of this public display of religion does not mask "a secularization from within," a privatization of faith and an insistence on individual self-expression that undermines organized religion even as people pay lip service to religion.[11]

In short, there is much disagreement over the future direction of religion in America as well as over the remedies for an ailing religious life. Certainly, there is always room for modest speculation about the near-term future, but given the complexity of religious experience, coupled with the unrelenting and rapid change that characterizes life in the twentieth century, grand statements about the future are foolhardy. Moreover, as Jewish communal leaders recognize the challenges to continuity and religious unity, they will reshape the communal agenda and thereby rechannel American Judaism. This conclusion will therefore not offer prophecies but will instead highlight the salient patterns that have emerged from our examination of Judaism in contemporary America. For only with a clear understanding of the present can policy makers plan intelligently for the future.

UNDERSTANDING THE PRESENT

Increasing levels of disunity and heightened polarization have been central themes in our discussion of American Judaism. Jewish religious behavior is assuming a bipolar constellation, with a large population of Jews moving toward religious minimalism and a minority gravitating toward greater participation and deepened concern for religion. The latter include newly committed Jews and converts to Judaism, whose conscious choice of religious involvement has infused all branches of American Judaism with new energy and passion; rabbinic and lay leaders of the official denominations, who continue to struggle with issues of continuity and change within their respective movements; and groups of Jews who are experimenting with traditional forms in order to reappropriate aspects of the Jewish past. These articulate and vocal Jews have virtually transformed American Judaism during the past two decades. At the same time an even larger population of American Jews has drifted away from religious participation. Such Jews have not articulated the sources of their discontent but have voted with their feet, by absenting themselves from synagogues and declining to observe religious rituals that require frequent attention. Many are incapable of or unwilling to transmit a strong religious commitment to their children.

As for organized religious life, the official movements of American Judaism struggle with internal dissent, even as they wage ever harsher campaigns against their denominational foes. All of the denominations of American Judaism are in fact coalitions, straining to maintain internal unity. There are conservative and liberal factions in all four movements, and there are divisions that cannot be reduced to a simple matter of right and left. Perhaps to compensate for such internal disunity and to create a common cause against external foes, each of the movements has embarked on a program of more overt competition and criticism directed at other Jewish movements.

Some choose to view this fragmentation as primarily a matter of increased diversity, rather than as an issue of antagonism and communal divisiveness. We are creating a pluralistic Judaism, they contend. As laudable as this goal may be, it has not been attained and religious incivility characterizes relations between many sectors of American Judaism. Whereas more traditional groups insist that only their way is correct and therefore feel impelled to attack their opponents openly, there is also much intolerance among the champions of pluralism. Many feminists have no tolerance for synagogues or institutions that maintain traditional definitions of women's status; proponents of havurot do not simply absent themselves from formal synagogues, they scorn them; and Reform leaders, for all their talk of religious pluralism, harbor strong triumphalist views and do not hide their disdain for other types of Jews. Shrill divisiveness, rather than pluralism, is the order of the day.

These patterns mirror developments within Christian America. As Stephen Warner writes: "It isn't as if American religion had simply moved to the right. It was moving in several directions, becoming both noisy to the public outside and divisive to itself."[12] American religious life has fragmented, spawning a diversity of special-purpose groups and new forms of religion, even as hundreds of formal denominations continue to attract adherents. Moreover, as is the case with Judaism, Christian denominations embrace a wide range of practices; it is impossible to anticipate the type of religious service one will encounter from one congregation to the next within a given Protestant denomination. Even in the more centralized Catholic Church, there is much greater diversity today, as the historian Jay Dolan writes: "There is no longer one way to do theology, to worship at Mass, to confess sin, or to pray. There are various ways of being Catholic, and people are choosing the style that best suits them."[13]

Religious fragmentation and diversity is the result of fundamental changes in the way Americans view religious questions. Since the 1960s three features of American life have particularly reshaped religious life and detonated explosions within the denominations of Christianity and Judaism.

First, the interrelated *sexual and feminist revolutions* have challenged all American religious groups by raising profound questions about both gender roles and sexual mores. Few organized religious groups have been able to ignore the feminist agenda. In both churches and synagogues, women have demanded inclusion as religious celebrants and congregational leaders, as well as revisions of liturgy to reflect their experiences and rites of passage. These challenges to tradition have polarized churches in the last quarter of the century, dividing religious conservatives and religious liberals. Each of the Jewish religious movements has reacted, with the most liberal and most conservative responding with the greatest alacrity. Not surprisingly, the movement in the center of the spectrum, Conservative Judaism, was torn in two directions by an issue that so directly pits tradition against change.

Hierarchical religious categories have also evoked sharp criticism. Both feminism and the gay rights movement march under the banner of egalitarianism, a concept that is unknown to traditional forms of Western religions. Both seek to level distinctions between categories of religious adherents that are critical to the traditional teachings of Judaism and Christianity. Not surprisingly, the struggle between liberals and conservatives on these issues has been protracted. And after a quarter of a century most denominations in Christianity and Judaism have still not resolved all the provocative questions posed by the sexual and feminist revolutions.

In Jewish religious life, as in Christian America, gender and sexual issues have been at the center of much of the maelstrom—within each of the movements and between them. The centrality of gender issues was manifest already in the middle decades of the century, when the decision to eliminate the physical barrier separating men and women in the synagogue became the symbolic breaking point between Conservatism and Orthodoxy; in the closing decades of the century some of the movements have been internally divided over gender or sexual issues, the Orthodox over women's prayer groups, the Conservatives over egalitarianism; and they have disagreed with each other over the religious status of homosexuals and gender neutral liturgy.

A second catalyst in American life is the deeply ingrained heritage of voluntarism, which has in recent decades fostered *a spirit of religious individualism* that challenges all organized religion. On the most basic level it encourages every person to make a personal decision about religious involvement. Ascriptive loyalties to the religion of one's family, ethnic group, or community have drastically declined in recent decades. Instead, according to Wade Clark Roof and William McKinney,

> what surfaces under these conditions is the peculiarly American practice of claiming a "religious preference." Faith comes to be expressed as an opinion or point of view, something that can be easily modified or even discarded if one so chooses. Put simply, religion becomes even more privatized, more anchored in the personal and subjective sphere, and less bound by custom or social bonds.[14]

Judaism, a religion that depends upon ascribed loyalty—one is born a Jew—and that has traditionally imposed an elaborate set of customs and social bonds, has been particularly hard hit by this brave new world of American religion. The two most Americanized versions of Judaism, Reform and Reconstructionism, have repositioned themselves to accommodate highly individualized versions of Judaism. They have taken steps to accept the American way of defining religious identity as primarily a matter of personal belief and observance, rather than of descent: according to their decisions on patrilineal descent, a Jew must demonstrate commitment to Judaism before the presumption of Jewishness conferred by his or her birth to a Jewish parent can be confirmed. Hence, ascribed Jewish identity is no longer enough; each Jew must now become a "Jew by choice." The Conservative and Orthodox movements insist on the more traditional view that Judaism is not chosen but imposed by the accident of birth; as a result they find themselves swimming against the powerful current of American individualism. According to survey research, 80 percent of Americans agree that individuals should arrive at their own religious beliefs independent of any church or synagogue, and fewer than half of adult Americans have an unbroken record of involvement with their present denomination.[15] "It is decreasingly satisfying," writes Stephen Warner, "to respond to a query that one has one's religion 'because that's how I was brought up.' One is supposed to be more self-actualized than that."[16]

The new American belief that religious identification is achieved, rather than ascribed from birth, also encourages a far more individualistic approach: each individual is expected to tailor religion to meet personal needs and sensibilities. There is much talk in all religious traditions of "pick and choose religion," "smorgasbord theology," "cafeteria religion."[17] By elevating the autonomy of the individual or the community to a central tenet, by sanctioning an approach to religion that encourages each Jew to select from the tradition as he or she sees fit, Reform and Reconstructionist Judaism have demonstrated just how attuned they are to the new American individualism. Like their counterparts in liberal versions of Christianity, they are challenged by traditionalists who castigate such an approach as pandering to the pick-and-choose mentality.

In its most extreme forms, American individualism encourages a highly privatized version of religion that leaves little room for any form of organized religion. This privatism, which was personified by "Sheilaism" in the widely remarked study entitled *Habits of the Heart*, places "the locus of moral and religious decision making . . . within an autonomous self, dislodged from any meaningful social and institutional context."[18] Religious privatism may prove the key to understanding the growing population of Jews who practice only a minimalistic form of Judaism but continue to think of themselves as Jewish by religion.

Third, even as American individualism has encouraged some to reject religion as an ascribed and regulated system, it has encouraged *a quest for community and personal meaning* in others. This is one of the primary reasons given for the growth of conservative religious congregations in America: they offer their members respite and comfort from the chaos and rootlessness of American society. Among Jews as well, the search for meaning and community has propelled a minority to greater activism and religious involvement. It is not accidental that an important study of Havurah Judaism was entitled "Making Judaism Meaningful."[19] Certainly all the special-purpose versions of Judaism, as well as of Christianity, appeal to specific subpopulations because they offer fellowship among kindred spirits—feminists, Havurah types, gay Jews, and so forth. And within denominational Judaism, the most successful congregations have also worked to create a community. It is difficult to imagine that Orthodoxy, especially in its more right-wing forms, could have flourished in an environment that did not leave space for religious and communal exploration in the name of individual self-expression. American individualism has thus also fostered religious involvement. "The bonding that goes on in a vital religious community is of a kind of brotherhood or sisterhood," writes Stephen Warner. "In this way, the breakdown of ascriptive ties to religion can enhance, rather than reduce, the elemental nature that believers attribute to their experiences. . . . Not religion, but social ascription that denies one's true being, is seen as arbitrary."[20]

These new approches to religion are likely to continue to disrupt Jewish unity in the future both at home and abroad. The international solidarity of Jews will suffer as Judaism in America and Israel, the two largest centers of Jewish civilization today, diverge, making it harder for Jews in those two environments to respond sympathetically to each other. It has been difficult enough for these two Jewries to empathize with each other given the vast differences in their physical circumstances: Israeli and American Jews inhabit neighborhoods where conflict is resolved in vastly different ways; the economic and political power of Jews in the United States and Jews living in their own state are not comparable; and each Jewry employs different building blocks in the construction of its identity so that they differ in their attitudes toward land, the non-Jewish world, the family of the Jewish people, and their visions of the Jewish future.

A recent examination of these "two worlds of Judaism" concluded optimistically that even though Israeli and American Jews construct their Jewish identities and worldviews differently, they ultimately share many commonalities.[21] But as American Judaism continues to Americanize, it appears that the two worlds of Judaism will become further estranged. The revolutionary transformations in American religious life during the past few decades, which are so much a reflection of the singularly American ethos, have virtually no echo in Israeli Judaism. Only Orthodox Jews, who have strong ties to the religious establishment in Israel and who send most of their youngsters for sustained study at yeshivas there, share strong religious commonalities with their counterparts in Israel. For the rest of American Jews, religion is a barrier to their attachment to Israel. And it appears that Israeli Jews of all stripes cannot relate to the non-Orthodox versions of Judaism that attract the vast majority of American Jews.[22]

The political consequences of these divisions are potentially great, for if Jews cannot identify with each other—if they regard each other as alien—they will find it harder to rally to each other's side. Survey research already illustrates that for some American Jews, identification with Israel declines when they perceive a strong link between the government of Israel and its Orthodox religious establishment. Furthermore, criticism of religious intolerance in Israel may well legitimize other types of criticism directed at the Jewish state. Serious differences in religious outlook may further weaken already frayed ties.

The second likely consequence of the patterns we have discussed affects domestic Jewish life: religious divisions may adversely affect the ability of the American Jewish community to act in concert. On the most basic level, Jewish groups are increasingly competing with one another for the allegiance of the minority of Jews who affiliate. American ideals of voluntarism and individualism, coupled with the rejection of ascribed identity, all encourage individual Jews to pursue religious activities that they find personally meaningful. Just as Christianity in America continues to splinter into new denominations, special-purpose groups, and cults, so too will the Jewish community. And as organized religious groups compete for the allegiance of the declining numbers of Jews who are engaged, it is also likely that relations between them will grow even more strained. To some observers, such competition is healthy because it reminds organized groups to pay attention to their constituents and prods them to invest more resources and creativity in the services they provide. But Judaism is not a commercial enterprise that necessarily improves with competition.

Moreover, religious competition and polarization drive wedges between the minority of Jews who exhibit a strong Jewish identity. It is especially troubling when these committed Jews are riven in two over the question of "who is a Jew?" And yet, two numerically small groups that contribute disproportionately to the energy, finances, and leadership of the American Jewish community—Orthodox and observant Conservative Jews—cannot recognize growing populations of patrilinear Jews accepted by the majority of the American Jewish community.

As the "who is a Jew?" debacle of 1988 made clear, those disagreements can affect levels of giving to pan-Jewish causes such as the United Jewish Appeal and the campaigns of local federations of Jewish philanthropy.

Unresolved questions of Jewish personal status will also complicate efforts by local federations and their agencies to identify their constituents. There is no longer a consensus on the boundaries of the Jewish community and, therefore, community institutions will have difficulty defining whom they should serve and how they should allocate their resources. Community-wide institutions have already begun to debate whether to invest in winning back mixed-marriage families or to concentrate their energies only on endogamous families.[23] These questions will become even more explosive as rates of mixed marriage spiral and community resources shrink.

Jewish religious divisions are also hampering the ability of the Jewish community to project a unified stance within American society. Since the mid-1980s, Conservative and Orthodox organizations have established their own public policy commissions and at least two Orthodox groups have opened lobbying offices in Washington, D.C., to represent their distinctive positions.[24] These new arms parallel and compete with the Reform movement's Religious Action Center. They add to the cacophony of Jewish voices seeking the attention of Washington lawmakers. As each denomination stakes out its own distinctive position on questions of public policy, the American Jewish community will find itself even more hard-pressed to speak with coherence in the American public square.

There is even evidence that religious divisions are subverting Jewish unity concerning the one cause that consistently brought American Jews together—the struggle against anti-Semitism. In response to attacks upon Hasidic Jews in New York City in the early 1990s, Orthodox groups have begun to organize their own defense efforts because they feel abandoned by nondenominational agencies that combat anti-Semitism.[25] Religious differences now threaten to fragment the community relations activities of American Jewry.

Tensions over religious questions thus intrude into all spheres of Jewish communal life. They color social relations between Jews of different denominations and outlooks. They undermine the ability of the American Jewish community to act in concert regarding domestic issues, such as the struggle against anti-Semitism. And they exacerbate estrangement between American and Israeli Jews. It is no longer possible—or wise—to dismiss religious polarization as peripheral to Jewish life. The divided world of Judaism imperils the unity of the Jewish people in America.

NOTES

Introduction

1. Hundreds of articles appeared in Jewish newspapers on this subject between mid-November and mid-December 1988. For an overview, see Lawrence Grossman, "Jewish Communal Affairs," *American Jewish Yearbook* 90 (1990), pp. 276–77.

2. Arthur J. Magida, "'Who Is a Jew' Dominates Assembly," *Jewish News* (Detroit), November 25, 1988, pp. 1ff.

3. Gary Rosenblatt, "Separating the Historical from the Hysterical," *Baltimore Jewish Times*, December 9, 1988, pp. 29ff., offers a helpful introduction to the controversy.

4. "A Call to 'Every Jew'—and Some Responses," *Jewish Observer*, January 1985, p. 37.

5. "The People of the State of Illinois vs. Elchonon Ebert." The stenographic transcript of this case is in the Ratner Center for the Study of Conservative Judaism, the Jewish Theological Seminary of America. See esp. p. 12.

6. *CCAR Yearbook* 97 (1987), pp. 175–76.

7. *Intermountain Jewish News*, December 2, 1983, special section on Conversion and Patrilineality.

8. Steven M. Cohen and Paul Ritterband, "Will the Well Run Dry? The Future of Jewish Giving in America," *Response*, Summer 1979, pp. 9–16; and

Steven M. Cohen, "Trends in Jewish Philanthropy," *American Jewish Year-book* 80 (1980), pp. 40–44.

9. Sidney Goldstein, "Profile of American Jewry," *American Jewish Yearbook* 92 (1992), p. 141.

10. Sam Allis, "In Vermont: When Woody Allen Meets L. L. Bean, *Time*, September 26, 1988, pp. 10–11; Lis Harris, "Holy Days," *New Yorker*, September 16, 23, 30, 1985.

11. Michael Specter, "The Oracle of Crown Heights," *New York Times*, March 15, 1992, pp. 36ff.

12. Rabbi Sanford Seltzer, quoted in "The Search for Spirituality in Reform Judaism," *Moment*, June 1992, pp. 29–35, esp. p. 35.

13. Michael Shapiro, "Building the Future: Six Hebrew Schools That Break the Mold," *Baltimore Jewish Times*, May 29, 1992, pp. 52–58.

14. Ira Rifkin, "The G.A.: Feeling the Crunch," *Baltimore Jewish Times*, November 15, 1991, pp. 66–80; and idem, "Angst over Assimilation," *Baltimore Jewish Times*, November 29, 1991, pp. 32–34.

15. For different assessments of American Jewish religious polarization, see Irving Greenberg and Steven M. Cohen, "The One in 2000 Controversy," *Moment*, March 1987, pp. 11–22.

16. Martin E. Marty, *A Nation of Behavers* (Chicago: University of Chicago Press, 1976), p. 18.

17. For a survey of the field, see Nathan Glazer, "New Perspectives in American Jewish Sociology," *American Jewish Yearbook* 87 (1987), pp. 3–19. Some recent works that examine the ethnic cohesiveness of Jews are Calvin Goldscheider, *Jewish Continuity and Change: Emerging Patterns in America* (Bloomington: Indiana University Press, 1986); Steven M. Cohen, *American Assimilation or Jewish Revival?* (Bloomington: Indiana University Press, 1988); and Sergio DellaPergola and Uziel O. Schmelz, "Demographic Transformations of American Jewry: Marriage and Mixed-Marriage in the 1980s," *Studies in Contemporary Jewry*, vol. 5 (New York: Oxford University Press, 1989), pp. 169–200.

18. For an elaboration upon some of these questions, see Todd M. Endelman, "The Legitimization of the Diaspora Experience in Recent Jewish Historiography," *Modern Judaism*, May 1991, pp. 195–209.

Chapter 1

1. For a lively account of the postwar suburban expansion and the "drive-in" culture it engendered, see Kenneth T. Jackson, *Crabgrass Frontier: The Suburbanization of the United States* (New York: Oxford University Press, 1985), chaps. 13–15.

2. For a contemporaneous account of the Jewish move to suburbia, see Albert Gordon, *Jews in Suburbia* (Boston: Beacon Press,1959). On the geographic relocation of American Jews in the postwar era, see Marshall Sklare, *America's Jews* (New York: Random House, 1971), pp. 44–47.

3. For an extended discussion of Jewish associationalism that characterized second-generation Jews, see Deborah Dash Moore, *At Home in America: Second Generation Jews in New York* (New York: Columbia University Press, 1981).

4. The role of World War II in the Americanization of second-generation

Jews and their Judaism has been insufficiently appreciated. Two essays written shortly after the war emphasize this point: Abraham Duker, "On Religious Trends in American Life," *YIVO Annual* 4 (1949), p. 63; and Moses Kligsberg, "American Jewish Soldiers on Jews and Judaism," *YIVO Annual* 5 (1950), pp. 256–65. The latter emphasizes anti-Semitism in the military as a factor promoting chapel attendance by servicemen and servicewomen.

5. Morris Freedman, "A New Jewish Community in Formation," *Commentary*, January 1955, pp. 36–47.

6. Gordon, *Jews in Suburbia*, p. 98.

7. There is ample evidence from this period, in synagogue brochures as well as survey responses, that parents regarded the synagogue primarily as a vehicle for the education of youth. See, for example, Leonard Fein et al., *Reform Is a Verb: Notes on Reform and Reforming Jews* (New York: UAHC, 1972), chap. 5, esp. p. 90; and Marshall Sklare and Joseph Greenblum, *Jewish Identity on the Suburban Frontier: A Study of Group Survival in an Open Society* (Chicago: University of Chicago Press, 1967), p. 190.

8. See Sklare and Greenblum, *Jewish Identity*, chap. 5.

9. For congregational growth in the Conservative movement, see the *Biennial Reports of the United Synagogue of America* (1952), p. 52; (1957), p. 97; (1959), p. 140; (1961), p. 3; (1963), pp. 184–85; (1965), p. 6.

10. On the growth of the UAHC, see Marc Lee Raphael, *Profiles in American Judaism* (San Francisco: Harper and Row, 1984), pp. 71, 198.

11. On the spread of Orthodox synagogues, see Charles S. Liebman, "Orthodoxy in American Jewish Life," *American Jewish Yearbook* 66 (1965), pp. 22–40, 59–60.

12. Jacob K. Shankman. "The Changing Role of the Rabbi," in *Retrospect and Prospect*, ed. Bertram W. Korn (New York: Central Conference of American Rabbis, 1965), p. 246.

13. Enrollment figures are taken from Uriah Z. Engelman, "Educational and Cultural Activities" *American Jewish Yearbook* 46 (1946), p. 137; idem, "Jewish Education," *American Jewish Yearbook* 64 (1963), pp. 152–53; Walter Ackerman, "Jewish Education," in *Movements and Issues in American Judaism*, ed. Bernard Martin (Westport, Conn.: Greenwood Press, 1978), p. 196.

14. Uriah Z. Engelman, "Jewish Education," *American Jewish Yearbook* 64 (1963), pp. 152–53, 161–62.

15. Freda Imrey, "Religion," *American Jewish Yearbook* 64 (1963), p. 146. Protestant churches faced similar shortages of pastors, with vacancy rates hovering between 20 and 40 percent. See Robert Wuthnow, *The Restructuring of American Religion: Society and Faith since World War II* (Princeton: Princeton University Press, 1988), pp. 28–29.

16. "Survey of Synagogue Finances," issued by the Department of Synagogue Administration, United Synagogue of America, November 1963, p. 21.

17. Many observers of Jewish life have remarked on the reliance of parents on the synagogue rather than on the home to provide their children with Jewish identity and knowledge. The frustration of rabbis over this state of affairs was summed up in Rabbi Arthur Hertzberg's cynical quip that the synagogue in America is "to a large degree, a parent-teacher association of the religious school." Quoted in Carolyn L. Wiener, "A Merger of Synagogues in San Francisco," *Jewish Journal of Sociology* 14 (December 1972), p. 189.

18. On the relationship between synagogue schools and congregational membership, see Marshall Sklare, *Conservative Judaism: An American Religious Movement* (Glencoe, Ill.: Free Press, 1955), pp. 77ff.

19. *Jewish Identity: Facts for Planning*, Council of Jewish Federations (supervised by Fred Masaryk), December 1974, pp. 2–4. Local surveys also bore out these findings for many communities. See, for example, Sidney Goldstein and Calvin Goldscheider, *Jewish Americans: Three Generations in a Jewish Community* (Englewood Cliffs, N.J.: Prentice-Hall, 1968), pp. 176–77.

20. See Sklare, *Conservative Judaism*.

21. Philip Bernstein wrote at the conclusion of World War II that Jewish chaplains subordinated their ideologies to the needs of Jewish soldiers. "This led to more observance of tradition by the Reform, a liberalization of the Orthodox, and an expansion of Conservatism." See Bernstein, "Jewish Chaplains in World War II," *American Jewish Yearbook* 47 (1945–46), p. 174.

22. Gordon, *Jews in Suburbia*, p. 97.

23. Jack Wertheimer, "The Conservative Synagogue," in *The American Synagogue: A Sanctuary Transformed*, ed. Jack Wertheimer (New York: Cambridge University Press, 1987), pp. 111–47.

24. Shuly Rubin Schwartz, "Camp Ramah: The Early Years, 1947–52," *Conservative Judaism*, Fall 1987, pp. 12–42.

25. Walter Ackerman, "The Day School in the Conservative Movement," *Conservative Judaism*, Winter 1961, pp. 50ff.

26. Marc Tannenbaum, "Religion," *American Jewish Yearbook* 60 (1959), p. 64.

27. The prayer book was edited by Rabbi Morris Silverman under the direction of a joint committee of the Rabbinical Assembly and the United Synagogue of America, headed by Rabbi Robert Gordis.

28. Sidney Schwarz, "Law and Legitimacy: An Intellectual History of Conservative Judaism, 1902–1973" (Ph.D. diss., Temple University, 1982), pp. 221–22, 255–56.

29. Jacob Neusner, "Religion," *American Jewish Yearbook* 61 (1960), p. 57.

30. Morris S. Goodblatt, "Synagogue Ritual Survey," *Proceedings of the Rabbinical Assembly* 8 (1942), pp. 105–9.

31. Wuthnow, *The Restructuring of American Religion*, p. 138.

32. On the institutional growth of the Reform movement, see Raphael, *Profiles in American Judaism*, pp. 71, 75, 198.

33. Leon A. Jick, "The Reform Synagogue," in Wertheimer, *The American Synagogue*, pp. 102–3.

34. On institutional growth within the Reform movement, see Raphael, *Profiles in American Judaism*, pp. 71, 75, 198.

35. On the UAHC's controversial relocation to New York, see Maurice Eisendrath, "The Union of American Hebrew Congregations: Centennial Reflections," *American Jewish Historical Quarterly* 63 (December 1973), pp. 144–45.

36. Morris N. Kertzer, "Religion," *American Jewish Yearbook* 53 (1952), p. 155.

37. See Jick, "The Reform Synagogue," p. 104; Stephen Sharot, *Judaism: A Sociology* (New York: Holmes and Meier, 1976), pp. 164–71; and Benjamin Efron and Alvan D. Rubin, "The Reality of Bar Mitzvah," *CCAR Journal* 8 (October 1960), pp. 31–33.

38. Michael A. Meyer, *Response to Modernity: A History of the Reform Movement in Judaism* (New York: Oxford University Press, 1988), p. 355.

39. The outlook of Classical Reform was enunciated most clearly in the Pittsburgh Platform of 1885 and revised in the Columbus Platform of 1937.

40. Morris N. Kertzer, "Religion," p. 155.

41. Marcus's address is quoted by Alan Tarshish, "How 'Central' is the CCAR?" *CCAR Journal* 8 (January 1960), p. 32.

42. On the impact of Orthodox refugees from Nazism on American Orthodoxy, see Shubert Spero, "Orthodox Judaism," in Bernard Martin, ed., *Movements and Issues in American Judaism* (Westport, Conn.: Greenwood Press, 1978), pp. 86–87; and Charles Liebman, "Religion, Class, and Culture in American Jewish Life," *Jewish Journal of Sociology* 9 (December 1967), pp. 239–40. A careful analysis of this group's immigration history and impact on American Jews and Judaism is urgently needed.

43. For a discussion of the impact of immigrants upon the Orthodox rabbinate, see Jeffrey S. Gurock, "Resisters and Accommodators: Varieties of Orthodox Rabbis in America, 1886–1983," *American Jewish Archives* 35 (1983), pp. 150–56.

44. Joshua Trachtenberg, "Religious Activities," *American Jewish Yearbook* 47 (1946), pp. 216–17.

45. On the ban, see Tannebaum, "Religion," p. 59; and "Religious Pluralism at Home: A Hundred Years of the N.Y. Board of Rabbis," *Jewish Observer*, May 1981, pp. 44–47.

46. Jacob Sloan, "Religion," *American Jewish Yearbook* 58 (1957), p. 153.

47. For good introductions to the separatist ideologies in Central Europe, see Robert Liberles, *Religious Conflict in Social Context: The Resurgence of Orthodox Judaism in Frankfurt am Main, 1838–1877* (Westport, Conn.: Greenwood Press, 1985); and Michael K. Silber, "The Emergence of Ultra-Orthodoxy: The Invention of a Tradition," in *The Uses of Tradition: Jewish Continuity in the Modern Era*, ed. Jack Wertheimer (New York and Cambridge, Mass.: Jewish Theological Seminary and Harvard University Press, 1993), pp. 23–85.

48. On the defection to Conservatism, see Wertheimer, "The Conservative Synagogue," pp. 124–25. On the issue of separate seating as a boundary issue for Orthodoxy, see Louis Bernstein, "The Emergence of the English Speaking Orthodox Rabbinate" (Ph.D diss., Yeshiva University, 1977), pp. 289–97; and Bernard Litvin, *The Sanctity of the Synagogue* (New York: Spero Foundation, 1959), pp. 49–77. See also Morris N. Kertzer, "Religion," *American Jewish Yearbook* 56 (1955), p. 235; and Marc Tannenbaum, "Religion," pp. 60–62.

49. See, for example, in *Tradition*: Eliezer Berkovits, "Reconstructionist Theology: A Critical Evaluation," Fall 1959, pp. 20–66; Norman Lamm, "Separate Pews in the Synagogue: A Social and Psychological Approach," Spring 1959, pp. 141–64; Emanuel Rackman, "Arrogance or Humility in Prayer," Fall 1958, pp. 13–26; and Walter Wurzburger, "The Oral Law and the Conservative Dilemma," Fall 1960, pp. 82–90.

50. Shubert Spero, "Orthodox Judaism," in Martin, *Movements and Issues in American Judaism*, pp. 86–87.

51. For an early article noting the revolution in the Kosher food industry, see Morris Kertzer, "Religion," *American Jewish Yearbook* 65 (1964), p. 81, which reports on a survey conducted in 1963 claiming that two thousand products certified as kosher were manufactured by four hundred companies, compared with half the number of both just a few years before.

52. On the residual and nonobservant Orthodox, see Liebman, "Orthodoxy in American Jewish Life," pp. 30–36.

53. Abraham Duker, "On Religious Trends in American Life," *YIVO Annual* 4 (1949), pp. 54–55.

54. Sklare, *Conservative Judaism*, p.43. A continuing high rate of defection from Orthodoxy was also predicted on the basis of surveys of younger Jews. The Riverton study, for example, found that most adolescents from Orthodox homes planned to identify as Conservative. Marshall Sklare, Marc Vosk, and Mark Zborowski, "Forms and Expression of Jewish Identification," *Jewish Social Studies* 17 (July 1955), p. 209.

55. Kaplan is quoted in Jacob Neusner, "Religion," p. 58.

56. Will Herberg, *Protestant, Catholic, Jew: A Study in American Religious Sociology* (Garden City, N.Y.: Doubleday, 1955), p. 260; and idem, "The Triple Melting Pot," *Commentary*, August 1955, pp. 101–8.

57. According to a Gallup poll in 1964, 71 percent of Catholics, 37 percent of Protestants, and only 17 percent of Jews claimed to have attended a religious service during the previous week. By 1970 these figures were 60 percent, 38 percent, and 19 percent, respectively. See *Yearbook of American and Canadian Churches* (1972), p. 257.

58. For an evocative overview of changing practices in Jewish popular religion at midcentury, see Abraham G. Duker, "The Emerging Patterns in American Jewish Life," in *The Jewish Experience in America*, vol. 5, ed. Abraham J. Karp (Waltham, Mass.: American Jewish Historical Society, 1969), originally published in the *Publication of the American Jewish Historical Society* 39 (1950). Duker details the many traditional rituals that fell into disuse but also notes the emergence of new or altered customs, for example: the custom of visiting cemetery plots shifted from the month of Elul prior to the Jewish New Year to Mother's Day and Father's Day; new wedding rituals were adopted, as were new stringencies such as kosher certification for mineral water.

59. For an especially sober assessment, see Victor B. Geller, "How Jewish Is Jewish Suburbia," *Tradition*, Spring 1960, pp. 318–30.

60. *Time*, October 15, 1951, pp. 52–57. The importance of these interfaith activities were recognized by New York's Cardinal Spellman, who dubbed Finkelstein the "father of ecumenism." Jessica Feingold, "Up from Isolation: Intergroup Activities at the Seminary," *Judaism*, Summer 1978, p. 291.

61. Herberg, *Protestant, Catholic, Jew*. For an extended discussion of the new respectability of Jews since 1945, see Edward S. Shapiro, "World War II and American Jewish Identity," *Modern Judaism*, February 1990, pp. 65–84.

62. Herberg, *Protestant, Catholic, Jew*, p. 23.

63. Ibid., p. 84.

64. Quoted in Sidney E. Ahlstrom, *A Religious History of the American People*, vol. 2 (Garden City, N.Y.: Doubleday, 1975), p. 450.

65. Arthur Hertzberg estimated that three-fifths of all Jews in America affiliated with a synagogue. But a communal survey of Jews in Washington, D.C., found that half the Jews attended synagogue only on the High Holidays, a figure that held true for all three denominations of Judaism. See Hertzberg, "Religion," *American Jewish Yearbook* 59 (1958), p. 114.

66. For comparable developments in American Catholicism, see Jay P. Dolan, *The American Catholic Experience: A History from Colonial Times to the Present*

(Garden City, N.Y.: Doubleday, 1985), p. 381. On Protestantism, see Wuthnow, *The Restructuring of American Religion*, pp. 16–17, 49.
67. Martin E. Marty, *A Nation of Behavers* (Chicago: University of Chicago Press, 1976), p. 256.

Chapter 2

1. Robert Wuthnow, *The Restructuring of American Religion: Society and Faith since World War II* (Princeton: Princeton University Press, 1988) p. 49.
2. Sidney E. Ahlstrom, *A Religious History of the American People*, vol. 2 (Garden City, N.Y.: Doubleday, 1975), p. 600.
3. Ibid., p. 486.
4. For an analysis of the changing social and political climate during the 1960s, see Allen J. Matusow, *The Unraveling of America: A History of Liberalism in the 1960s* (New York: Harper and Row, 1984); and Stewart Burns, *Social Movements of the 1960s: Searching for Democracy* (Boston: Twayne, 1990). For a cultural history, see William L. O'Neill, *Coming Apart: An Informal History of America in the 1960s* (New York: Quadrangle/N.Y. Times Books, 1971).
5. Morris N. Kertzer, "Religion," *American Jewish Yearbook* 65 (1964), p. 75.
6. Historian Michael A. Meyer suggests that this shift to the left was made possible by the rising influence of lay leaders of East European extraction who were prone to "more liberal social views." See Meyer, *Response to Modernity: A History of the Reform Movement in Judaism* (New York: Oxford University Press, 1988), p. 364.
7. On Reform activism, see Meyer, *Response to Modernity*, pp. 364–66. The enthusiasm of southern rabbis for the civil rights movement has entered the mythical realm. Judging from a survey conducted in 1967, many Reform rabbis in the South shied away from the issue of black rights. A minority did assume a high profile; the outspoken Jacob Rothschild of Atlanta was one such individual. See the results of a survey conducted by P. Allen Krause, "Rabbis and Negro Rights in the South, 1954–1967," *American Jewish Archives* 21 (April 1969), pp. 20–47.
8. Meyer, *Response to Modernity*, pp. 366–67. For an illuminating discussion of how modern Orthodox faculty and students at Yeshiva University responded to the protest movements during the 1960s, see Jeffrey S. Gurock, *The Men and Women of Yeshiva: Higher Education, Orthodoxy, and American Judaism* (New York: Columbia University Press, 1988), pp. 214–26.
9. Meyer, *Response to Modernity*, p. 367.
10. Bill Novak, "On Relevance, and Beyond," *Judaism*, Summer 1971, p. 321. For a gripping account of the rise and decline of political activism in one church, see R. Stephen Warner, *New Wine in Old Wineskins: Evangelicals and Liberals in a Small-Town Church* (Berkeley: University of California Press, 1989), esp. chapters 4–8.
11. For an overview of the early history of Jewish feminism, see Sylvia Barack Fishman, "The Impact of Feminism on American Jewish Life," *American Jewish Yearbook* 89 (1989), p. 6.
12. For a succinct overview of the origins of the contemporary feminist movement and an analysis of how it differed from earlier women's movements for

suffrage, see Steven M. Buechler, *Women's Movements in the United States: Woman Suffrage, Equal Rights, and Beyond* (New Brunswick, N.J.: Rutgers University Press, 1990), pp. 23–40.

13. These developments are surveyed by Fishman, "The Impact of Feminism," pp. 7–9. Weiss-Rosmarin's essay appeared in *Jewish Spectator*, October 1970, pp. 2–6; and Adler's in *Davka*, Summer 1971, pp. 6–11.

14. For some background on the gradual efforts of the Conservative movement to educate girls and introduce the Bat Mitzvah celebration, see Paula E. Hyman, "The Introduction of Bat Mitzvah in Conservative Judaism in Postwar America," *YIVO Annual* 19 (1990), pp. 133–46.

15. Alan Silverstein, "The Evolution of Ezrat Nashim," *Conservative Judaism*, Fall 1975, pp. 44–45.

16. Anne Lapidus Lerner, "'Who Hast Not Made Me a Man': The Movement for Equal Rights for Women in American Jewry," *American Jewish Yearbook* 77 (1977), pp. 6–7.

17. Ibid., pp. 11–12.

18. Ibid., pp. 16–20.

19. For an incisive analysis of the counterculture and its impact on Christian groups in America, see Steven M. Tipton, *Getting Saved from the Sixties: Moral Meaning in Conversion and Cultural Change* (Berkeley: University of California Press, 1982), esp. chap. 1.

20. Representative views may be found conveniently in James A. Sleeper and Alan L. Mintz, eds., *The New Jews* (New York: Vintage Books, 1971).

21. Much of the ensuing discussion of the Jewish counterculture and the early Havurah movement is based on chapter 2 of Riv-Ellen Prell's illuminating anthropological study, *Prayer and Community: The Havurah in American Judaism* (Detroit: Wayne State University Press, 1989).

22. Alan L. Mintz, "Along the Path to Religious Community," in Sleeper and Mintz, *The New Jews*, p. 32. The essay originally appeared in *Midstream*, March 1970.

23. Prell, *Prayer and Community*, p. 80.

24. Ibid., p. 84.

25. Ibid., p. 92.

26. On the founding of the Germantown minyan, see Lenore Eve Weissler, "Making Judaism Meaningful: Ambivalence and Tradition in a Havurah Community" (Ph.D. diss., University of Pennsylvania, 1982), pp. 48–59. See chap. 4 in this volume for a discussion of the minyan groups that evolved out of the early havurot.

27. William Novak, "From Somerville to Savanah . . . and Los Angeles . . . and Dayton," *Moment*, January–February 1981, p. 19.

28. This entire discussion is based on Prell, *Prayer and Community*, chap. 2.

29. Ibid., pp. 69–72.

30. Ibid., pp. 102–4.

31. Already in early 1970 the nascent havurot were the subject of a generally favorable article by Stephen C. Lerner, "The Havurot," *Conservative Judaism*, Spring 1970, pp. 2–15. Lerner regarded the havurot as a challenge to Jewish communities and especially to Conservative Judaism from whence most members derived. For other early assessments, see William Novak, "The Greening of American Jewry," *Judaism*, Spring 1971, pp. 213–17; and the symposium, "The New Jews: A Reality," *Congress Bi-Weekly*, September

8, 1972. Shraga Arian, a leading Conservative educator, viewed "the new Jews" as "pockets" of activism rather than a movement; but he regarded the activists as "the best thing that's happened in American Jewish life in the last thirty years" (p. 24).

32. Lerner, "The Havurot," p. 15.

33. Richard Siegel, Sharon Strassfeld, and Michael Strassfeld, eds., *The Jewish Catalogue: A Do-It-Yourself Kit* (Philadelphia: Jewish Publication Society of America, 1973); Sharon Strassfeld and Michael Strassfeld, eds., *The Second Jewish Catalogue: Sources and Resources* (Philadelphia: Jewish Publication Society, 1976); idem, *The Third Jewish Catalogue: Creating Community* (Philadelphia: Jewish Publication Society, 1980).

34. Rabbi Jacob Weinstein, then president of the Reform rabbinic organization, summed up the predicament when he declared before the CCAR: "We must not be embarrassed by the charge that we are doves on Vietnam and hawks on Israel." But of course some Jews were embarrassed and confused by the ambiguity of their stance. Meyer, *Response to Modernity*, p. 367.

35. Wade Clark Roof and William McKinney, *American Mainline Religion: Its Changing Shape and Future* (New Brunswick, N.J.: Rutgers University Press, 1987), pp. 18–20.

36. Ibid., p. 21.

37. Fred Masaryk, *Jewish Identity: Facts for Planning* (Pamphlet issued by the Council of Jewish Federations, New York, 1976), pp. 2–4.

38. Dean M. Kelley, *Why Conservative Churches Are Growing* (New York: Harper and Row, 1972).

39. Quoted in Roof and McKinney, *American Mainline Religion*, p. 22.

40. Kelley, *Why Conservative Churches Are Growing*, pp. 85–90.

41. Wuthnow, *The Restructuring of American Religion*, assigns critical importance to changes in patterns of education as a means to explain declining religious involvement among younger Americans. Our discussion is based upon pp. 153–64.

42. Roof and McKinney, *American Mainline Religion*, pp. 11–15.

43. John H. Simpson, quoted by Richard L. Rubenstein, "God and Caesar in Conflict in the American Polity," in Jeffrey K. Hadden and Anson Shupe, eds., *Secularization and Fundamentalism Reconsidered*, vol. 3 (New York: Paragon House, 1989).

44. Steven M. Cohen and Leonard J. Fein, "From Integration to Survival: American Jewish Anxieties in Transition," *Annals of the American Academy of Political and Social Science* (July 1985), p. 76.

45. The emergence of a consciousness of the Holocaust and scholarship on the destruction of the Jews are described by Michael R. Marrus, *The Holocaust in History* (Hanover, N.H.: University Press of New England, 1987), pp 4–6.

46. Quoted by Haskel Lookstein, *Were We Our Brother's Keepers?* (New York: Hartmore House, 1985), p. 21.

47. Melvin Urofsky, *We Are One: American Jewry and Israel* (Garden City, N.Y.: Doubleday, 1978), p. 351.

48. Lucy Dawidowicz, "American Public Opinion," *American Jewish Yearbook* 67 (1968), p. 205.

49. Urofsky, *We Are One*, p. 358. In their study of "Lakeville" Jews a decade earlier, Marshall Sklare and Joseph Greenblum found a strong identification with Israel but an unwillingness to sacrifice for Israel. Less then 15 percent

believed that Israel's financial needs should take precedence over local Jewish needs, and fewer than one third approved of affiliation with a Zionist organization. *Jewish Identity on the Suburban Frontier: A Study of Group Survival in an Open Society* (Chicago: University of Chicago Press, 1967), pp. 214–49.

50. Quoted from the *Village Voice*, June 15, 1967, by Lucy Dawidowicz, "American Public Opinion," *American Jewish Yearbook* 69 (1968), p. 211. For a fine analysis of how the experience of converting to a new ideology (which often involves a rejection of religion) is still verbalized in a religious idiom, see Virginia Lieson Brereton, *From Sin to Salvation: Stories of Women's Conversions, 1800 to the Present* (Bloomington: Indiana University Press, 1991), chap. 8.

51. Quoted in Dawidowicz, "American Public Opinion," p. 209.

52. Dawidowicz, "American Public Opinion," p. 208.

53. Ibid., p. 207. Dawidowicz describes the increasing importance of synagogues as centers for fund-raising activities after the Six-Day War.

54. The letter appeared in the July 7, 1967, issue and is quoted by Dawidowicz, "American Public Opinion," p. 221.

55. Quoted in Urofsky, *We Are One*, p. 364.

56. Quoted by Dawidowicz, "American Public Opinion," p. 224. See also Meyer, *Response to Modernity*, on the decline in ecumenical activities after the Six-Day War (p. 368).

57. Maurice Eisendrath, "The U.A.H.C.: Centennial Reflections," *Publications of the American Jewish Historical Society* 63 (December 1973), pp. 147–48.

58. Meyer, *Response to Modernity*, p. 368. See also David Polish, "The Changing and the Constant in the Reform Rabbinate," *American Jewish Archives* 35 (November 1983), p. 314, on the growing disaffection of Reform rabbis with civil rights movement in the late 1960s and their shift to Zionist/Israel concerns.

59. Erich Rosenthal, "Acculturation without Assimilation?" *American Journal of Sociology* 66 (November 1960), pp. 275–289, quoted in *Intermarriage and Jewish Life in America*, ed. Werner Cahnman (New York: Herzl Press, 1963), pp. 15–16.

60. Arthur Hertzberg cited this survey published in the *National Review* (Oct. 8, 1963) in "The American Jew and His Religion," in *The American Jew: A Reappraisal*, ed. Oscar I. Janowsky (Philadelphia: Jewish Publication Society, 1964), p. 103.

61. Marshall Sklare, "Intermarriage and Jewish Survival," *Commentary*, March 1970, p. 52. Sklare's fears were dismissed by some as needless panic because, after all, Boston was not representative since so many of its Jews were students at local universities, an argument that overlooked the ominous implications of so high a rate of intermarriage among young Jews. See Arnold Schwartz, "Intermarriage in the United States," *American Jewish Yearbook* 71 (1970), p. 108.

62. Hertzberg, "The American Jew and His Religion," p. 102. For the findings of the National Jewish Population Study on intermarriage, see *Intermarriage: Facts for Planning*, Council of Jewish Federations, N.Y., n.d., p. 10.

63. On the results of the National Jewish Population Survey of 1971, see the series of pamphlets entitled "Facts for Planning" issued in the mid-1970s by the Council of Jewish Federations; and Sidney Goldstein, "Jews in the

United States: Perspectives from Demography," *American Jewish Yearbook* 81 (1981), pp. 3–60.

64. Elihu Bergman, "The American Jewish Population Erosion," *Midstream*, October 1977, pp. 9–19.

65. Sefton Temkin, "Religion," *American Jewish Yearbook* 65 (1964), p. 176.

66. Wolfe Kelman, "The American Synagogue: Present Prospects," *Conservative Judaism*, Fall 1971, p. 13.

67. Oscar Rosenfeld, "Membership Survey and Statistics," United Synagogue of America *Biennial Report*, New York, 1965, p. 95.

68. Kelman, "The American Synagogue," p. 13.

69. Mordecai M. Kaplan, *Judaism as a Civilization* (New York: Macmillan Publishing, 1934); and Charles S. Liebman, "Reconstructionism in American Jewish Life," *American Jewish Yearbook* 71 (1970), pp. 3–99. The Jewish Reconstructionist movement is not to be confused with Christian Reconstructionism, a far-right variation of fundamentalism. See Nancy T. Ammerman, "North American Jewish Fundamentalism," In *Fundamentalisms Observed*, eds. Martin E. Martin and R. Scott Appleby (Chicago: University of Chicago Press, 1990), pp. 49–54.

70. On Kaplan's allegiance to JTS and his refusal to found a separate movement, see Sidney Schwarz, "Law and Legitimacy," pp. 191–96, 400–404; and Liebman, "Reconstructionism in American Jewish Life," pp. 30–39.

71. On the founding of the Reconstructionist Rabbinical College, see Liebman, "Reconstructionism in American Jewish Life," pp. 41–45.

72. In 1955 the Reconstructionist Foundation launched a Reconstructionist Fellowship of Congregations consisting of four affiliates. See Jacob Sloan, "Religion," *American Jewish Yearbook* 57 (1956), p. 190.

73. There may also have been a negative reason for the decision of Reconstructionists—the need to shore up Kaplan's influence, which had been eclipsed by others in the 1960s. Whereas in the immediate postwar era, Kaplan's religious naturalism was regarded by rabbis as "the single greatest influence on American Jewish thought," it was evident by the mid-1960s that Kaplan had been superseded by Buber and Rosenzweig. Within the American Jewish community other figures, such as Abraham Joshua Heschel, Joseph B. Soloveitchik, and Emil Fackenheim, were acknowledged as dominant. Robert G. Goldy, *The Emergence of Jewish Theology in America* (Bloomington: Indiana University Press, 1990), p. 5.

74. This is the way Stephen C. Lerner, editor of a symposium on the Sklare essay in *Conservative Judaism*, characterized the new assessment. See Lerner, "Morale and Commitment," *Conservative Judaism*, Fall 1972, p. 12. Sklare's essay formed the concluding chapter of a revised edition of his book *Conservative Judaism: An American Religious Movement* (New York: Schocken Books, 1972), pp. 253–82.

75. In the symposium "The RA Faces the Seventies," in *Proceedings of the Rabbinical Assembly* 34 (1970), p. 99.

76. William Greenfeld, quoted by Hillel Silverman in *Proceedings of the Rabbinical Assembly* 34 (1970), p. 111.

77. Jordan S. Ofseyer, *Conservative Judaism*, Fall 1972, p. 16.

78. Borowitz is quoted in Leon Jick, "The Reform Synagogue," in *The American Synagogue: A Sanctuary Transformed*, ed. Jack Wertheimer (New York: Cambridge University Press, 1987), p. 105.

79. Leonard J. Fein et al., *Reform Is a Verb: Notes on Reform and Reforming Jews* (New York: UAHC, 1972), pp. 140–52.
80. Theodore I. Lenn et al., *Rabbi and Synagogue in Reform Judaism* (New York: Central Conference of American Rabbis, 1972), p. 396; emphasis in orginal.
81. Ibid., pp. 395, 400, 184.
82. Ibid., p. 392.
83. Norman Mirsky, "Mixed Marriage and the Reform Rabbinate," *Midstream*, January 1970, pp. 40–46.
84. Lenn et al., *Rabbi and Synagogue*, p. 187.
85. Richard N. Levy, "The Reform Synagogue: Plight and Possibility," *Judaism*, Spring 1969, p. 159.
86. These were the findings of the National Jewish Population Study of 1971. See Bernard Lazerwitz, "Past and Future Trends in the Size of American Jewish Denominations," *Journal of Reform Judaism*, Summer 1979, pp. 77–82. Fourteen percent of the sample population indicated no religious affiliation.
87. Charles S. Liebman, "Changing Social Characteristics of Orthodox, Conservative and Reform Jews," *Sociological Analysis* 27 (Winter 1966), pp. 210–22.
88. Charles S. Liebman, "Orthodoxy in American Jewish Life," *American Jewish Yearbook* 66 (1965), pp. 89–91, 92.
89. Quoted by Urofsky, *We Are One*, p. 400.
90. Temkin, "Religion," *American Jewish Yearbook* 65 (1964), p. 177.
91. Rodney Stark and Charles Y. Glock, *American Piety: The Nature of Religious Commitment* (Berkeley: University of California Press, 1968), p. 55.

Chapter 3

1. Robert Wuthnow, *The Struggle for America's Soul: Evangelicals, Liberals, and Secularism* (Grand Rapids, Mich.: Eerdmans, 1989), p. xiv.
2. Martin E. Marty, "Transpositions: American Religion in the 1980s," *Annals of the American Academy of Political and Social Science* 480 (July 1985), p. 12. See also idem, "Religion in America, 1935–1985," in *Altered Landscapes: Christianity in America, 1935–85*, ed. David W. Lotz (Grand Rapids, Mich.: Eerdmans, 1989), pp. 1–18.
3. R. Stephen Warner, "The Place of the Congregation in the Contemporary American Religious Configuration" (Typescript), p. 10. Forthcoming in *The Congregation in American Life*, eds. James Lewis and James P. Wind (Chicago: University of Chicago Press.)
4. "A Time to Seek," *Newsweek*, December 17, 1990, p. 50.
5. Wade Clark Roof and William McKinney, *American Mainline Religion: Its Changing Shape and Future* (New Brunswick, N.J.: Rutgers University Press, 1987). p. 40.
6. Robert N. Bellah et al., *Habits of the Heart: Individualism and Commitment in American Life* (Berkeley: University of California Press, 1985), pp. vii, 220–21.
7. Bruce A. Greer and Wade Clark Roof, "'Desperately Seeking Sheila': Locating Religious Privatism in American Society," *Journal for the Scientific Study of Religion* 31 (1992), pp. 350–51.

8. Robert Wuthnow distinguishes between Protestant teachings, which understand religious identity as a matter of choice, and Catholicism and Judaism, in which religious identity is acquired by birth. "The 'new voluntarism,'" writes Wuthnow, "that encourages people to pick and choose until they find the religion best suited to their tastes is evidence of the growing emphasis on achieved rather than ascribed religious identities." Wuthnow, "Forum," *Religion and American Culture* 2 (Winter 1992), p. 5.

9. Roof and McKinney, *American Mainline Religion*, p. 32.

10. The following population studies conducted under the auspices of local federations of Jewish philanthropies were utilized in the compilation of data for this chapter (relevant page numbers for data on religious issues follow). Unless noted otherwise, all data cited in this section are taken from these reports. (I thank Jeffrey Scheckner, administrator, North American Jewish Data Bank, for graciously making these studies available to me.) ATLANTA: Metropolitan Atlanta Jewish Population Study, *Summary of Major Findings* (Atlanta Jewish Federation, 1983), pp. 8–9. BALTIMORE: Gary A. Tobin, *Jewish Population Study of Greater Baltimore* (Associated Jewish Charities and Welfare Fund, 1985), sec. 6, and *Summary Report*, pp. 21–32. BOSTON: Sherry Israel, *Boston's Jewish Community: The 1985 CJP Demographic Study* (Combined Jewish Philanthropies of Greater Boston, 1985), chap. 3. CHICAGO: Peter Friedman, *A Population Study of the Jewish Community of Metropolitan Chicago* (Jewish Federation of Metropolitan Chicago, 1982) pp. 42–45. Additional data that did not appear in the published report were generously provided to the author by Dr. Mark A. Zober, senior planning and research associate at the Jewish United Fund of Metropolitan Chicago. CLEVELAND: Ann Schorr, *From Generation to Generation*, and *Survey of Cleveland's Jewish Population* (Jewish Community Federation of Cleveland, 1981), pp. 42–49; DADE COUNTY, FLA.: Ira M. Sheskin, *Population Study of the Greater Miami Jewish Community* (Greater Miami Jewish Federation, 1982), pp. 157–211, 227–44. DENVER: Bruce A. Phillips, *Denver Jewish Population Study* and *Supplement to the Denver Jewish Population Study* (Allied Jewish Federation of Denver, 1981), pp. iii–iv, 44, 55, and pp. 14–25, respectively. HARTFORD: *Highlights from the Greater Hartford Jewish Population Study* (Greater Hartford Jewish Federation, 1981), p. 8. KANSAS CITY: Gary A. Tobin, *A Demographic Study of the Jewish Community of Greater Kansas City: Executive Summary* (Jewish Federation of Greater Kansas City, 1985), pp. 3–19, 36, 41. LOS ANGELES: Steven Huberman and Bruce A. Phillips, *Jewish Los Angeles: Synagogue Affiliation. Planning Report* (Jewish Federation Council of Greater Los Angeles, 1979), pp. 3–32, 37–51. Also Bruce A. Phillips, "Los Angeles Jewry: A Demographic Portrait," *American Jewish Yearbook* 86 (1986), pp. 126–95. METRO WEST, N.J.: Michael Rappeport and Gary A. Tobin, *A Population Study of the Jewish Community of Metro West, New Jersey* (United Jewish Federation of Metro West, N.J., 1985), pp. 61–96. MILWAUKEE: Bruce A. Phillips and Eve Weinberg, *The Milwaukee Jewish Population: Report of a Survey* (Milwaukee Jewish Federation, 1984), pp. iv, 1–17; also *Summary Report*, pp. 1–5. MINNEAPOLIS: Lois Geer, *Population Study: The Jewish Community of Greater Minneapolis* (Minneapolis Federation for Jewish Service, 1981), chap. 5, pp. 1–19; also *Executive Summary*, pp. 8–9. NASHVILLE: Nancy Hendrix, *A Demographic Study of the Jewish Community of*

Nashville and Middle Tennessee (Jewish Federation of Nashville and Middle Tennessee, 1982), p. 20. NEW YORK: Steven M. Cohen and Paul Ritterband, *The Jewish Population of Greater New York, A Profile* (Federation of Jewish Philanthropies of N.Y., 1981), pp. 22–34; Additional data were provided to me directly by Paul Ritterband. PALM BEACH COUNTY, FLA.: Ira M. Sheskin, *Jewish Demographic Study* (Jewish Federation of Palm Beach County, 1987), pp. 101–40. PHILADELPHIA: William Yancey and Ira Goldstein, *The Jewish Population of the Greater Philadelphia Area* (Federation of Jewish Agencies of Greater Philadelphia, 1983), pp. 109–62, 172–208. PHOENIX: Bruce A. Phillips and William S. Aron, *The Greater Phoenix Jewish Population Study: Jewish Identity, Affiliation, and Observance* (Greater Phoenix Jewish Federation, 1983), pp. 3–10. PITTSBURGH: Ann Schorr, *Survey of Greater Pittsburgh's Jewish Population* (United Jewish Federation of Greater Pittsburgh, 1984), sec. 4; also *Community Report*, pp. 6–15. RICHMOND: Ann Schorr, *Demographic Study of the Jewish Community of Richmond* (Jewish Federation of Richmond, 1984), pp. 9, 30, 31, 42, 48. ROCHESTER: Gary A. Tobin and Sylvia B. Fishman, *The Jewish Population of Rochester, N.Y. (Monroe County)* (Jewish Community Federation of Rochester, N.Y., 1980), pp. i–iii, 19–33. ST. LOUIS: Gary A. Tobin, *A Demographic and Attitudinal Study of the Jewish Community of St. Louis* (Jewish Federation of St. Louis, 1982), pp. iv–viii, 23, 42. SCRANTON: "Demographic Census" (Typescript report by Mrs. Seymour Bachman, Scranton-Lackawanna Jewish Federation, 1984). SEATTLE: James McCann with Debra Friedman, *A Study of the Jewish Community in the Greater Seattle Area* (Jewish Federation of Greater Seattle, 1979), pp. 8–11, 67–73. TAMPA: Ray Wheeler, *A Social and Demographic Survey of the Jewish Community of Tampa, Florida* (Tampa Jewish Federation, 1980), pp. 60–66. WASHINGTON, D.C.: Gary A. Tobin, Janet Greenblatt, and Joseph Waksberg, *A Demographic Study of the Jewish Community of Greater Washington, 1983* (United Jewish Appeal Federation of Greater Washington, D.C., 1983), pp. 25, 39, 97–101, 139–50. WORCESTER, MASS.: Gary A. Tobin and Sylvia Barack Fishman, *A Population Study of the Greater Worcester Jewish Community* (Worcester Jewish Federation, 1986), pp. 91–112.

11. On the 1971 survey, see Sidney Goldstein, "The Jews in the United States: Perspectives from Demography," *American Jewish Yearbook* 81 (1981), pp. 3–59. The results of the National Jewish Population Study were published in a series of pamphlets issued by the Council of Jewish Federations and Welfare Funds during the 1970s. On the 1990 survey, see Barry A. Kosmin et al., *Highlights of the National Jewish Population Survey* (New York: Council of Jewish Federations, 1991); and Sidney Goldstein, "Profile of American Jewry: Insights from the National Jewish Population Survey," *American Jewish Yearbook* 92 (1992), pp. 77–173.

12. Peter Friedman and Mark Zober, "Factors Influencing Synagogue Affiliation: A Multi Community Analysis," *North American Jewish Data Bank, Occasional Papers* no. 3 (May 1987), pp. 11–23.

13. In this regard, American Jews are much like their Christian neighbors: church affiliation and attendance increase dramatically when families have school-age children, prompting the observation that "without a little child to lead them, most of the sixties generation would still be spending Sabbath morning in bed." "A Time to Seek," *Newsweek*, December 17, 1990, p. 52.

14. George Gallup, Jr., and Jim Castelli, *The People's Religion: American Faith in the 90's* (New York: Macmillan, 1989), p. 116.

15. Kosmin et al., *Highlights of the National Jewish Population Survey*, p. 36. By comparison, only 13 percent of mixed Jewish-Gentile households maintained synagogue membership. It is worth noting that even with a rate of synagogue affiliation hovering near 40 percent, membership figures since World War II exceed those for earlier decades in this century. Thus, Stephen Sharot estimates synagogue affiliation in 1939 at between 25 and 33 percent. Admittedly, the Great Depression may have accounted for part of this low rate, but by 1939 the worst of the economic crisis had passed. See Sharot, *Judaism: A Sociology* (New York: Holmes and Meier, 1976), p. 146.

16. *Yearbook of American and Canadian Churches* 52 (1985), pp. 283–84.

17. See Marshall Sklare and Joseph Greenblum, *Jewish Identity on the Suburban Frontier: A Study of Group Survival in an Open Society* (Chicago: University of Chicago Press, 1967), p. 52; and Sidney Goldstein and Calvin Goldscheider, *Jewish Americans: Three Generations in a Jewish Community* (Englewood Cliffs, N.J.: Prentice-Hall, 1968), p. 201. Regarding fasting on Yom Kippur there is a puzzling discrepancy between local surveys and the national survey of 1990: the latter found that only 48 percent of core Jews claimed to have fasted; 48 percent reported they did not fast; the rest claimed they were unable to fast. Goldstein, "Profile of American Jewry," *American Jewish Yearbook* 92 (1992), p. 137. In community surveys, fasting on Yom Kippur appeared much more widespread.

18. Sklare, *America's Jews* (New York: Random House, 1971), p. 114.

19. On the history of Hanukkah's elevation by American Jews to a holiday of great significance, see Jenna Weissman Joselit, "'Merry Chanuka': The Changing Holiday Practices of American Jews, 1880–1950," in Jack Wertheimer, ed., *The Uses of Tradition: Jewish Continuity in the Modern Era* (New York and Cambridge, Mass.: Jewish Theological Seminary of America and Harvard University Press, 1993), pp. 303–29.

20. It is still too soon to analyze the patterns of observance among fourth-generation Jews, as compared with the practice of their parents and grandparents. For a preliminary attempt that utilizes data from the New York survey, see Steven M. Cohen, *American Assimilation or Jewish Revival?* (Bloomington: Indiana University Press, 1988), pp. 54, 56, 129–30.

21. Goldstein, "Profile of American Jewry," *American Jewish Yearbook* 92, (1992), p. 172.

22. Goldstein, "Profile of American Jewry" (1992), pp. 136–37. In a significant departure from their usual pattern of maintaining high levels of Jewish observance, half the households containing a Jew by Choice have Christmas trees. As Goldstein notes, some of these Jews by Choice never underwent a formal conversion and therefore may still be attached to some Christian traditions. Alternatively, some may have a tree to maintain contact with their families.

23. Paul Ritterband, "The Social Basis of American Jewish Religious Organization," *Studies in Jewish Demography, 1989* (Jerusalem: Institute for Contemporary Jewry, forthcoming), p. 5 of typescript provided by the author.

24. Goldstein, "Profile of American Jewry," *American Jewish Yearbook* 92 (1992), pp. 129–130.

25. See Fred Masaryk, *Jewish Identity: Facts for Planning* (New York: Council of Jewish Federations, December 1974), pp. 2–4.
26. For the 1971 findings, see Sherry Israel, *Boston's Jewish Community: The 1985 CJP Demographic Study.* The 1991 figures may have undercounted the Orthodox, since some Hasidic groups were recorded as "miscellaneous Jewish."
27. Kosmin et al., *Highlights of the National Jewish Population Survey*, p. 37, Table 29.
28. Ibid., pp. 32 and 34, Tables 22 and 26.
29. Goldstein, "Profile of American Jewry" (1992), p. 132.
30. In most surveys Reconstructionists were deemed numerically negligible and therefore were not listed separately. Even in Philadelphia, where the central institutions of the Reconstructionist movement are located, only 1.5 percent of respondents identified with Reconstructionism.
31. Steven M. Cohen and Paul Ritterband, "The Social Characteristics of the New York Area Jewish Community, 1981," *American Jewish Yearbook* 84 (1984), p. 153 and Table 3.3.
32. Orthodoxy will also face the challenge of holding the allegiance of its young as the generations pass. In a sample of the nine largest Jewish communities during the 1980s, it was striking that the Orthodox population, unlike its counterparts, was drawn preponderantly from immigrants and their children: 46 percent were first generation; 43 percent second generation; 10 percent third generation; and 2 percent fourth generation.

    In order to obtain detailed data on religious behavior, I have utilized two merged samples created by the North American Jewish Data Bank: (1) The Nine City Sample provides weighted data from surveys conducted in the 1980s in the largest Jewish communities—Baltimore, Boston, Chicago, Cleveland, Los Angeles, Miami, New York, Philadelphia, and Washington, D.C. These are not representative communities and they do not reflect small-town Jews. The Nine City Sample, however, covers approximately three-quarters of the Core Jewish Population in the United States. (2) A Ten City Sample was also compiled to include cities of varying sizes in a weighted fashion. This sample includes fewer Jews but is more representative of the varieties of Jewish populations in the U.S. Since only the Ten City Sample included data on intermarriage and visits to Israel, I will use that sample when discussing those two measures of Jewish identity.
33. A strong case for the defection scenario has been made by Charles Liebman and Saul Shapiro, "A Survey of the Conservative Movement: Some of Its Religious Attitudes" (Manuscript, September 1979), p. 22. Steven M. Cohen has argued that identification is tied to family status. See Cohen, "The American Jewish Family Today," *American Jewish Yearbook* 82 (1982), pp. 145–53.
34. Goldstein, "Profile of American Jewry" (1992), p. 130 and p. 170, Table 20.
35. These data are drawn from a sample of the nine largest Jewish communities surveyed during the early 1980s. We must note that fourth-generation samples were relatively small in the 1980s, comprising only 56,000 individuals, compared with over 450,000 second-generation Jews in the sample. Accordingly, data on fourth-generation Jews is not very reliable.
36. Readers should bear in mind two important caveats regarding this blanket assertion. First, there are exceptions to the rule: there are Conservative and

Reform Jews who are considerably more Jewishly engaged than some Orthodox Jews and there are some Reform Jews who are more Jewishly active than their Conservative counterparts. We are describing the patterns of the aggregates. Second, the actual behavior of Jews who identify with a movement does not necessarily conform with the ideology of that movement. Most Jews apparently claim a denominational label because it conforms with their degree of involvement, not because they agree with or even know the denominational ideology.

37. Data on synagogue membership are from the Nine City Sample.

38. Nine City Sample, North American Jewish Data Bank.

39. Synagogue attendance twice a year or *less* by self-defined Conservative Jews increases from 49 percent of third-generation Jews to 71 percent of the fourth generation. Among Reform Jews, 70 percent of third-generation Jews claim to attend twice or less as do 75 percent of fourth-generation Jews. These data on generational shifts derive from the Nine City Sample.

40. See Table 7 of Wertheimer, "Recent Trends in American Judaism," *American Jewish Yearbook* 89 (1989), pp. 94–95.

41. The source of these data are the Ten City Sample. They are confirmed by a survey of American Jewish attitudes toward Israel conducted by Steven M. Cohen. Cohen concluded that "the extent of Orthodox Jews' attachment to Israel, however measured, significantly exceeded that of other denominations, and Conservative Jews consistently scored higher than Reform or nondenominational Jews. Moreover, differences between Orthodox and non-Orthodox were sharpest on the most demanding measures of involvement—receptivity to aliyah (settling in Israel) versus just pro-Israel feelings, familiarity with several Israelis versus only a few, or fluency rather than rudimentary knowledge of Hebrew." Orthodox Jews also traveled to Israel more frequently: over a third of the Orthodox Jews in his sample population had been to Israel twice or more compared with only one Conservative Jew in eight and fewer than one in ten Reform and nondenominational Jews who had been to Israel twice.

42. Paul Ritterband has found that in New York, "among the varieties of synagogues, those associated with the Conservative movement are the most likely to participate in pan-Jewish campaign efforts while many of the Orthodox maintain and support specifically Orthodox charities . . . , some in exclusion of nondenominational Jewish charities. The Jewish household most likely to be solicited is older, affiliated with a Conservative synagogue as well as being affiliated with other Jewish organizations, and earns a high income." Ritterband, "The Determinants of Jewish Charitable Giving in the Last Part of the Twentieth Century," in *Contemporary Jewish Philanthropy in America*, eds. Barry A. Kosmin and Paul Ritterband (Savage, Md.: Rowman and Littlefield, 1991), p. 67. On Orthodox giving, see in the same volume Samuel Heilman, "*Tzedakah*: Orthodox Jews and Charitable Giving," p. 139.

43. These data from the Ten City Sample are probably much outdated since rates of intermarriage have continued to escalate.

44. It is symptomatic of the distinction Jews draw between their own religious identity and that of their spouse that 4 percent of intermarried Jews in Los Angeles identified themselves as Orthodox.

45. *Intermarriage: Facts for Planning* (Council of Jewish Federations, n.d.), p. 10.

For a critique of these figures, see Charles Silberman, *A Certain People: American Jews and Their Lives Today* (New York: Summit Books, 1985), pp. 289–92. Silberman pooh-poohed the grim conclusions drawn by pessimistic sociologists from the 1971 survey. By contrast, the demographer Sidney Goldstein concludes twenty years later that the 1971 survey was interpreted too optimistically because that survey "underestimated the levels of intermarriage and overestimated the gains to Judaism through conversion." Goldstein, "Profile of American Jewry" (1992), p. 126.

46. Goldstein, "Profile of American Jewry" (1992), p. 127.

47. In his study of intermarriage rates of three American groups—Japanese Americans, African Americans, and American Jews—Paul Spickard noted the lowest rates for each group "near centers of ethnic concentration: for Blacks, the South and, in later years, northern industrial cities; for Jews, eastern cities; for Japanese, California and Hawaii. . . . In each case, it was the presence or absence of an ethnic community that was crucial. . . . This pattern of low intermarriage near points of ethnic concentration and a high rate where ethnic fellows were few was followed by every other American ethnic group on record." For example, Puerto Ricans in Boston were twice as likely as those in New York City to intermarry. And "Italians married non-Italians much less frequently at their centers of concentration in northeastern cities than they did in other parts of the country." Spickard, *Mixed Blood: Intermarriage and Ethnic Identity in Twentieth-Century America* (Madison: University of Wisconsin Press, 1989), pp. 347–48.

48. Bethamie Horowitz and Jeffrey R. Solomon, "Why Is This City Different from Other Cities: New York and the 1990 National Jewish Population Survey," *Journal of Jewish Communal Service* 68 (Summer 1992), p. 316.

49. Peter Medding et al., "Jewish Identity in Conversionary and Mixed Marriages," *American Jewish Yearbook* 92 (1992), pp. 9–10.

50. Egon Mayer, *Love and Tradition: Marriage between Jews and Christians* (New York: Schocken, 1985), p. 157.

51. Medding et al., "Jewish Identity in Conversionary and Mixed Marriages," p. 127.

52. Ibid., p. 10. For an analysis of the impact of rabbinic officiation at mixed marriages, see Egon Mayer, *Intermarriage and Rabbinic Officiation* (New York: American Jewish Committee, 1989).

53. Mark L. Winer, Sanford Seltzer, and Steven Schwager, *Leaders of Reform Judaism: A Study of Jewish Identity, Religious Practices and Beliefs, and Marriage Patterns* (New York: Union of American Hebrew Congregations, 1987), p. 66.

54. The nature of the debate over outreach to mixed married families is well captured by Peter Steinfels, "Debating Intermarriage, and Jewish Survival," *New York Times*, October 18, 1992, p. A1; and Egon Mayer, "The Case for a New Intermarriage Policy," *Jewish Week*, September 4–10, 1992, p. 18.

55. Egon Mayer, *Children of Intermarriage: A Study in Patterns of Identification and Family Life* (New York: American Jewish Committee, 1983), pp. 7, 11, 15–18. For a more recent discussion of the consequences of out marriage, see U. O. Schmelz and Sergio DellaPergola, *Basic Trends in American Jewish Demography* (New York: American Jewish Committee, 1988), pp. 20–24.

56. The 1990 national survey provides ample information about the absence

of ritual practices in the homes of high percentages of mixed-married families and thereby further explains the tenuous connection to Judaism of children raised in such homes. See Goldstein, "Profile of American Jewry" (1992), p. 134.

57. Goldstein, "Profile of American Jewry" (1992), p. 127.

58. Medding et al., "Jewish Identity in Conversionary and Mixed Marriages," p. 39.

59. Another term that is often employed in such a context and that is intentionally absent from this book is "secularization." Particularly in light of the renewed interest in religion since the 1970s, sociologists of religion have debated the so-called secularization thesis, with its assumptions about the inevitable turn to secularity by modern societies. For a succinct discussion of the thesis, see Thomas Robbins and Dick Anthony, eds., *In Gods We Trust: New Patterns of Religious Pluralism in America*, 2d ed. (New Brunswick, N.J.: Transaction Books, 1990), pp. 7–8; and for a good overview of how this debate applies to the case of American Jewry, see Stephen Sharot, "Judaism and the Secularization Debate," *Sociological Analysis* (Fall 1991), pp. 255–73. Sharot supports a modified version of the secularization thesis regarding Jews and writes of "the secularized majority and the traditionalist minority." I avoid the term secular because it forces an either/or analysis that fails to do justice to the complexity of human religious strivings.

60. Jonathan D. Sarna, "Interreligious Marriage in America," in *The Intermarriage Crisis: Jewish Communal Perspectives and Responses* (New York: American Jewish Committee, 1992), p. 2; emphasis in original.

61. Richard D. Alba, *Ethnic Identity: The Transformation of White America* (New Haven: Yale University Press, 1990), p. 13.

62. Ibid., p. 15. A more recent estimate by a church official placed the rate at 40 percent. Frank Hannigan, director of the Office of Family Ministries with the archdiocese of Chicago, quoted in the *New York Times*, October 23, 1992, p. B16.

63. Sarna, "Interreligious Marriage in America," p. 3.

64. Gallup and Castelli, *The People's Religion*, p. 116.

65. Ibid., pp. 33–35.

66. Theodore Caplow et al., *All Faithful People: Change and Continuity in Middletown's Religion* (Minneapolis: University of Minnesota Press, 1983), p. 29.

67. Steven M. Cohen, *Content or Continuity? Alternative Bases for Commitment: The 1989 National Survey of American Jews* (New York: American Jewish Committee, 1991), p. 67. Cohen's sample was selected from a consumer mail panel and therefore probably does not as accurately reflect the gamut of American Jewry as do some demographic surveys. But the broader patterns it traces are highly suggestive and probably close to the mark. On American religious beliefs, see Andrew W. Greeley, *Religious Change in America* (Cambridge, Mass.: Harvard University Press, 1989), pp. 13–14.

68. Cohen, *Content or Continuity?* p. 68; and Gallup and Castelli, *The People's Religion*, p. 36.

69. Gallup and Castelli, *The People's Religion*, found that approximately 85 percent of Protestants and Catholics believed that "even today miracles are performed by God," compared with 46 percent of Jews; over 80 percent of Christians claimed they were "sometimes very conscious of God's pres-

ence," compared with 61 percent of Jews (pp. 58–59). And Cohen (*Content or Continuity*) found that "only a narrow minority believe God is active and personal" (p. 51).

70. Greeley, *Religious Change in America*, pp. 115–16. See also Caplow et al., *All Faithful People*, pp. 34–45; and Gallup and Castelli, *The People's Religion*, p. 20. Robert Wuthnow concludes that while on most indices there is stability in levels of religion expression, the intensity of religious activities in the 1950s was not recaptured in the 1970s and 1980s. See Wuthnow, "Indices of Religious Resurgence in the United States," in Richard T. Antoun and Mary E. Hegland, eds., *Religious Resurgence* (Syracuse, N.Y.: Syracuse University Press, 1987), pp. 16–17.

71. Cohen, *Content or Continuity?*, p. 40.

72. Ibid., p. 51.

73. Kosmin et al., *Highlights of the National Jewish Population Survey*, p. 28.

74. Quoted by Raanan Gerberer, "It's Time to Market Judaism," *LI Jewish World*, December 20, 1991, p. 21.

75. Ritterband, "The Determinants of Jewish Charitable Giving," pp. 59–60.

Chapter 4

1. Riv-Ellen Prell, *Prayer and Community: The Havurah in American Judaism* (Detroit, Mich: Wayne State University Press, 1989), pp. 71–72.

2. David Glanz review in *Congress Bi-Weekly*, June 21, 1974, p. 21. For sales figures of the three catalogs, see Charles Silberman, *A Certain People: American Jews and Their Lives Today* (New York: Summit, 1985), p. 269.

3. William Novak, "The Future of Havurah Judaism," *Moment*, January 1977, p. 56.

4. From *The Second Jewish Catalogue*, quoted by Novak, "The Future of Havurah Judaism," p. 56.

5. Novak, "The Future of Havurah Judaism," p. 56.

6. Shira Weinberg Hecht, "Religious Practice and Organization in an Egalitarian Minyan Setting" (Paper delivered at the annual meeting of the Society for the Scientific Study of Religion, October 1988), p. 28, n. 14 (emphasis added). I thank the author for graciously sharing this paper and information on her research.

7. Alan Mintz, in the symposium, "Have You Sold Out?" *Response*, Spring 1976, p. 43.

8. Novak, "The Future of Havurah Judaism," p. 59. For a hard-hitting critique of Havurah Judaism by an outsider, see Marshall Sklare, "The Greening of Judaism," *Commentary*, December 1974, pp. 51–57. Sklare was particularly incensed over the rejection of Jewish norms in favor of the "youth culture," and the sense of "superiority toward the conventional forms of American Jewish life" (p. 57).

9. Harold Schulweis, "Restructuring the Synagogue," *Conservative Judaism*, Summer 1973, p. 19.

10. William Novak, "From Somerville to Savannah . . . and Los Angeles . . . and Dayton," *Moment*, January–February 1981, p. 19.

11. I am indebted to Rabbi Rubin for sharing some of his survey findings with me. As far as I know, they have not been published. On havurot on the West

Coast, see Gerald B. Bubis and Harry Wasserman, *Synagogue Havurot: A Comparative Study* (Philadelphia: Center for Jewish Community Studies, 1983).

12. "Havurah Failures and Successes," *Proceedings of the Rabbinical Assembly* 41 (1979), pp. 55–75. There is no Havurah movement within Orthodoxy, perhaps because many Orthodox synagogues are small and function as intimate communities.

13. Daniel Elazar and Rela Geffen Monson, "The Synagogue Havurah: An Experiment in Restoring Adult Fellowship to the Jewish Community," *Jewish Journal of Sociology* 21 (June 1979), pp. 72–74.

14. Jeffrey Oboler, "The First National Havurah Conference," *Congress Monthly*, December 1979, pp. 12–13.

15. In Boston, however, Shira Weinberg Hecht found that many Havurah members send their children to day schools, thereby obviating the need to join a synagogue to obtain a Hebrew school education for their children. See Hecht, "Religious Practice and Organization," p. 26, n. 3.

16. Ibid., p. 6.

17. Lenore Eve Weissler, "Making Judaism Meaningful: Ambivalence and Tradition in a Havurah Community" (Ph.D. diss., University of Pennsylvania, 1982), cited in Hecht, "Religious Practice and Organization," p. 8.

18. For some debate over this issue, see Steven M. Cohen, "Conflict in the Havurot: Veterans vs. Newcomers," *Response*, Summer 1979, pp. 3–4; and Michael Strassfeld, "Too Many for a Minyan," *Response*, Spring 1980, pp. 21–28.

19. For a discussion of the principle of egalitarianism in Havurah Judaism, see Novak, "From Somerville . . . ," pp. 58–59. For a case study of the struggle for egalitarianism within one havurah, see Prell, *Prayer and Community*, chap. 7.

20. Quoted in Prell, *Prayer and Community*, p. 317. Describing his own work, *The Jewish Catalogue*, as "a codification of the *Havurah*'s oral tradition, which, like all such codifications, also then marks the end of a period of significant creativity and innovation," one of the editors of the catalogs lamented the "tiredness" and loss of creativity of Havurah Judaism by the end of the 1980s. Michael Strassfeld, "Twenty Years of the Havurah Movement," *Sh'ma*, November 24, 1989, p. 9.

21. Our discussion of denominational life noted the struggles for increased women's participation within established institutions such as synagogues and seminaries. The present section is concerned with less formal and institutionalized expressions of feminist Judaism, many of which transcend ideology and denomination.

22. The absence of coordination and formal communication attests to the nature of feminist Judaism as "a welling up of popular religion," according to the historian Shulamit S. Magnus. "Despite the fact that much of it is taking place outside established Judaism, the sheer breadth of 'second stage' feminist Judaism is making it a central rather than a peripheral phenomenon." See Magnus, "Re-inventing Miriam's Well: Feminist Jewish Ceremonials," in *The Uses of Tradition: Jewish Continuity in the Modern Era*, ed. Jack Wertheimer (New York and Cambridge, Mass.: Jewish Theological Seminary of America and Harvard University Press, 1993), p. 334.

23. Much of the source material utilized in this section was gathered by Rabbi

Debra Cantor, who as a student at the Jewish Theological Seminary compiled "A Compendium of New Jewish Women's Rituals" for a course I taught on contemporary American Judaism. The most important repository of materials on Jewish women's activities in the religious and other spheres is the Jewish Women's Resource Center housed at the headquarters of the National Council of Jewish Women in New York.

24. Over fifty different birth ceremonies for girls are on file at the Jewish Women's Resource Center. See also Susan Weidman Schneider, *Jewish and Female* (New York: Simon and Schuster, 1984), pp. 121–30; an issue of *Sh'ma* devoted to these rituals and liturgies (December 23, 1983); Daniel I. Leifer and Myra Leifer, "On the Birth of a Daughter," in *The Jewish Woman: New Perspectives*, ed. Elizabeth Koltun (New York: Schocken, 1976), pp. 91–100; and "The Covenant of Washing," *Menorah: Sparks of Jewish Renewal*, April–May 1983, pp. 22ff.

25. Chava Weissler, "New Jewish Birth Rituals for Baby Girls" (Manuscript, Jewish Women's Resource Center, 1985), p. 6.

26. Copies of such ceremonies are on file at the Jewish Women's Resource Center. For a survey, see Schneider, *Jewish and Female*, which contains a section entitled "Rituals for the Landmarks of Our Lives," pp. 117–48.

27. For a ceremony marking the onset of menarche, see Penina V. Adelman, *Miriam's Well: Rituals for Jewish Women around the Year* (Fresh Meadows, N.Y: Biblio Press, 1986), section on "Sivan." See also *Siddur Nashim*, comp. Maggie Wenig and Naomi Janowitz (Unpublished, Providence, 1976), for a "Prayer on Menstruation."

28. On the reappropriation of the *mikveh*, Evelyn Hutt v'Dodd's contribution in "The Ways We Are," *Lilith*, Winter 1976–77, pp. 7–9.

29. Cynthia Ozick, "Bima: Torah as a Matrix for Feminism," *Lilith*, Winter–Spring 1985, pp. 48–49.

30. For the survey of thirteen feminist Haggadot, see *JWRC Newsletter*, Winter–Spring 1981, pp. 1–2. See also Reena Friedman, "How Was This Passover Different from All Other Passovers?" *Lilith*, Spring–Summer 1977, pp. 33–36. For a new prayer to mark the pre-Passover cleaning, see Lynn Gottlieb, "Spring Cleaning Ritual on the Eve of Full Moon Nissan," in *On Being A Jewish Feminist: A Reader*, ed. Susannah Heschel (New York: Schocken, 1983), pp. 278–80.

31. For a good introduction to the historical as well as the contemporary observance of Rosh Hodesh by women, see Arlene Agus, "This Month Is for You: Observing Rosh Khodesh as a Woman's Holiday," in Koltun, *The Jewish Woman*, pp. 84–93.

32. Magnus, "Re-inventing Miriam's Well," p. 337. See also Carol Glass, "A Festival of Joy," *JWRC Newsletter*, Winter–Spring 1981, which reports on Rosh Khodesh groups. Numerous texts on the celebration of this ritual in different localities are on file at the Jewish Women's Resource Center.

33. This is central to the larger feminist predicament that goes under the rubric of "equality versus difference." See the review of Joan W. Scott's *Gender and the Politics of History* by William H. Sewell, Jr., in *History and Theory* 29 (1990), pp. 73–74.

34. For a sampling of views in this debate, see the essays by Judith Plaskow, Rita M. Gross, and Arthur Green in Heschel, *On Being a Jewish Feminist*, pp. 217–60. See also Naomi Janowitz and Maggie Wenig, "Selections from a

Prayerbook Where God's Image Is Female," *Lilith*, Fall–Winter 1977–78, pp. 27–29.

35. This discussion of theological concerns is based on an unpublished paper written by Rabbi Rona Shapiro when she was a student of mine. Entitled "From Jewish Feminism to Feminist Judaism," the paper contrasts presentations offered at two conferences on feminist Judaism separated by fifteen years. For the most expansive reflections on these issues, one that urges a radical rethinking of Jewish theology and liturgy, see Judith Plaskow, *Standing Again at Sinai* (San Francisco: Harper and Row, 1990).

36. On Congregation Beth Simchat Torah and its new rabbi, see Yosef I. Abramowitz, "Rabbi Takes on Congregation's Risks, Challenges," *LI Jewish World*, April 10–16, 1992, p. 12.

37. Barry Alan Mehler, "Gay Jews," *Moment*, March 1977, p. 22; Henry Rabinowitz, "Talmud Class in a Gay Synagogue," *Judaism*, Fall 1983, pp. 433–43; Janet R. Marder, "Getting to Know the Gay and Lesbian Shul," *Reconstructionist*, October–Novenber 1985, pp. 20–25. At the twelfth International Conference of Gay and Lesbian Jews held in 1991, separate services were held to accommodate Reform, Conservative, and Orthodox religious sensibilities. When asked how he reconciled being Orthodox and gay, one participant shrugged and said, "We observe 612" commandments, instead of the requisite 613. Tamar Kaufman, "Gays, Lesbians Show Their Pride," *Jewish Week*, June 7–13, 1991, p. 33.

38. Michael Rankin and Gary Koenigsberg, "Let the Day Come Which Is All Shabbat: The Liturgy of the 'Gay-Outreach' Synagogue," *Journal of Reform Judaism*, Spring 1986, p. 70.

39. I have learned of these ceremonies and liturgies from a research paper written by my former student Abby Aaron, who collected materials from several gay congregations, including Beth Chayim Chadashim in Los Angeles.

40. "Editor's Chair," *Jewish Post and Opinion*, April 29, 1992, p. 2.

41. Some five thousand Jewish families in rural New England are linked by mailings from the K'fari Center. Dinah Wisenberg Brin, "Keeping the Faith in the Outposts," *Jewish Exponent* (Philadelphia), December 27, 1991, p. 18.

42. Sam Allis, "In Vermont: When Woody Allen Meets L. L. Bean," *Time*, September 26, 1988, pp. 10–11.

43. *P'nai Or*, undated brochure issued in 1989. Most affiliates call themselves P'nai or B'nai Or; one in Berkeley is called the Aquarian Minyan. There are two affiliates in Europe.

44. *Adventures in Jewish Renewal*, a publication of the P'nai Or Outreach Bureau (n.d., c. 1988), p. 2.

45. See "An Interview with Zalman Schachter-Shalomi," *New Traditions*, Fall 1985, pp. 9–25. His own account of some of his earlier experimentation is in "The Conscious Ascent of the Soul," in *The Ecstatic Adventurer*, ed. Ralph Metzner (New York: Macmillan, 1968), pp. 96–123.

46. Shira Dicker, "Renewing Ties at a Jewish Woodstock," Baltimore *Jewish Times*, September 25, 1992, p. 102.

47. *P'nai Or*, 1989; *Adventures in Jewish Renewal*.

48. Draft copy of *Or Chadash: A New Light–New Paths for Shabbat Morning*, July 1989.

49. *Adventures in Jewish Renewal*, p. 2.

50. *New Menorah*, Pessach 5749, pp. 6, 10. For more on Waskow's views, see Waskow, *These Holy Sparks: The Rebirth of the Jewish People* (San Francisco: Harper and Row, 1983).

51. Rabbi Jeff Roth, executive director of Elat Chayyim, a new retreat center, explained that the renewal movement "is trying to be somewhere between non-denominational and post-denominational." Quoted by Dicker, "Renewing Ties at a Jewish Woodstock," p. 81.

52. Naomi Godfrey, "Taking the Theism out of Judaism," *Jewish Week*, April 8, 1988, p. 28. See also letter from Rabbi Duskin Feldman, *Jewish Post and Opinion*, June 12, 1991, p. 15. The poem is from *Meditation Services for Humanistic Jews* (Farmington Hills, Mich.: Society for Humanistic Judaism, 1976), p. 13.

53. Steven J. Mason, "Where No Congregation Has Gone Before," *Jewish Post and Opinion*, January 15, 1992, p. 9.

54. The sociologist Harold Himmelfarb has raised the provocative question of whether participants in innovative religious programs have expanded the pool of involved Jews or are merely drawn from among those already engaged. Himmelfarb claims that those Jews who are "higher in traditional forms of Jewish identification are also higher in the so-called non-traditional forms such as organizational participation." Himmelfarb, "The Solace of Sociology," *American Jewish History* 74 (June 1985), p. 441.

55. Several articles in the *New York Times*, citing the Reform movement's Rabbi Alexander Schindler, set the annual conversion figure at between ten thousand and twelve thousand. This figure was then repeated in the Jewish press. *New York Times*, December 9, 1981, and March 23, 1984, p. A14.

56. Silberman, *A Certain People*, pp. 318–21.

57. Barry A. Kosmin et al., *Highlights of the National Jewish Population Survey*, (New York: Council of Jewish Federations, 1991), p. 6. The survey also reported an even larger population of Jews who had converted out, numbering some 210,000.

58. Sidney Goldstein, "Profile of American Jewry," *American Jewish Yearbook* 92 (1992), pp. 134–38. One glaring exception to the high patterns of Jewish religious observance among converts is that conversionary households are far more likely to have Christmas trees. We do not know whether that is done to maintain ties with the Christian families of Jews by Choice or for other reasons.

59. Goldstein, "Profile of American Jewry," p. 141.

60. Alyssa Gabbay, "Jews by Choice," *Baltimore Jewish Times*, June 1, 1990, pp. 52ff.

61. Cited in David Holzel, "Children of Ruth," *Atlanta Jewish Times*, January 12, 1990, pp. 10–11.

62. A 1978 study of Reform converts in Boston concluded that "as a group [converts] define their Judaism in religious rather than ethno-communal terms." Quoted in Egon Mayer, "Jews by Choice: Their Impact on the Contemporary American Jewish Community," *Proceedings of the Rabbinical Assembly* 45 (1983), p. 63.

63. For a discussion of some of these issues, see Peter Medding et al., "Jewish Identity in Conversionary and Mixed Marriages," *American Jewish Yearbook* 92 (1992), pp. 26–27, 35–37.

64. Jonathan Sarna, "Reform Jewish Leaders, Intermarriage, and Conversion," *Journal of Reform Judaism*, Winter 1990, esp. pp. 6–8, which reacts to the equanimity displayed by Reform converts when asked their feelings about the possibility of their own children's intermarriage.

65. Gabbay, "Jews by Choice," pp. 52ff.

66. Charles Liebman has offered a slightly different definition of the *baal teshuvah* as "anyone of college age or older who is more observant than his or her parents, teachers, or childhood friends would have predicted." Quoted in Silberman, *A Certain People*, p. 244.

67. Lis Harris, "Holy Days," *New Yorker*, September 16, 23, 30, 1985.

68. Anne R. Roiphe, *Lovingkindness: A Novel* (New York: Simon and Schuster, 1987).

69. For a brief historical overview of Orthodox outreach programs, see M. Herbert Danzger, *Returning to Tradition: The Contemporary Revival of Orthodox Judaism* (New Haven: Yale University Press, 1989), chaps. 3, 4. Two studies of women *baalot teshuvah* are Lynn Davidman, *Tradition in a Rootless World: Women Turn to Orthodox Judaism* (Berkeley: University of California Press, 1991); and Debra Renee Kaufman, *Rachel's Daughters: Newly Orthodox Jewish Women* (New Brunswick, N.J.: Rutgers University Press, 1991).

70. Paul Cowan, *An Orphan in History* (Garden City, N.Y.: Doubleday, 1982). For other such works, see Anne R. Roiphe, *Generation without Memory: A Jewish Journey in Christian America* (New York: Simon and Schuster, 1981); and Letty Pogrebin, *Deborah, Golda, and Me: Being Jewish and Female in America* (New York: Crown Publishing, 1991).

71. Among the most popular are Blu Greenberg, *How to Run a Traditional Jewish Household* (Northvale, N.J.: Jason Aaronson, 1989); Irving Greenberg, *The Jewish Way: Living the Holidays* (New York: Summit Books, 1988); Hayim Donin, *To Be a Jew: A Guide to Jewish Observance in Contemporary Life* (New York: Basic Books, 1972); Roselyn Bell, ed., *The Hadassah Jewish Parenting Book* (Northvale, N.J.: Jason Aaronson, 1989).

We may even speculate as to the impact of *baalei teshuvah* upon the Americanization of kosher cuisine: with their experience of nonkosher eating, the newly observant may well be concocting kosher variations of forbidden foods, such as seafood and pâté de foie gras.

72. Robert Alter, "What Jewish Studies Can Do," *Commentary*, October 1974, pp. 71–75.

73. "Jewish Studies after College: An Exchange," *Response*, Spring 1974, pp. 92–108; and Gershon D. Hundert in *AJS Newsletter*, Fall 1988, p. 1.

74. Quoted in Alter, "What Jewish Studies Can Do," p. 75.

75. For a study of such yeshivas in Israel, see Janet Aviad, *Return to Judaism: Religious Renewal in Israel* (Chicago: University of Chicago Press, 1983).

76. Aryeh Davidson and Jack Wertheimer, "The Next Generation of Conservative Rabbis," in *The Seminary at 100*, ed. Nina Cardin and David W. Silverman (New York: Rabbinical Assembly, 1986), pp. 37, 40.

77. Allie A. Dubb and Sergio DellaPergola, *First Census of Jewish Schools in the Diaspora, 1981/83* (Jerusalem: Institute for Contemporary Jewry, 1986), pp. 1, 4.

78. Quoted by Bernard Reisman, *Informal Jewish Education in North America*, (Cleveland: Commission on Jewish Education, Mandel Associated Founda-

tions North America, 1990), p. 29. For a devastating portrait of a Hebrew school, see David L. Schoem, *Ethnic Survival in America: An Ethnography of a Jewish Afternoon School* (Atlanta, Ga.: Scholar's Press, 1989).

79. Harold S. Himmelfarb, "The Impact of Religious Schooling: The Effect of Jewish Education upon Adult Religious Involvement," (Ph.D. diss., University of Chicago, 1974).

80. Reisman, *Informal Jewish Education in North America*, pp. 44–46.

81. On the Reform network of summer camps, see Jeffrey K. Salkin, "NFTY at Fifty: An Assessment," *Journal of Reform Judaism*, Fall 1989, pp. 17–25. On the Conservative movement's Ramah camps, see Sylvia Ettenberg and Geraldine Rosenfeld, eds., *The Ramah Experience: Continuity and Commitment* (New York: Jewish Theological Seminary of America, 1989).

82. For a good overview of outreach activities, see Steven Bayme, *Outreach to the Unaffiliated: Communal Context and Policy Direction* (New York: American Jewish Committee, 1992).

83. For a discussion of the theory and practice of Jewish family education, see Reisman, *Informal Jewish Education in North America*.

84. Cowan, *An Orphan in History*.

85. Vicki Brower, "The Greening of Judaism," *Hadassah Magazine*, October 1992, pp. 16–20.

86. Lee D. Cranberg, "Sanctuary in the Synagogue," *Response*, Winter 1990.

87. Rahel Musleah, "AIDS: How Can Judaism Help?" *Hadassah Magazine* August–September 1992, pp. 24–27.

88. Stephen Chaim Listfield, "Turning Singles into Spouses," *Moment*, October 1988, pp. 20–25; and "Friday-Night Fervor Fills D.C. Synagogue," *Washington Post*, October 4, 1984, p. 5B. See also John L. Rosove, "A Synagogue Model for the Single Jew," *Journal of Reform Judaism*, Winter 1986, pp. 29–36; and Richard Bono, "Traditional Jewish Values Back in Vogue," *Atlanta Jewish Times*, April 15, 1988, p. 1.

89. Rela Geffen Monson, "The Impact of the Jewish Woman's Movement on the American Synagogue, 1972–1985," in *Daughters of the King: Women and the Synagogue*, eds. Susan Grossman and Rivka Haut (Philadelphia: Jewish Publication Society, 1992), pp. 227–36.

90. On the adult Bat Mitzvah programs that have come into vogue in American synagogues, see Stuart Schoenfeld, "Integration into the Group and Sacred Uniqueness: An Analysis of Adult Bat Mitzvah," in *Persistence and Flexibility: Anthropological Studies of American Jewish Identities and Institutions*, ed. Walter Zenner (Albany: SUNY Press, 1989), pp. 117–33; and idem, "Ritual and Role Transition: Adult Bat Mitzvah as a Successful Rite of Passage," in *The Uses of Tradition*, ed. Wertheimer, pp. 349–75.

91. Quoted in Susan Gilman, "Bat Mitzvah Ceremonies Not Just Kid Stuff," *Jewish Week*, May 27, 1988, p. 30.

92. See the program materials on the "Yad Hazakah" program of Beth El Synagogue in Minneapolis.

93. Rebecca T. Alpert and Jacob J. Staub, *Exploring Judaism: A Reconstructionist Approach* (New York: Reconstructionist Press, 1985), p. 82.

94. Harvey J. Fields, "Creating the Sharing Worship Community," *Journal of Reform Judaism*, Winter 1984, pp. 75–80.

95. My colleague Aryeh Davidson and I organized a pilot study of eight Conservative congregations in New Jersey to learn more about regular syna-

gogue goers—what attracts them, how they differ from fellow congregants who do not attend regularly, and so forth. We are preparing a report on our findings, which sheds new light on religiously committed Jews who are not Orthodox.

96. Robert Wuthnow, *The Restructuring of American Religion: Society and Faith since World War II* (Princeton: Princeton University Press, 1988), chap. 6.

97. Ibid., p. 121.

98. R. Stephen Warner, "The Place of the Congregation in the Contemporary American Religious Configuration," in *The Congregation in American Life*, eds. James Lewis and James P. Wind (Chicago: University of Chicago Press, forthcoming).

99. Dolan, *The American Catholic Experience: A History from Colonial Times to the Present* (Garden City, N.Y.: Doubleday, 1985), p. 438.

100. Quoted in *Religion in America: 50 Years, 1935–1985*, Gallup Report no. 236, May 1985, p. 13.

101. Wuthnow, *The Restructuring of American Religion*, p. 305.

Chapter 5

1. Walter Jacob, ed., *American Reform Responsa: Collected Responsa of the CCAR, 1983–1989*. (New York: CCAR, 1983), pp. 1–4.

2. On the history of the UPB, see Lou H. Silberman, "The Union Prayer Book: A Study in Liturgical Development," in *Retrospect and Prospect*, ed. Bertram Korn (New York: CCAR, 1965), pp. 46–80.

3. For an extended discussion of the problems posed by the UPB, see the symposium in the *CCAR Journal* 14 (January and October 1967); and Edward Graham, "Winds of Liturgical Reform," *Judaism*, Winter, 1974, pp. 53–54.

4. On the creative liturgies of the 1960s, see Jeffrey K. Salkin, "NFTY at Fifty: An Assessment," *Journal of Reform Judaism*, Fall 1989, pp. 17–18; and Marc Lee Raphael, *Profiles in American Judaism* (San Francisco: Harper and Row, 1984), pp. 66–67.

5. Eric Friedland, "Reform Liturgy in the Making," *Jewish Spectator*, Fall 1987, pp. 40–42. On polydoxy, see Alvin Reines, "Polydox Judaism: A Statement," *Journal of Reform Judaism*, Fall 1980, pp. 47–55; and idem, *Polydoxy: Explorations in a Philosophy of Liberal Religion* (Buffalo, N.Y.: Prometheus Books, 1987). On the confusion regarding theism, see David Polish, "An Outline for Theological Discourse in Reform," *Journal of Reform Judaism*, Winter 1982, pp. 2–3.

6. Michael A. Meyer, *Response to Modernity: A History of the Reform Movement in Judaism* (New York: Oxford University Press, 1988), p. 375.

7. On the widespread acceptance of the *Gates of Prayer*, see *CCAR Yearbook* 89 (1979), p. 39, which claims that within four years of its appearance, it had been adopted by 75 percent of Reform temples.

8. See the symposium on "*Gates of Prayer*: Ten Years Later," *Journal of Reform Judaism*, Fall 1985, pp. 13–61.

9. Samuel M. Silver's letter in *Journal of Reform Judaism*, Spring 1986, p. 83. The writer refers sarcastically to rituals such as the donning of a skullcap and prayer shawl and the frequenting of a ritual bath.

10. The Centenary Perspective, as well as analysis provided by members of the

committee that drafted the statement, appears in *CCAR Journal* 24, (Spring 1977), pp. 3–80.

11. The entire debate appears in *CCAR Yearbook* 83, 1973, pp. 59–97. For the original resolution, see pp. 63–64. See also David Polish, "Enough," *CCAR Journal* 20 (Winter 1973). It is not entirely clear why the issue arose in 1973, but certainly one precipitating factor was the circulation within the CCAR in August 1969 of a list of colleagues who officiated at mixed marriages. This list confirmed for the first time that over one hundred Reform rabbis participated in such ceremonies and made their names available to colleagues who wished to refer their congregants to them. As noted by Professor Norman Mirsky of HUC, the circulation of this list "removed the matter from the realm of private to that of social dissent," and it made it easier for rabbis who had desisted from officiating at such ceremonies to change their policies. "Mixed Marriage and the Reform Rabbinate," *Midstream*, January 1970, pp. 40–60.

12. *CCAR Yearbook* 83 (1973), pp. 96, 64–70.

13. David Polish, "The Changing and the Constant in the Reform Rabbinate," *American Jewish Archives* 35 (November 1983), p. 327.

14. Ibid.

15. Judah Cahn, "The Struggle within Reform Judaism," *CCAR Journal*, Summer 1975, p. 65. For more on this association, see Sylvin L. Wolf, "Reform Judaism as Process: A Study of the CCAR, 1960–75" (Ph.D. diss., St. Louis University, 1978), pp. 269–71; and Eugene Mihaly, *Teshuvot on Jewish Marriage with Special Reference to "Reform Rabbis and Mixed Marriage"* (Cincinnati: privately published, 1985). By the early 1990s a list of Reform and Reconstructionist rabbis who perform intermarriages included 223 names. See *Jewish Post and Opinion*, June 19, 1991, p. 2.

16. *Gates of Prayer* (1975); *Gates of Repentance* (1977); *Gates of Mitzvah* (1979); *Gates of Seasons* (1983); *The Five Scrolls* (with services, 1983); *Songs and Hymns* (for *Gates of Prayer*, 1987); *Gates of Forgiveness-Selichot* (1987); *Gates of Understanding (Commentary to Gates of Prayer)* (1987). For a thoughtful assessment of *The Torah: A Modern Commentary*, ed. W. Gunther Plaut and Bernard Bamberger, see Robert Alter, "Reform Judaism and the Bible," *Commentary*, February 1982, pp. 31–35. (All of these volumes were published by the Central Conference of American Rabbis, New York.)

17. Simeon Maslin, ed., *Gates of Mitzvah* (New York: CCAR, 1979), pp. 3–5, 40. It is noteworthy that the term "mitzvah" does not appear in the Centenary Perspective; the operative term there is "obligation."

18. Norman Mirsky, "Nathan Glazer's *American Judaism* after 30 Years: A Reform Opinion," *American Jewish History* 77 (December 1987), pp. 237–38.

19. It is noteworthy in this context that HUC has become the least sectarian of the major rabbinical seminaries in its recruitment of faculty. Whereas the College had once fired faculty members who did not agree with Reform doctrine, particularly regarding nonsupport of Zionism, it now has faculty members from across the denominational spectrum. This is far less true of either Yeshiva University or the Jewish Theological Seminary of America or even the more eclectic Reconstructionist Rabbinical College.

20. Mirsky, "Nathan Glazer's *American Judaism*," p. 241; David Polish, "The Changing and the Constant," p. 330. On the dissatisfaction of Reform Rabbis with the Bar and Bat Mitzvah due to their deleterious impact upon Sab-

bath morning attendance, see Herman Snyder, "Is Bar-Bat Mitzvah Destroying Attendance at Synagogue Service," *Journal of Reform Judaism*, Winter 1980, pp. 9–12.

21. "Reform Temples Return to Customs, Ceremonies," *Jewish Post and Opinion*, November 7, 1990, p. 1; and Diane Winston, "Searching for Spirituality: Reform Judaism Responds," *Moment*, June 1992, p. 35.
22. Michael Zeldin, "Beyond the Day School Debate," *Reform Judaism*, Spring 1986, pp. 10–11.
23. Raphael, *Profiles in American Judaism*, p. 69.
24. "A Rabbinical First," *Jewish Week*, July 31–August 6, 1992, p. 8.
25. Laurie S. Senz, "The New Cantors," *Reform Judaism*, Fall 1986, p. 18.
26. Daniel Elazar and Rela Geffen Monson, "Women in the Synagogue Today," *Midstream*, April 1981, pp. 25–26.
27. See the symposium on "Judaism and Homosexuality," in *CCAR Journal* 20 (Summer 1973), esp. p. 33, on Freehof's decision, and pp. 33–41, on the founding of Beth Chayim Chadashim at the Leo Baeck Temple in Los Angeles.
28. John Hirsch, "Don't Ghettoize Gays," *Reform Judaism*, Spring 1988, p. 15. By 1990 there were five predominantly homosexual congregations in the UAHC. *Jewish Post and Opinion*, July 25, 1990, p. 3.
29. The text of the statement was printed in the *Jewish Post and Opinion*, June 27, 1990, p. 1. For press coverage of the convention that approved the policy statement, see the report by Tom Tugend in the *Jewish Week*, June 1, 1990, p. 2.
30. *Jewish Post and Opinion*, June 27, 1990, p. 1.
31. Debra Nussbaum Cohen, "Reform Movement Torn by Gay Rabbi Issue," *Jewish Week*, July 5–11, 1991, p. 9.
32. Janet Marder, "Our Invisible Rabbis," *Reform Judaism*, Winter 1990, pp. 5–12.
33. This was the proud characterization offered by the outgoing vice president of the UAHC, Albert Vorspan. *Intermountain Jewish News*, June 30, 1989, p. A9.
34. Alexander Schindler during the debate on the resolution concerning patrilineal descent, *CCAR Yearbook* 93 (1983), p. 149; and Mark L. Winer, "Jewish Demography and the Challenges to Reform Jewry," *Journal of Reform Judaism*, Winter 1984, p. 9.
35. Joseph A. Edelheit and Arthur Meth, "Accepting Non-Jews as Members of Synagogues," *Journal of Reform Judaism*, Summer 1980, pp. 87–92.
36. *JTA Community News Reports*, July 25, 1969, report on the School for Converts sponsored by the UAHC.
37. Kenneth Briggs, "Reform Jews to Seek Conversion of Non-Jews," *New York Times*, December 9, 1981, p. 18.
38. For the complete text of the "Report of the Committee on Patrilinear Descent on the Status of Children of Mixed Marriages," see Walter Jacob, *American Reform Responsa* (New York: CCAR, 1983), pp. 546–50.
39. *CCAR Yearbook* 93 (1983), pp. 144–60.
40. These issues have been raised during most recent debates over policy as well as at lay and rabbinic conventions. See, for example, Marder, "Our Invisible Rabbis," p. 12; Larry Yudelson, "Reform Judaism: Moving toward Spirituality . . . ," *LI Jewish World*, February 16–22, 1990; Arthur J. Magida, "Reform

Judaism: Stretching the Limits," *Baltimore Jewish Times*, November 1, 1991, pp. 60–63.

41. Arthur J. Magida, "A Movement Searching for Its Soul," *Baltimore Jewish Times*, November 8, 1991, p. 50.

42. See the responsum and dissenting opinions in "Reform Responsum: Humanistic Congregation," *CCAR Journal* 38, (Fall 1991), pp. 55–61.

43. *New York Times*, November 16, 1991, p. 26.

44. Debra Nussbaum Cohen, "Reform Grapple with Role of Non-Jews in Synagogue," *Jewish Week*, November 15–21, 1991, p. 6.

45. "Another Temple Opens to Interfaith Weddings," *Jewish Post and Opinion*, January 10, 1990, p. 1; Marilyn Silverstein, "Non-Jews in the Synagogue: Setting the Limits," *Philadelphia Jewish Exponent*, December 13, 1991, pp. 58ff.

46. "Should Jews Worship on Sunday?" *Chicago Tribune*, December 4, 1988. According to the *Jewish Post and Opinion*, March 18, 1992, p. 3, only three American congregations still held their Sabbath services on Sunday.

47. Jakob Petuchowski, "Reform Judaism: Undone by Revival," *First Things: A Monthly Journal of Religion and Public Life*, January 1992, pp. 6–7. See also idem, "Reform Judaism's Diminishing Boundaries: The Grin That Remains," *Journal of Reform Judaism*, Fall 1986, pp. 15–24.

48. Quoted by Winston, "Searching for Spirituality," p. 34.

49. Winston, "Searching for Spirituality," p. 35.

50. Ibid.

51. See Moshe Zemer, "An Halachic and Historical Critique of *Responsa on Jewish Marriage*," *Journal of Reform Judaism* 35 (Spring 1988), pp. 31–47. On the number of Reform rabbis officiating at mixed marriages, see Hershel Shanks, "Rabbis Who Perform Intermarriages," *Moment*, January–February 1988, p. 14, a report on a survey taken by Rabbi Irwin Fishbein. See also the "Forum" section of *Moment*, June 1988, for a discussion of the survey's reliability, as well as the letter from Rabbi David Ostrich, which suggests that rabbinical students at HUC now overwhelmingly opt to participate at mixed marriages, for "not to officiate would render the rabbi left out of the life of the congregation" (p. 7). By 1992 Fishbein's list had grown to 225 Reform and Reconstructionist rabbis. *Jewish Post and Opinion*, January 1, 1992, p. 2.

52. *Jewish Post and Opinion*, June 28, 1989, pp. 8–9.

53. Winer, "Jewish Demography and the Challenges to Reform Jewry," p. 14.

54. On the emergence of new leadership and the considerable controversy surrounding their appointments, see Eugene Borowitz, "Reform Judaism's Coming Power Struggle," *Sh'ma*, March 19, 1971, pp. 75–78; and Mark Winer, "The Crisis in the Reform Movement," *Response*, Fall 1971, pp. 112–20.

    In contrast to Maurice Eisendrath, his predecessor, Schindler emphasized survivalist rather than social-action issues—ritual, Jewish education, and Israel. See the assessment of him offered by Michael A. Meyer in Yudelson, "Reform Judaism," p. 14. On Gottschalk's stewardship of HUC, see Ezra Goldstein's profile in *LI Jewish World*, March 8–14, 1991, pp. 3ff.

55. Winer, "Jewish Demography and the Challenges to Reform Jewry," p. 25.

56. Alexander Schindler, "Remarks by the President of the UAHC," *CCAR Yearbook* 92 (1982), p. 63.

57. Lance Sussman, "Further Reflections on Jewish Demography and Reform Judaism," *Journal of Reform Judaism*, Fall 1984, p. 32.
58. Daniel Jeremy Silver, "The Aging of Reform," in *Approaches to Modern Judaism*, vol. 2, ed. Marc Lee Raphael (Chico, Calif.: Scholar's Press, 1984), p. 57.

Chapter 6

1. Charles S. Liebman, "Orthodoxy Faces Modernity," *Orim*, Spring 1987, p. 13.
2. Our discussion of Orthodoxy does not distinguish between non-Ashkenazic and Ashkenazic Jews. Virtually all non-Ashkenazic synagogues come within the orbit of the Orthodox world. Yeshiva University has tried to cultivate various non-Ashkenazic groups. But some sectors of the Sephardic community are participating in the shift to the right. While some leaders, such as Rabbi Marc Angel of the Spanish Portuguese Synagogue in New York, have worked to moderate the positions of the Orthodox community, much of the Sephardic community is now dominated by the views of Israeli Sephardic rabbis. For the flavor of this orientation, see the *Sephardic Voice International*, published in Brooklyn. For reports on Syrian, Moroccan, and other non-Ashkenazic Jews in New York City, see "Three New York Communities" and "Yeshiva U. a Center for Sephardic Life," *Jewish Week*, August 7–13, 1992, pp. 3, 15. The many non-Ashkenazic Jews who are not Orthodox join congregations sponsored by the major denominations of American Judaism and therefore are not treated separately in this volume.
3. For an interesting account of such fears in one modern Orthodox community, see Edward Shapiro, "Orthodoxy in Pleasantdale . . . " *Judaism*, Spring 1985, p. 170. Shapiro notes the irony in this congregation's importation of ultra-Orthodox disciples of Rabbi Moses Feinstein to supervise construction of their *eruv* in order to ensure that everything be done according to the strictest norms; but once the *eruv* was operating, they feared that "black hatters" such as the supervisor would move into their community. (An *eruv* encloses a public domain, within which Jews may carry objects and push strollers, actions that would be forbidden in the absence of an *eruv*.)
4. Louis Bernstein, "Orthodoxy: Flourishing but Divided," *Judaism*, Spring 1987, p. 175.
5. Note the views of Rabbi Moses Feinstein, who differentiated between *Shomrei Mitzvot*, observers of the commandments, and the community of "God Fearers," sectarians. See Ira Robinson, "Because of Our Many Sins: The Contemporary Jewish World as Reflected in the Responsa of Moses Feinstein," *Judaism*, Winter 1986, pp. 38–39.
6. The most important English-language periodical of the Orthodox right is the *Jewish Observer*, which espouses the views of Agudath Israel. (See vol. 1, September 1963, p. 3.) Its approach has been characterized by one modern Orthodox intellectual as one of "unrelieved negativism. Rather than articulating its own positive approach to issues, it is in most instances content merely to inveigh against positions adopted by others." See David Singer, "Voices of Orthodoxy," *Commentary*, July 1974, p. 59.
7. Orthodox rabbinic organizations include the Rabbinical Council of Amer-

ica, Agudath HaRabbonim, the Rabbinical Alliance of America, Agudath Ha'Admorim, and Hitachduth Harabbonim HaHaredim. See Marc Lee Raphael, *Profiles in American Judaism* (San Francisco: Harper and Row, 1984), p. 155. Among synagogue bodies there are the Union of Orthodox Jewish Congregations of America and the National Council of Young Israel. For the various rabbinical seminaries, aside from the Rabbi Isaac Elchanan Theological Seminary of Yeshiva University, see William Helmreich, *The World of the Yeshiva: An Intimate Portrait of Orthodox Jewry* (New York: Free Press, 1982).

8. Charles S. Liebman, "Orthodoxy in American Jewish Life," *American Jewish Yearbook* 66 (1965), pp. 21–98.

9. Lynn Davidman, "Accommodation and Resistance to Modernity: A Comparison of Two Contemporary Orthodox Jewish Groups," *Sociological Analysis* 51 (1990), pp. 35–51, esp. 41, 47, 49.

10. See, for example, Emanuel Feldman, "Observant Jews and Religious Jews," *Tradition*, Winter 1992, p. 3.

11. Letter to the *Jewish Week*, July 27, 1990, p. 22.

12. See Natalie Gittelson, "American Jews Rediscover Orthodoxy," *New York Times Magazine*, September 30, 1984, pp. 41ff.

13. *New York Times*, June 29, 1984, p. B5.

14. *Jewish Journal* (New York), March 11–18, 1988, p. 4.

15. Joan Nathan, "Kosher Goes Mainstream," *New York Times*, September 7, 1988, p. C1.

16. On the rise of this phenomenon, see Raphael, *Profiles in American Judaism*, p. 170. For a report on one such community, see *Jewish Observer*, September 1983, p. 37.

17. See, for example, Joe Kubert's cartoon strip entitled, "An Act of Resistance," *Moshiach Times*, September 1985, pp. 12–13. On the introduction of "Dial-A-Shiur" and Jewish cable television programs featuring study, see advertisements in *Good Fortune Magazine*, January–February and March 1988.

18. Ira Robinson, "That Marvelous Midos Machine: Audio Tapes as an Orthodox Educational Medium," in *Essays in the Social Scientific Study of Judaism and Jewish Society*, eds. Simcha Fishbane and Stuart Schoenfeld, vol. 2 (Hoboken, N.J.: Ktav, 1992), p. 162.

Orthodox Jews have used other new technologies to popularize traditional practices. The *Wall Street Journal* ran a report about decorating yarmulkes with drawings of cartoon characters, such as Batman and the Teenage Mutant Ninja Turtles (February 4, 1992, p. 1).

19. Barbara Sofer, "Bringing Artscroll to Israel," *Good Fortune: The Magazine about Jewish Personalities*, April 1987, p. 13. The Feinstein biography sold over sixty thousand copies in three years. Abby Mendelson, "Behind the Scenes at Artscroll," *Good Fortune*, January 1990, p. 13.

20. On the scholarly perspective of Artscroll publications, see B. Barry Levy, "Artscroll: An Overview," *Approaches to Modern Judaism*, vol. 1 (Chico, Calif.: Scholars Press, 1983), pp. 111–40. For a more polemical version of this essay, which offers a scathing critique of Artscroll books for their lack of scholarly rigor, mistranslations, and failure to address modern critical thinking, see B. Barry Levy, "Judge Not a Book by Its Cover," *Tradition*, Spring 1981, pp. 89–95.

21. On the audience for Artscroll books, see Sofer, "Bringing Artscroll to Israel," pp. 13–14.

22. On the Glatt Yacht controversy, see Ari Goldman, "Jews Debate Who Will Define the Nature of Orthodoxy," *New York Times*, November 28, 1990, p. B1.; an advertisement in the *LI Jewish World* announces the comedy club (August 14, 1992, p. 3).

23. On the founding of New Square by followers of the Skverer Rebbe, see *New York Times*, July 18, 1975, p. 33. And on the Satmar enclave of Kiryas Joel, see *New York Times*, October 22, 1986, p. B1.

24. "Are You a Jew," *Time*, September 2, 1974, pp. 56–57; "Jewish Tanks," *Newsweek*, July 15, 1974, p. 77.

25. M. Herbert Danzger, *Returning to Tradition: The Contemporary Revival of Orthodox Judaism* (New Haven: Yale University press, 1989), p. 2. See also two recent studies of women who have become *baalot teshuvah*: Lynn Davidman, *Tradition in a Rootless World: Women in Orthodox Judaism* (Berkeley: University of California Press, 1991); and Debra Renee Kaufman, *Rachel's Daughters: Newly Orthodox Jewish Women* (New Brunswick, N.J.: Rutgers University Press, 1991).

26. On the appropriation of traditional rituals within the federation world, see Jonathan Woocher, *Sacred Survival: The Civil Religion of American Jews* (Bloomington: Indiana University Press, 1986), p. 153. The battle to introduce religious observances into Jewish public life was not monopolized by Orthodox Jews; Conservative rabbis often played a pioneering, though unheralded role. See Wolfe Kelman, "Defeatism, Triumphalism, or Gevurah?" *Proceedings of the Rabbinical Assembly* 42 (1980), p. 20.

27. For examples of earlier reports emphasizing the exotic world of Hasidic communities, see Harvey Arden and Nathan Benn, "The Pious Ones," *National Geographic*, August 1955, pp. 276ff., which explores "the closed world of Brooklyn's Hasidic Jews—a bit of old Hungary transplanted to a tenement neighborhood in America's largest city." See also Ray Schultz, "The Call of the Ghetto," *New York Times*, November 10, 1974. For a very different kind of reportage, see Lis Harris, *Holy Days: The World of a Hasidic Family* (New York: Summit Books, 1985), which originally appeared in three installments in the *New Yorker*.

For other examples of media attention devoted to the Orthodox world, see Dorit Phyllis Gary, "The Chosen," *New York Magazine*, June 28, 1982, pp. 24–31. See also Jan Hoffman, "Back to Shul: The Return of Wandering Jews," *Village Voice*, April 21, 1987, which unlike most other reports recognizes that the movement of return to Judaism cuts across the spectrum of Jewish religious life and is not monopolized by Orthodoxy (pp. 13ff.).

Finally, we should note the reverence of American neoconservative and conservative groups, which see Orthodoxy as an upholder of "family values." See, for example, the glowing article on "Thriving Families in Urban America: The Lubavitch Hasidim," in the neoconservative *First Things*, October 1990, pp. 1ff.

28. For data on the proliferation of day schools and the rise in enrollments, see Egon Mayer and Chaim I. Waxman, "Modern Jewish Orthodoxy in America: Toward the Year 2000", *Tradition*, Spring 1977, p. 99. For more recent estimates, see Alvin I. Schiff, "The Centrist Torah Educator Faces Critical Ideological and Communal Challenges," *Tradition*, Winter 1981, pp.

278–79. Samuel Heilman and Steven M. Cohen conclude that attendance at day schools is becoming virtually universal in Orthodox circles. See Heilman and Cohen, *Cosmopolitans and Parochials: Modern Orthodox Jews in America* (Chicago: University of Chicago Press, 1989).

29. Joseph Heimowitz, "A Study of the Graduates of the Yeshiva of Flatbush High School" (Ph.D. diss. Yeshiva University, 1979), pp. 102–3.

30. Two surveys illustrating higher levels of education and observance among younger Orthodox Jews are: Egon Mayer, "Gaps between Generations of Orthodox Jews in Boro Park, Brooklyn, N.Y.," *Jewish Social Studies* 39 (Spring 1977), p. 99; and Heilman and Cohen, *Cosmopolitans and Parochials*, chap. 5.

31. Heilman and Cohen, *Cosmopolitans and Parochials*, chap. 4.

32. Charles Liebman noted this shift in the economic status of Orthodox Jews already in the mid-1960s. Liebman, "Changing Social Characteristics of Orthodox, Conservative and Reform Jews," *Sociological Analysis* 27 (Winter 1966), pp. 210–22. See also Bertram Leff's study of the occupational distribution of Young Israel members, cited in Gershon Kranzler, "The Changing Orthodox Jewish Community," *Tradition*, Fall 1976, p. 72 n. 8; almost two-thirds of male members were professionals.

33. In New York City, Jewish Y's set aside special swim times for Orthodox Jews who require sex-segregated swimming; and other federation-sponsored agencies provide special clinics and programs for Orthodox Jews, such as a program for developmentally handicapped Orthodox youth.

34. According to Lynn Davidman's study of women *baalot teshuvah*, the primary motivation of such women, particularly in the Lubavitch programs, is the desire to find refuge in the more wholesome atmosphere of an Orthodox yeshiva. High percentages of her sample population in the Lubavitch yeshiva had been victims of abuse by their parents or husbands. Davidman, *Tradition in a Rootless World*.

35. Liebman, "Orthodoxy Faces Modernity," pp. 13–14.

36. On the treatment of deviance within the Orthodox setting, see Egon Mayer, *From Suburb to Shtetl: The Jews of Boro Park* (Philadelphia: Temple University Press, 1979), pp. 134–35; and Helmreich, *The World of the Yeshiva*, chap. 8. For a sweeping history of such self-policing within the Orthodox synagogue, see Jeffrey Gurock, "The Orthodox Synagogue," in *The American Synagogue: A Sanctuary Transformed*, ed. Jack Wertheimer (New York: Cambridge University Press, 1987), pp. 37–84.

37. See, for example, Aaron Twerski's essay in the *Young Israel Viewpoint*, June 1985, p. 16. Twerski denounces the Denver conversion program. Note the broader observation of Gershon Kranzler that the Young Israel movement, once a center for moderate Zionism, now is "solidly right-wing Agudah." Kranzler, "The Changing Orthodox Synagogue," *Jewish Life*, Summer–Fall 1981, p. 50.

38. Lawrence Kaplan, letter, *Judaism*, Summer 1981, pp. 382–83.

39. Walter Wurzburger, "Centrist Orthodoxy: Ideology or Atmosphere," *Journal of Jewish Thought* 1 (1985), p. 67.

40. Ibid., p. 68, where Wurzburger describes the new reading of Hirsch and labels it "absurd."

41. The registrar is quoted by William Helmreich in a letter published by *Judaism*, Summer 1981, p. 380.

42. Quoted in Jeffrey S. Gurock, *The Men and Women of Yeshiva: Higher Education, Orthodoxy, and American Judaism* (New York: Columbia University Press, 1988), pp. 254–55.

43. The most revealing evidence of a Modern Orthodox rabbinate under siege is provided by the symposium "The State of Orthodoxy," which appeared in *Tradition*, Spring 1982, pp. 3–83. The editor of that symposium, Walter Wurzburger, states explicitly that "considerable segments of modern Orthodoxy are in retreat," and he framed questions that underscore the challenge he perceives: "How do you view the resurgence of right-wing Orthodoxy? Does it portend the eclipse of modern Orthodoxy? Do you regard modern Orthodoxy as a philosophy of compromise or an authentic version of Judaism?" The thoughtful and pained answers of his respondents provide ample evidence that Wurzburger had identified very real issues that confront the Modern Orthodox rabbinate.

44. David Singer, "Is Club Med Kosher? Reflections on Synthesis and Compartmentalization," *Tradition*, Fall 1985, p. 34.

45. Bernard Rosensweig, "The Rabbinical Council of America: Retrospect and Prospect," *Tradition*, Summer 1986, pp. 8–10.

46. On the charisma of noncompromisers, see Mayer and Waxman, "Modern Jewish Orthodoxy in America," pp. 109–10.

47. See Joshua Berkowitz, "The Challenge to Modern Orthodoxy," *Judaism*, Winter 1984, pp. 101–6; and Shubert Spero, "A Movement in Search of Leaders," *Journal of Jewish Thought* 1 (1985): 83–101. See also the symposium in *Tradition*, Spring 1982.

48. The new RCA siddur also adds a brief preface by an RCA member who invokes the name of Rabbi Joseph B. Soloveitchik, the mentor of rabbis ordained at Yeshiva University (p. xii), and for the prayer for Israel (pp. 450–51). Other than these changes, the RCA siddur is identical to *The Complete Artscroll Siddur* (Brooklyn: Mesorah Publications, 1984); even pagination has been retained by adding pages 448a and 449b. David Singer has identified Agudath Israel as "the largest organized force within the Orthodox world" since World War II and has characterized its ideology as combining "an unswerving attachment to the traditional world of East European *yeshivot* with a bow to the exigencies of Western culture"; it also "continues to reject totally any form of secular Zionist ideology." See Singer, "Voices of Orthodoxy," *Commentary*, July 1974, p. 58.

49. On defections to *shtieblach* and *hashkomah* services, see Rosensweig, "The Rabbinical Council of America," p. 10; and Shlomo Riskin, "Where Orthodoxy Is At: And Where It Is Going," *Jewish Life*, Spring 1976, p. 27. See also Gershon Kranzler, "The Changing Orthodox Synagogue," pp. 43–51.

50. Shubert Spero, "Orthodox Judaism," in *Movements and Issues in Modern Judaism*, ed. Bernard Martin (Westport, Conn.: Greenwood Press, 1978), p. 89 describes the prevalence of mixed dancing; for a case study of one congregation, see Edward Shapiro, "Orthodoxy in Pleasantdale," *Judaism*, Spring 1985, p. 169.

51. Ari Goldman, "Jews Debate Who Will Define the Nature of Orthodoxy," *New York Times*, p. B2.

52. Jokes about the *"Chumrah* [stringency] -of-the-Month Club"* abound; the term appears in Charles Silberman, *A Certain People: American Jews and Their Lives Today* (New York: Summit, 1985), p. 260. For a serious attempt

to address the phenomenon, see Moshe Weinberger, "Keeping Up with the Katzes: The Chumra Syndrome: An Halachic Inquiry," *Jewish Action* 48 (1988) pp. 10–19.

53. The loss of authority by pulpit rabbis to the heads of yeshivas is noted by academic observers such as Egon Mayer and Chaim Waxman, "Modern Jewish Orthodoxy in America," p. 105; as well as by pulpit rabbis such as Rosensweig, "The Rabbinical Council of America," p. 10; and Riskin, "Where Orthodoxy Is At," p. 27.

54. On the triumph of the Agudah position at the expense of moderate religious Zionism, see Kranzler, "The Changing Orthodox Synagogue," p. 50. B'nai Akiva is a Zionist youth movement allied to Israel's National Religious Party.

55. For an analysis of the parallel destruction of folk traditionalism by *Haredi* leaders in Israel, see Menachem Friedman, "The Lost *Kiddush* Cup: Changes in Ashkenazic Haredi Culture—A Tradition in Crisis," in *The Uses of Tradition: Jewish Continuity in the Modern Era*, ed. Jack Wertheimer (New York and Cambridge, Mass.: Jewish Theological Seminary of America and Harvard University Press, 1993), pp. 175–85.

56. David Singer, "Thumbs and Eggs," *Moment*, September 1978, p. 36.

57. Lawrence Kaplan, letter, *Judaism*, Summer 1981, p. 382.

58. See Charles Liebman, "Extremism as a Religious Norm," *Journal for the Scientific Study of Religion* 22 (March 1983), pp. 82–85.

59. *On Women and Judaism* (Philadelphia: Jewish Publication Society, 1981), pp. 76–77.

60. "Tsena-Rena," *Lilith*, Fall–Winter 1979, pp. 46–47.

61. Ibid.; and *Lilith*, Fall–Winter 1985, pp. 5–6.

62. "Tsena-Rena," 1979; and "Orthodox Women's Prayer Groups," *Lilith*, Fall–Winter 1985, pp. 5–6.

63. Rivkeh Haut quoted in *Lilith*, Fall–Winter, 1985, p. 6.

64. Ibid. See also the article by Herschel (Zvi) Schachter in *Beit Yitzhak* 17 (1985), as well as the essays by Schachter and Aryeh Frimer in *Or Mizrach*, September 1985, pp. 64ff., which conveys the contempt of these rabbis for the aspirations of women.

65. On the founding of the Fellowship (FOTR), see *Jewish Week*, September 7, 1988, p. 6; and Gilbert L. Shoham, "There Is No Reason for the RCA to Fear the FOTR," *Jewish Week*, July 5–11, 1991, p. 16. Most of the founding members of this group were rabbis serving Traditional congregations which have mixed seating of men and women, a practice frowned upon by centrist Orthodox groups, let alone those on the right.

66. Jonathan Mark, "Modern Orthodox Rabbis Claim Assault from RCA Right Wing," *Jewish Week*, July 13, 1990, p. 4. See also idem, "Orthodox Rabbis Disciplining 8," *Jewish Week*, June 7–13, 1990, p. 4; Irving Greenberg, "Fighting for the Soul of Orthodoxy," *Jewish Week*, July 13, 1990, p. 20; idem, "Conflict in Orthodoxy: A Shame on All of Us," *Jewish Week*, July 27, 1990, p. 18; and the numerous letters on "The RCA Controversy," *Jewish Week*, July 27, 1990, p. 22.

67. "Spotlight on Centrism," an advertisement in the *Jewish Week*, February 9, 1990, p. 39.

68. Mark, "Modern Orthodox Rabbis Claim Assault from RCA Right Wing," p. 29.

69. Gary Rosenblatt, "Religious McCarthyism," *Baltimore Jewish Times*, November 22, 1991, p. 12.

70. Allan Nadler, "The Demise of Modern Orthodoxy," *Baltimore Jewish Times*, July 20, 1990, p. 11.

71. Press release by the Rabbinical Council of America, "Orthodoxy Should Follow a Policy of 'Creative Engagement' with Conservative and Reform, Says President of RCA," May 20, 1987.

72. Walter Wurzburger, "Orthodox Cooperation with Non-Orthodoxy," *Jewish Life*, Summer–Fall 1981, pp. 25–27; and ibid.

73. For the unequivocal condemnation of non-*mechitsa* synagogues by Rabbi Joseph B. Soloveitchik, see the letters quoted in "A Call to 'Every Jew' and Some Responses," *Jewish Observer*, January 1985, pp. 37–39.

74. The ruling by Moses Feinstein was intended as a leniency, so as to reduce the numbers of *mamzerim*, a category of children whose parents had remarried without a proper Jewish divorce. According to rabbinic law, non-*mamzerim* may not marry *mamzerim*. See David Ellenson, "Representative Orthodox Responsa on Conversion and Intermarriage in the Contemporary Era," *Jewish Social Studies* 47 (Summer–Fall 1985), pp. 215–18.

75. Joseph Berger, "Split Widens on a Basic Issue: What Is a Jew?" *New York Times*, February 28, 1986, p. 1. See also Solomon Freehof, "The Non-Observant Orthodox," *Journal of Reform Judaism*, Winter 1986, p. 43.

76. *Jewish Week*, September 20, 1988, p. 12.

77. Menachem Friedman, "Life Tradition and Book Tradition in the Development of Ultraorthodox Judaism," in *Judaism from Within and Without: Anthropological Perspectives*, ed. Harvey Goldberg (Albany: SUNY Press, 1987), pp. 235–55.

78. Note the observation of Norman Lamm, president of Yeshiva University: "Witness the readiness of our fellow Orthodox Jews to turn exclusivist, to the extent that psychologically, though certainly not halakhically, many of our people no longer regard non-Orthodox Jews as part of *Kelal Yisrael*." Lamm, "Some Comments on Centrist Orthodoxy," *Tradition*, Fall 1986, p. 10.

79. Reuven Frank, "Why Are Young Israel Children Going Astray?" *Young Israel Viewpoint*, September 1984, p. 24.

80. *Young Israel Viewpoint*, September–October 1988, p. 20.

81. Emanuel Feldman, "Observant Jews and Religious Jews," *Tradition*, Winter 1992, pp. 1–3.

Chapter 7

1. Mordecai Waxman, "Conservative Judaism Confronts Its Future," *Judaism*, Spring 1987, p. 180.

2. Ismar Schorsch, "Zacharias Frankel and the European Origins of Conservative Judaism," *Judaism*, Summer 1981, p. 344.

3. Marshall Sklare, *Conservative Judaism: An American Religious Movement* (New York: Schocken, 1972, rev. edition), p. 229.

4. Elliot N. Dorff, *Conservative Judaism: Our Ancestors to Our Descendants* (New York: United Synagogue of America, 1977), esp. pp. 110–57.

5. Sklare, *Conservative Judaism*, p. 190.

6. Neil Gillman, "Mordecai Kaplan and the Ideology of Conservative Judaism," *Proceedings of the Rabbinical Assembly* 48 (1986), p. 64.

7. Hershel Matt, "On Leaving the Congregational Rabbinate," *Beineinu,* November 1975, pp. 6–7.

8. Shalom Lewis, "The Rabbi Is a Lonely Person," *Conservative Judaism,* Winter 1983–84, pp. 40–41.

9. On attrition within the rabbinate in general, see "Rabbis and Their Discontents," *Commentary,* May 1985, pp. 55–58, esp. pp. 55–56, on Conservative rabbis. Singer, like most observers, focuses on departures from the pulpit for other fields of work within Jewish life. Since the overwhelming majority of rabbis who left the pulpit continued to work within the orbit of Jewish communal service—teaching Jewish studies at universities, working in Jewish education, serving as administrators for Jewish communal agencies, or living in Israel—it is not clear whether the rabbinate suffered attrition or merely a rechanneling of personnel due to the diversification of career options that became available to rabbis.

10. Routtenberg, quoted by William Lebeau, "The RA Faces the Seventies," *Proceedings of the Rabbinical Assembly* 34 (1970), p. 99.

11. Stephen C. Lerner, "2001: Blueprint for the Rabbinate in the 21st Century," *Proceedings of the Rabbinical Assembly* 41 (1979), p. 122.

12. William Greenfeld, quoted by Hillel Silverman in *Proceedings of the Rabbinical Assembly* 34 (1970), p. 111.

13. See the concluding chapter in Sklare's revised version of *Conservative Judaism: An American Religious Movement,* rev. ed. (New York: Schocken, 1972), pp. 253–82.

14. Charles S. Liebman and Saul Shapiro, "Survey of the Conservative Movement" (Unpublished, 1979) and Saul Shapiro, "The Conservative Movement" (Unpublished, November 13, 1979). For critiques of the survey design and its assumptions, see Harold Schulweis, "Surveys, Statistics and Sectarian Salvation," *Conservative Judaism,* Winter 1980, pp. 65–69; and Rela Geffen Monson, "The Future of Conservative Judaism in the United States: A Rejoinder," *Conservative Judaism,* Winter 1983–84, esp. pp. 10–14.

15. Stephen C. Lerner, "The Havurot," *Conservative Judaism,* Spring 1970, pp. 3–7; William Novak, "Notes on Summer Camps: Some Reflection on the Ramah Dream," *Response,* Winter 1971–72, p. 59. See also the symposium on Ramah in *Conservative Judaism,* Fall 1987, which points up the relationship between the camping movement and Havurah Judaism.

16. Jacob Neusner, *Contemporary Judaic Fellowship in Theory and Practice* (New York: Ktav, 1972).

17. Novak, "Notes on Summer Camps," p. 59.

18. On the complex relationship between the Conservative movement and Havurah Judaism, see Robert Goldenberg, "The Seminary and 'Havurah Judaism': Some Thoughts," in *The Seminary at 100,* ed. Nina Beth Cardin and David Wolf Silverman (New York: Rabbinical Assembly, 1987), pp. 155–63, esp. the footnotes.

19. Richard Siegel, "Futuristic Jewish Communities," *Proceedings of the Rabbinical Assembly* 36 (1974), p. 80.

20. Susannah Heschel, "Changing Forms of Jewish Spirituality," *Proceedings of the Rabbinical Assembly* 42 (1980), p. 146.

21. A central theme in Riv-Ellen Prell's study of a havurah in Los Angeles is the

emergence of high percentages of haverim from Conservative institutions and their ongoing acceptance of the belief system and ideology of Conservatism, even as they rejected its organizations and structure. See Prell, *Prayer and Community: The Havurah in American Judaism* (Detroit, Mich.: Wayne State University Press, 1989), esp. chaps. 1, 3. There is growing evidence that members of independent havurot came to rely on Conservative institutions for their children's education.

22. Aryeh Davidson and Jack Wertheimer, "The Next Generation of Conservative Rabbis," in *The Seminary at 100*, eds. Cardin and Silverman, p. 36. Other essays in that volume also point up the ability of the Conservative movement to recruit from within; see, for example, Burton I. Cohen, "From Camper to National Director: A Personal View of the Seminary and Ramah," pp. 125–34.

23. Robert Chazan, "Tribute to Ramah on Its 25th Anniversary," *Beineinu*, May 1973, p. 31.

24. Mayer Rabinowitz, "Toward a Halakhic Guide for the Conservative Jew," *Conservative Judaism*, Fall 1986, pp. 18, 22, 26, 29; see also Aaron H. Blumenthal, "The Status of Women in Jewish Law," *Conservative Judaism*, Spring 1977, pp. 24–40.

25. On publicity surrounding the Law Committee's actions, see Sidney Schwarz, "Law and Legitimacy: An Intellectual History of Conservative Judaism, 1902–1973," (Ph.D. Diss., Temple University, 1981), pp. 335–40.

26. I. Usher Kirshblum headed these two committees; his correspondence with rabbinic colleagues spanning the period from 1975 until 1983 are in the archives of the Ratner Center for the Study of Conservative Judaism at the Jewish Theological Seminary of America, New York.

27. For a more detailed account of the protracted struggle over women's ordination in the Conservative movement, see Jack Wertheimer, "Recent Trends in American Judaism," *American Jewish Yearbook* 89 (1989), pp. 130–34.

28. The "Final Report of the Commission for the Study of the Ordination of Women as Rabbis" was compiled by Gordon Tucker, executive director of the commission, and is printed in Simon Greenberg, ed., *The Ordination of Women as Rabbis: Studies and Responsa* (New York: Jewish Theological Seminary of America, 1988), pp. 5–30. See also the position papers of Seminary faculty members in the Greenberg volume. Several of the most forceful papers presented in opposition to women's ordination are not included in Greenberg's volume but appeared in a booklet entitled "On the Ordination of Women as Rabbis" (Mimeo, JTS, early 1980s). See especially the papers of David Weiss Halivni, Gershon C. Bacon, and David A. Resnick.

29. Greenberg, ed., *The Ordination of Women as Rabbis*, pp. 12–30. The minority report emphasized four key issues: most crucially, opponents of ordination argued that halakhic considerations had not been sufficiently resolved, particularly to the satisfaction of many congregations within the movement, as well as for many Jews outside of the movement "who may be affected by practices in connection with testimony relating to marriage and divorce." Second, fears were expressed concerning the divisiveness of such an action, which might impel some Conservative rabbis to reject the marriages and divorces supervised by colleagues. Third, the action might create such a deep rift that opponents of egalitarianism would feel driven out of the movement. And last, ordination would symbolically represent a break with

tradition, particularly for those young Conservative Jews most committed to halakhah.

30. On the background to the faculty vote of 1979, see David Szonyi, "The Conservative Condition," *Moment,* May 1980, esp. pp. 38–39.

31. Some supporters of Magidson's admission voted against her on the grounds that a woman ordained by the Seminary should be the first female admitted to the RA. Others felt that such a momentous decision should be reserved for a convention that drew a broader cross section of the membership. The convention met in Dallas and attendance was lower than usual.

32. For the debate over Magidson's application, see *Proceedings of the Rabbinical Assembly* 45 (1983), pp. 218–51, and p. 247 for the vote tally.

33. See Francine Klagsbrun, "At Last, A Conservative Rabbi," *Congress Monthly,* May–June 1985, p. 11; and Abraham Karp, " A Century of Conservative Judaism," *American Jewish Yearbook* 86 (1986), p. 52.

34. David Novak, in *Proceedings of the Rabbinical Assembly* 45 (1983), p. 223.

35. Aaron Gold in *Proceedings of the Rabbinical Assembly* 45 (1983), p. 237.

36. Ibid., pp. 229–30.

37. Benjamin Kreitman, "What Does Halakha Mean to Us?" *Proceedings of the Rabbinical Assembly* 40 (1978), p. 16.

38. For reflections on the role of the Seminary's faculty during the ordination debate and on the shifting role of Kaplan's views, see Gillman, "Mordecai Kaplan and the Ideology of Conservative Judaism," esp. pp. 64–65.

39. *Mahzor for Rosh Hashanah and Yom Kippur* (New York: Rabbinical Assembly, 1972).

40. Isaac Klein, *Guide to Jewish Religious Practice* (New York: Jewish Theological Seminary of America, 1979).

41. *The Feast of Freedom Passover Haggadah* (New York: Rabbinical Assembly, 1982).

42. *Siddur Sim Shalom: A Prayerbook for Shabbat, Festivals, and Weekdays* (New York: Rabbinical Assembly, 1985).

43. Joel Roth, *The Halakhic Process: A Systemic Analysis* (New York: Jewish Theological Seminary, 1986).

44. *Proceedings of the Committee on Jewish Law and Standards of the Conservative Movement, 1980–1985* (New York: Rabbinical Assembly, 1988).

45. *Emet Ve-Emunah: Statement of Principles of Conservative Judaism* (New York: Jewish Theological Seminary, Rabbinical Assembly, United Synagogue, 1988).

46. Ibid., pp. 21–25.

47. Ismar Schorsch, "Reflections on *Emet Ve-Emunah*" (Address circulated in typescript, unpaged).

48. *Emet Ve-Emunah,* pp. 14, 40–41.

49. *Siddur Sim Shalom,* pp. 2–3, 144.

50. "Presidential Address," *Proceedings of the Rabbinical Assembly* 49 (1987), p. 45.

51. *Emet Ve-Emunah,* p. 49.

52. For the debate over adopting the matrilineal principle as a standard within the Rabbinical Assembly, see *Proceedings of the Rabbinical Assembly* 48 (1986), pp. 313–22.

53. Edya Arzt, "Our Rights to Rites," *Women's League Outlook,* Fall 1988, pp. 17–18; and idem, "Survey Update: Women's Rights to Rites," *Women's League Outlook,* Summer 1990, pp. 20–21. For some earlier surveys, see

Zelda Dick, "Light from Our Poll on Women's Role," *Women's League Outlook*, Summer 1975, pp. 14–15; Daniel Elazar and Rela Geffen Monson, "Women in the Synagogue Today," *Midstream*, April 1979, pp. 25–30; Anne Lapidus Lerner and Stephen C. Lerner, "Report," *Rabbinical Assembly News*, February 1984, pp. 1, 8. For two essays on the process by which individual congregations adopted egalitarianism, see Ruth R. Seldin, "Women in the Synagogue: A Congregant's View," *Conservative Judaism*, Winter 1979, pp. 80–88; and Esther Altshul Helfgott, "Beth Shalom's Encounter with the Woman Question," *Conservative Judaism*, Spring 1986, pp. 66–76.

54. Gerson D. Cohen, "The Seminary Today," *Proceedings of the Rabbinical Assembly* 42 (1980), p. 37, which reports on the beginnings of a "semi-egalitarian service" in one of the dormitories. By the mid-1980s, that minyan had moved into the main Seminary building.

55. Douglas Aronin, "Relief for Beleaguered Traditionalists," *Hagahelet*, Spring 1987, p. 4.

56. See the articles by Alan J. Yuter and David Novak in *Sh'ma*, May 3, 1985, pp. 97–101.

57. In a letter to the *Jewish Post and Opinion*, Ron Price, the executive director, made the claim about rabbinic and lay supporters (August 17, 1988, p. 15). See also *Hagahelet*, Fall 1986, p. 5.

58. See the Responsum by Alan J. Yuter in *Tomeikh keHalakhah*, vol. 1, ed. Wayne Allen (Mount Vernon, N.Y.: Union for Traditional Conservative Judaism, 1986), pp. 6–12.

59. See chap. 6 for a discussion of the responsum of the Yeshiva Five on women's prayer groups.

60. See the brochure of the Institute of Traditional Judaism (undated). The *Jewish Week* reports on the founding of the school March 2, 1990, p. 23; see also the *New York Times*, March 10, 1990, and January 6, 1991.

61. *Hagahelet*, Summer 1990, p. 1.

62. Rahel Musleah, "Parting from the Mainstream (and Meeting in the Middle?)" *LI Jewish World*, May 18–24, 1990, pp. 12–14. The Union also has entered discussion with a newly formed International Federation of Traditional Cantors, which claims to represent two hundred cantors who broke with the Cantors Assembly, a Conservative body that decided in 1991 to admit women as members. See *Jewish Week*, January 17–23, 1992, p. 39.

63. Lerner, "2001: Blueprint for the Rabbinate in the 21st Century," p. 122. This was the forecast of the Liebman/Shapiro report.

64. Gilbert Rosenthal, "The Elements That Unite Us," *Proceedings of the Rabbinical Assembly* 46 (1984), p. 23.

65. Jeffrey Bocarsly, *Hagahelet*, Fall 1986, p. 7.

66. *Proceedings of the Rabbinical Assembly* 52 (1990), p. 275.

67. "Gay and Lesbian Jews: A Teshuvah," submitted to the Committee on Law and Standards.

68. "Homosexuality" submitted to the Committee on Law and Standards, dated November 1, 1991. See also Stewart Ain, "Gay 'Marriage'?" *Jewish Week*, December 27–January 2, 1992, pp. 4ff.

69. Stewart Ain, "Conservatives Reject Bid to Grant Equality to Gay Jews," *Jewish Week*, April 3–9, 1992, p. 4.

70. *Jewish Telegraphic Agency Daily News Bulletin*, May 26, 1992, p.1.

71. On the debate among women rabbinical students at JTS over the possibili-

ties for egalitarianism in the ritual sphere, see the essays of Carolyn Braun, Lori Forman, and Pamela Hoffman in *Sh'ma*, May 31, 1985, pp. 113–15.

72. Robert Gordis, "To Move Forward, Take One Step Back: A Plea to the Reform Movement," *Moment*, May 1986, pp. 58–61.

73. Ismar Schorsch, "Centenary Thoughts: Conservatism Revisited," *Proceedings of the Rabbinical Assembly*, 48 (1986), p. 79. See also in the same volume the "Presidential Acceptance Speech" of Kassel Abelson, which points to Conservatism becoming a "more militant middle" (p. 76).

74. Schorsch, "Centenary Thoughts," p. 79.

Chapter 8

1. The first sentence of the movement's platform announces that Reconstructionism is "one of the four major Jewish religious movements." *FRCH Newsletter*, September 1986, p. D.

2. Ira Eisenstein, *Reconstructing Judaism: An Autobiography* (New York: Reconstructionist Press, 1986), p. 214.

3. Ibid., pp. 218–19.

4. Ibid., pp. 226–29.

5. Temple University had recently come under public auspices and was eager to develop its seminary into a department of religion. The head of this department, Bernard Phillips, developed a master plan to bring seminarians of the Protestant and Catholic, as well as Jewish, faiths to Temple. See Phillips, "Where Religion Meets Scholarly Dialogue," *Reconstructionist*, October 11, 1968, pp. 7–9.

6. Reconstructionist Rabbinical College brochure, undated and unpaged.

7. For an early description of the curriculum, see Fred Kazan, "An Innovation in Total Concept" (Provided by the author, 1973); see the subsequent bulletins of RRC for evidence of staff turnover.

8. Michael Weiss, "Of Seekers and Skeptics," *Detroit Jewish News*, November 1, 1991, pp. 27ff., refers to 120 rabbis ordained between 1973 and late 1991 (p. 30).

9. Sidney Goldstein, "Profile of American Jewry," *American Jewish Yearbook* 92 (1992), pp. 129–30, 170.

10. Arthur J. Magida, "The Road Less Traveled," *Baltimore Jewish Times*, July 17, 1992, pp. 47–49. On recent affiliates and the reference to two thousand families in New York, see *FRCH Newsletter*, March 1988, p. 1.

11. *Reconstructionist Newsletter*, September 1968, p. 1.

12. "RRA Guidelines on Intermarriage," *Reconstructionist*, November 1983, pp. 18–23. A survey sponsored by RRA found that 50 percent of the members wanted a strong statement against rabbinic officiation at mixed marriages; and 30 percent did or were prepared to officiate at such marriages; *Ra'ayonot*, Spring–Summer 1982, p. 8.

13. *Reconstructionist*, June 1978, p. 31.

14. "Reconstructionists and Jewish Unity," *Reconstructionist*, September 1987, p. 12. In 1980 the Reconstructionist Rabbinical Association implemented a procedure for women to give a *get* (a Jewish bill of divorce), but at the time, such an action could only be taken if the *Beit Din* (Jewish court) was "completely convinced that the husband is adamant and uncooperative; in other

words, he absolutely refuses to give the *get* to his wife." Thus, as of 1980, gender equality was not yet in place, since the movement only permitted a woman to divorce her husband, if he could not be forced to issue a *get*. See Ira Eisenstein, "Reconstructionist Rabbinical Association Introduces 'Egalitarian' Divorce," *Reconstructionist*, June 1980, pp. 28–29.

15. Arthur Green, "Where We Stand: Theory and Practice of Contemporary Reconstructionism," *Reconstructionist*, Autumn 1990, p. 15. The RRA introduced a female-initiated *get* in 1980. Communication from Richard Hirsh, *Journal of Reform Judaism*, Winter 1984, p. 89.

16. Arthur Green, "Where We Stand," p. 15.

17. David Teutsch, "Seeking the Words of Prayer," *Reconstructionist*, March 1988, pp. 9ff.

18. Debra Nussbaum Cohen, "Gender-Neutral Liturgy Entering the Mainstream of Judaism," *Jewish Week*, July 24–30, 1992, p. 4.

19. *Kol Haneshamah* (Wyncote, Pa.: Reconstructionist Press, 1989). *Kol Haneshamah* is noteworthy as well for its transliteration of virtually every prayer. It views transliteration as a bridge to Hebrew literacy, but it seeks to address Jews who have no Hebrew language skills. The siddur also displays a new openness to traditional beliefs that Kaplan found unappealing—miracles, such as the splitting of the sea; references to the messianic age; and the second paragraph of the *Shema*, the Jewish credo, which declares the power of God to "seal the heavens so no rain will fall." Ari Goldman, "Reconstructionist Jews Turn to the Supernatural," *New York Times*, February 19, 1989, p. 26.

20. *FRCH Newsletter*, September 1986, p. E.

21. *Reconstructionist*, November 1983, p. 19.

22. "Democracy and Lay-Rabbinic Relations in Reconstructionism," *Reconstructionist*, September 1985, p. 8. See also Sidney H. Schwarz, "A Synagogue with Principles," *Reconstructionist*, June 1985, pp. 21–25.

23. "Editor's Response," *Reconstructionist*, March 1989, p. 34.

24. Rebecca T. Alpert and Jacob J. Staub, *Exploring Judaism: A Reconstructionist Approach* (New York: Reconstructionist Press, 1985), p. 79.

25. Jacob Staub, "A Vision of Our Future," *Reconstructionist*, January–February 1985, p. 14; and Sidney H. Schwarz, "Reconstructionism as Process," *Reconstructionist*, June 1979, pp. 13–19. A typical congregational decision concerns the maintenance of a kosher kitchen. The congregational body of the movement, FRCH, does not require its affiliates to keep a kosher kitchen; but Mordechai Liebling of FRCH reports that "most congregations end up deciding to observe kashrut for the very Reconstructionist reason that Jewish peoplehood is the center of Judaism, and we want all Jews to feel comfortable coming to our synagogues. The synagogues should be places of inclusion, and having a kosher kitchen makes the synagogue more inclusive." Quoted in Weiss, "Of Seekers and Skeptics," p. 29.

26. See the symposium on "Democracy and Lay-Rabbinic Relations in Reconstructionism," and especially the remarks of Richard A. Hirsh "Clarifying Our Terms," *Reconstructionist*, September 1985, pp. 13–15. Hirsh is one of the few to object to this rejection of the traditional rabbinic model, noting that "while all Jews are *entitled* to an opinion, not all opinions are equally informed or equally valuable. I remain convinced that in lay-rabbinic interchange, a rabbi's perspective . . . is generally better informed (though not necessarily more correct) than that of a lay-person" (p. 15).

27. *FRCH Newsletter*, September 1986, p. E.
28. Nancy Fuchs-Kreimer, "Reconstructionism between the Generations," *Ra'ayonot*, Spring/Summer 1982, pp. 44–45.
29. Sidney Schwarz, "Neo-Hasidism and Reconstructionism: The Limits of Cooperation," *Ra'ayonot*, Summer 1984, p. 26; see also in the same issue the symposium on neo-Hasidism, which refers to Ira Eisenstein as another opponent of this trend (p. 2).
30. The former president of the college, Ira Silverman, and a leading administrator of the movement, David Teutsch, also advocated a reexamination of Kaplan's theology because "naturalism or transnaturalism doesn't adequately address this generation's theological needs." See Sidney Schwarz, "The Reconstructionist Symposium," *Reconstructionist*, March 1982, p. 21.
31. Ibid., p. 22.
32. "Prayerbook-Committee Progress Report," *Reconstructionist*, Spring 1983, p. 21; and the symposium on chosenness in the *Reconstructionist*, September 1984.
33. *Kol Haneshamah*, p. 128.
34. "The Temper of Reconstructionism," in *Jewish Life in America*, ed. Theodore Friedman and Robert Gordis (New York: Ktav, 1955), p. 74.
35. *Reconstructionist*, October–November 1984, p. 7.
36. Gary Rosenblatt, "Can a Reconstructionist Rabbi Go Too Far?" *Baltimore Jewish Times*, March 27, 1987, p. 66.
37. Rebecca T. Alpert and Arthur Waskow, "Toward an Ethical Kashrut," *Reconstructionist*, March–April 1987, p. 13.
38. Sissy Carpey, "Miklat Legerim: A Havurah for Sanctuary," *Reconstructionist*, May–June 1987, pp. 8–12.
39. Jane R. Litman, "Can Judaism Respond to Feminist Criticism," *Baltimore Jewish Times*, April 17, 1987, p. 7. Litman was responding to a story that evoked much criticism of the RRC for seeming to tolerate the worship of Canaanite goddesses. Rosenblatt, "Can a Reconstructionist Rabbi Go Too Far?" pp. 66–68. See also Jane Litman's letter in *Midstream*, October 1988, pp. 62–63.
40. Ed Stattmann, "Gays, Lesbians Still Problem Even for Reconstructionists," *Jewish Post and Opinion*, July 8, 1992, p. 3.

Chapter 9

1. On Irving Greenberg's views, see Gary Rosenblatt, "Judaism's Civil War: How Deep Is the Rift?" *Baltimore Jewish Times*, January 29, 1988, pp. 56–59; Greenberg, "Will There Be One Jewish People in the Year 2000?" *Moment*, June 1985; and idem, "The One in 2000 Controversy" *Moment*, March 1987.
2. The most complete account of this experiment, which includes interviews with all of the participating rabbis, appeared in a special section entitled, "Conversion and Patrilineality," *Intermountain Jewish News*, December 2, 1983.
3. Traditional synagogues and rabbis are largely a midwestern phenomenon; Traditional congregations permit men and women to sit together and utilize a microphone during religious services; their rabbis, mainly graduates of

the Hebrew Theological Seminary in Skokie, identify with Modern Orthodoxy.

4. For a history of the board written by the leading Reform rabbi in Denver, see Steven E. Foster, "The Community Rabbinic Conversion Board: The Denver Model," *Journal of Reform Judaism*, Summer 1984, esp. pp. 27–28.

5. Nisson Wolpin, "Compromise on the Great Divide: Questionable Conversions in Denver," *Jewish Observer*, January 1984, pp. 32–34.

6. Editorial on "The Synagogue Council of America," *Reconstructionist*, July–August 1986, p. 6.

7. When the CCAR placed a female candidate in the chaplaincy program, the commission was reconstituted as the Jewish Chaplains Council in 1986. See *JTA Bulletin*, August 29, 1985, p. 3; and *American Jewish Yearbook* 86 (1986), p. 399; and *American Jewish Yearbook* 87 (1987), p. 400, on the name change.

8. *New York Times*, February 28, 1986, p. A1.

9. Ibid.

10. For information on this conference, see *Materials from the Critical Issues Conference*, which includes press clippings from Jewish newspapers compiled by CLAL to publicize the discussions held in mid-March 1986.

11. Cardin is quoted in Arthur J. Magida, "'Who Is a Jew' Dominates Assembly," *Jewish News* (Detroit), November 25, 1988, p. 1. See also "'Who Is a Jew' Issue Threatens Funding," and "Leaders Protest 'Who Is,'" *Atlanta Jewish Times*, December 2, 1988, pp. 12, 13, as well as "'Who is a Jew' Furor Erupts," *Atlanta Jewish Times*, November 8, 1988, p. 16A.

12. The open letter appeared in the *New York Times*, December 19, 1988, p. B9. On Orthodox divisions over the issue, see Alan Richter and Walter Ruby, "Rift Develops among Orthodox over Law of Return," *LI Jewish World*, December 2–8, 1988, p. 3.

13. Marc D. Angel, "Leaders of U.S. Jewry Have Fear of Losing Power," *Jewish Week*, December 16, 1988, p. 26.

14. This is the summary offered by Irving Greenberg, "Will There Be One Jewish People by the Year 2000?—Further Reflections," in *Conflict or Cooperation: Papers on Jewish Unity* (New York: American Jewish Committee, 1989), pp. 9–10.

15. Steven M. Cohen, "Are Reform Jews Abandoning Israel," *Reform Judaism*, Spring 1988, pp. 4–5.

16. See the exchange between Greenberg and Steven M. Cohen in Greenberg, "The One in 2000 Controversy."

17. Steven M. Cohen, *Unity and Polarization in Judaism Today: The Attitudes of American and Israeli Jews* (New York: American Jewish Committee, 1988), p. 5.

18. Lawrence Grossman, "Jewish Communal Affairs," *American Jewish Yearbook* 91 (1991), p. 200.

19. Greenberg, "Will There Be One . . . Further Reflections," p. 10.

20. Ira Rifkin, "Intra-Jewish Tension Delays Papal Meeting," *Baltimore Jewish Times*, November 2, 1990, pp. 43–44.

21. Rahel Musleah, "Surgically Simple, Ritually Complex," *LI Jewish World*, January 19, 1990, p. 3; Debra Nussbaum Cohen, "Conservative Rabbis Get Training in Kashrut Supervision," *JTA Report*, July 23, 1992.

22. Lawrence Troster, "Conversion and *Mikveh*," *RA Newsletter*, Summer 1989, p. 4.

23. Alexander Schindler, "Remarks by the President of the UAHC," *CCAR Yearbook* 92 (1982), p. 63.

24. Alan J. Yuter, "Is Reform Judaism a Movement, a Sect, or a Heresy," *Tradition*, Spring 1989, p. 94; N. Wolpin, "One Straw, How Many Camels?" *Jewish Observer*, September 1986, p. 16.

25. Samuel Heilman, *Jewish Unity and Diversity: A Survey of American Rabbis and Rabbinical Students* (New York: American Jewish Committee, 1991), pp. 27–35.

26. Samuel Heilman and Steven M. Cohen, *Cosmopolitans and Parochials: Modern Orthodox Jews in America* (Chicago: University of Chicago Press, 1989), pp. 122–23.

27. Hints of this social stance appear occasionally. It is the subject of an editorial column written by Gary Rosenblatt, a journalist who identifies with Orthodoxy but has many contacts with the rest of the community. Rosenblatt claims that "Orthodox rabbis . . . tell their congregants not to associate with non-Jews, or even non-Orthodox families," and as a result these congregants "feel they have hardly any common points of reference or connection with their so-called brethren." Rosenblatt, "'Frum' Here to Modernity," *Baltimore Jewish Times*, September 25, 1992, p. 10.

28. Ira Robinson, "The Marvelous Midos Machine: Audio Tapes as an Orthodox Educational Medium," in *Essays in the Social Scientific Study of Judaism and Jewish Society*, vol. 2, ed. Simcha Fishbane and Stuart Schoenfeld (Hoboken, N.J.: Ktav, 1992), p. 165.

29. Steven M. Cohen, *Content or Continuity? Alternative Bases for Commitment* (New York: American Jewish Committee, 1990), p. 71.

    Few spokespersons for Orthodoxy will go on record with their views, but it is no secret that many regard non-Orthodox versions of Judaism as another religion. One right-wing activist has spoken as follows: "If we give them a test, use any standard recognized by the most uneducated, uninitated Gentile as to what would constitute Jewish affiliation—Sabbath observance, eating kosher, frowning on adultery, the Ten Commandments—these people would not match up in any way. So therefore I say that they are practicing a religion which is not Judaism." Quoted by James Davison Hunter, *Culture Wars: The Struggle to Define America* (New York: Basic Books, 1991), p. 15.

30. See the joint publication of CLAL and the AJC, *Conflict or Cooperation: Papers on Jewish Unity*.

31. See, for example, "A Message from Our Rabbis," *Community Review*, December 15, 1988, p. 1, which issues an appeal for unity in the name of all the rabbis in Harrisburg, Pa.

32. "An Open Letter to Our Brethren," *Jewish Week*, December 30, 1988, p. 19.

33. Heilman, *Jewish Unity and Diversity*, pp. 16–17.

34. Robert Wuthnow, *The Restructuring of American Religion* (Princeton: Princeton University Press, 1988), p. 6.

35. Hunter prefers the terms orthodox and progressivist for what others call religious conservatives and religious liberals.

36. Hunter, *Culture Wars*, pp. 44–45.

37. Wade Clark Roof and William McKinney, *American Mainline Religion: Its Changing Shape and Future* (New Brunswick, N.J.: Rutgers University Press, 1987), p. 37.

38. Jerry Falwell, "An Agenda for the 1980s," in *Piety and Politics: Evangelicals and Fundamentalists Confront the World*, ed. Richard J. Neuhaus and Michael

Cromartie (Lanham, Md.: University Press of America, 1987), pp. 113–14; Edward Hoffman, "Thriving Families in Urban America: The Lubavitcher Hasidim," *Family in America* (The Rockford Institute Center on the Family in America) 4 (October 1990), pp. 1ff.

39. See Grossman, "Jewish Communal Affairs," pp. 191–92, for a discussion of Jewish organizational responses when the U.S. Supreme Court took up a Missouri law denying public funding and facilities for abortion.

40. Sarah Gold, "Where Do Jews Stand in the Debate over Abortion," *LI Jewish World*, October 23–29, 1992, p. 3.

41. The claim of biblical inerrancy fundamentally asserts the literal truth of the Bible; such literalism was rejected by rabbinic Judaism, and even the most Orthodox of Jews believes in the necessity for rabbinic interpretations, which sometimes flatly contradict the literal words of the text. For a brief analysis of the theological meaning of inerrancy, see James D. Hunter, *Evangelicalism: The Coming Generation* (Chicago: University of Chicago Press, 1987), pp. 20–25.

42. Nancy Ammerman, *Bible Believers: Fundamentalism in the Modern World* (New Brunswick, N.J.: Rutgers University Press, 1987), p. 8. For a trenchant analysis of the early history of Jewish ultra-Orthodoxy in Europe, see Michael K. Silber, "The Emergence of Ultra-Orthodoxy: The Invention of a Tradition," in *The Uses of Tradition: Jewish Continuity in the Modern Era*, ed. Jack Wertheimer (New York and Cambridge, Mass.: Jewish Theological Seminary of America and Harvard University Press, 1993), pp. 23–84.

43. Martin E. Marty and R. Scott Appelby, eds., *Fundamentalisms Observed* (Chicago: University of Chicago Press, 1991), pp. ix–x.

44. Heilman and Cohen, *Cosmopolitans and Parochials*, pp. 160–73.

45. For the two most important works on the transformation of American religious life under the impact of these political/cultural battles, see Wuthnow, *The Restructuring of American Religion*; and Hunter, *Culture Wars*.

46. Hunter, *Culture Wars*, p. 13.

47. One area of public policy that has attracted Orthodox attention is the question of church/state separation, specifically regarding government support for parochial schools and the public display of religious symbols, such as the Hanukkah menorah. But here too they have pursued the matter out of narrow interest, rather than on broad principle. On other issues such as abortion rights, there is little unity, given the openness of traditional Judaism to abortion under certain circumstances. On separation issues, see Naomi W. Cohen, *Jews in Christian America: The Pursuit of Religious Equality* (New York: Oxford University Press, 1992), pp. 240–41; on abortion rights issues, see Grossman, "Jewish Communal Affairs," pp. 191–92; and Gold, "Where Do Jews Stand in the Debate over Abortion?" p. 3.

48. Samuel Heilman and Menachem Friedman, "Religious Fundamentalism and Religious Jews: The Case of Haredim," in Marty and Appelby, *Fundamentalisms Observed*, p. 258.

Conclusion

1. Simon Rawidowicz, "Israel: The Ever-dying People," in his *Studies in Jewish Thought* (Philadelphia: Jewish Publication Society of America, 1974), pp. 210–24.

2. Charles Silberman, *A Certain People: American Jews and Their Lives Today* (New York: Summit, 1985), p. 25.

3. Silberman, quoted in Gary Rosenblatt, "Even the Optimists Are Worried," *Baltimore Jewish Times*, August 16, 1991, p. 10.

4. Arthur Hertzberg, *The Jews in America: Four Centuries of an Uneasy Encounter* (New York: Simon and Schuster, 1989), p. 386. The author comes out of a tradition of Zionist writing that for the past century has issued similar pronouncements about diaspora Jewries. For a recent example, see David Vital, *The Future of the Jews: A People at the Crossroads* (Cambridge, Mass.: Harvard University Press, 1990).

5. Marshall Sklare, *Conservative Judaism: An American Religious Movement*, 2d ed. (New York: Schocken, 1972), pp. 43, 262–67.

6. Letter to the editor, "Orthodoxy Saves Judaism," *Jewish Week*, November 6–12, p. 22.

7. "1,000,000 Jews Can Now Be Rescued . . . Right Here in North America," advertisement in the *Jewish Week*, November 6–12, 1992, p. 25; and the sharp rejoinder by sociologist Egon Mayer, *Jewish Week*, November 13, 1992, p. 32.

8. On these issues, see Dean M. Kelley, *Why Conservative Churches Are Growing* (New York: Harper and Row, 1972); Dean R. Hoge, *Division in the Protestant House: The Basic Reasons behind Intra-Church Conflicts* (Philadelphia: Westminster Press, 1976), pp. 115–20; Wade Clark Roof and William McKinney, *American Mainline Religion: Its Changing Shape and Future* (New Brunswick, N.J.: Rutgers University Press, 1987), pp. 244–51; and Robin D. Perrin and Armand L. Mauss, "The Great Protestant Puzzle: Retreat, Renewal, or Reshuffle," in *In Gods We Trust: New Patterns of Religious Pluralism in America*, 2d ed., eds. Thomas Robbins and Dick Anthony (New Brunswick, N.J.: Transaction Books, 1990), pp. 158–65.

9. Eugene Kennedy, *Tomorrow's Catholics, Yesterday's Church: The Two Cultures of American Catholicism* (San Francisco: Harper and Row, 1990), pp. 8–37; James Castelli and George Gallup, Jr., *The American Catholic People: Their Beliefs, Practices and Values* (Garden City, N.Y.: Doubleday, 1987); and on a recent Gallup poll of Catholics, Ari L. Goldman, "Catholics Are at Odds with Bishops," *New York Times*, June 19, 1992, p. A16.

10. Arthur S. Parsons, "The Secular Contribution to Religious Innovation: A Case Study of the Unification Church," *Sociological Analysis* 49 (Fall 1989), p. 209.

11. Roof and McKinney, *American Mainline Religion*, p. 247.

12. R. Stephen Warner, "Change and Continuity in the U.S. Religious System: Perspectives from Sociology" (Paper delivered at Princeton Theological Seminary, February 6, 1989), pp. 5–6.

13. Jay Dolan, *The American Catholic Experience: A History from Colonial Times to the Present* (Garden City, N.Y.: Doubleday, 1985), p. 453.

14. Roof and McKinney, *American Mainline Religion*, p. 67.

15. These results of a Gallup survey conducted in 1988 are reported by Bruce A. Greer and Wade Clark Roof, "'Desperately Seeking Sheila': Locating Religious Privatism in American Society," *Journal for the Scientific Study of Religion* 31 (1992), p. 347.

16. Warner, "Change and Continuity in the U.S. Religious System," pp. 32–33.

17. Peter Steinfels, "Do We Live in an Era of 'Pick and Choose' Religion?" *New York Times*, April 13, 1991, p. 10.

18. Greer and Roof, "'Desperately Seeking Sheila,'" pp. 346–47.

19. Lenore Eve Weissler, "Making Judaism Meaningful: Ambivalence and Tradition in a Havurah Community" (Ph.D. diss., University of Pennsylvania, 1982).

20. Warner, "Change and Continuity in the U.S. Religious System," p. 35. See also R. Stephen Warner, "Work in Progress Toward a New Paradigm for the Sociological Study of Religion in the United States," *American Sociological Review* 98 (March 1993).

21. Charles S. Liebman and Steven M. Cohen, *Two Worlds of Judaism: The Israeli and American Experiences* (New Haven: Yale University Press, 1990).

22. The sense of alienation between these two worlds of Judaism was expressed poignantly by an American convert to Judaism who settled in Israel. Writing to cancel his subscription to the journal *Sh'ma*, the writer praised the quality of the journal but lamented the gap between his concerns in Israel and those matters explored in *Sh'ma*: "While I do appreciate *Sh'ma*'s dealing with issues that touch the Jewish American community, it saddens me to read that such are the issues, and such are the concerns of the Jew in America. . . . I can't help but suspect that the distance I feel between my own view and *Sh'ma*'s views reflects a difference between the Jew in Israel versus the Jew in America." *Sh'ma*, May 15, 1992, p. 110.

23. On the emerging policy debate within the organized Jewish community, see Egon Mayer, "The Case for a New Jewish Intermarriage Policy," *Jewish Week* (New York), September 4–10, 1992, p. 18; and Steven Bayme, *Outreach to the Unaffiliated: Communal Context and Policy Direction* (New York: American Jewish Committee, 1992).

24. On a new policy commission of the Conservative movement, see *The Jewish Week*, November 20–26, 1992, p. 42. Several centrist Orthodox groups have opened a lobbying office in Washington even as Agudath Israel maintains its separate office. (*The Jewish Journal* [New York], March 11, 1988, p. 4.)

25. On new Orthodox efforts to combat anti-Semitism on their own because "the non-Orthodox have deserted us," see Steven Lipman, "Orthodox Taking Off Gloves to Battle Anti-Semitism," *Jewish Week* (November 27–December 3, 1992), p. 11.

BIBLIOGRAPHY
OF SELECTED
SECONDARY WORKS

Ackerman, Walter. "The Day School in the Conservative Movement." *Conservative Judaism* 16 (Winter 1961).

Ahlstrom, Sidney E. *A Religious History of the American People.* 2 vols. Garden City, N.Y.: Doubleday, 1975.

Alba, Richard D. *Ethnic Identity: The Transformation of White America.* New Haven: Yale University Press, 1990.

Ammerman, Nancy. *Bible Believers: Fundamentalism in the Modern World.* New Brunswick, N.J.: Rutgers University Press, 1987.

Antoun, Richard T., and Mary E. Hegland, eds. *Religious Resurgence.* Syracuse, N.Y.: Syracuse University Press, 1987.

Arzt, Edya. "Our Rights to Rites." *Women's League Outlook* 58 (Fall 1988). pp. 17–18.

———. "Survey Update: Women's Rights to Rites." *Women's League Outlook* 6 (Summer 1990).

Aviad, Janet. *Return to Judaism: Religious Renewal in Israel.* Chicago: University of Chicago Press, 1983.

Bayme, Steven. *Outreach to the Unaffiliated: Communal Context and Policy Direction.* New York: American Jewish Committee, 1992.

Bellah, Robert N., et al. *Habits of the Heart: Individualism and Commitment in American Life.* Berkeley: University of California Press, 1985.

Bernstein, Louis. "The Emergence of the English Speaking Orthodox Rabbinate." Ph.D. diss., Yeshiva University, 1977.

Blumenthal, Aaron H. "The Status of Women in Jewish Law," *Conservative Judaism* 3 (Spring 1977).

Brereton, Virginia Lieson. *From Sin to Salvation: Stories of Women's Conversions, 1800 to the Present.* Bloomington: Indiana University Press, 1991.

Bubis, Gerald B., and Harry Wasserman. *Synagogue Havurot: A Comparative Study.* Philadelphia: Center for Jewish Community Studies, 1983.

Buechler, Steven M. *Women's Movements in the United States: Woman Suffrage, Equal Rights, and Beyond.* New Brunswick, N.J.: Rutgers University Press, 1990.

Burns, Stewart. *Social Movements of the 1960s: Searching for Democracy.* Boston: Twayne, 1990.

Caplow, Theodore, et al. *All Faithful People: Change and Continuity in Middletown's Religion.* Minneapolis: University of Minnesota Press, 1983.

Castelli, James, and George Gallup, Jr. *The American Catholic People: Their Beliefs, Practices and Values.* Garden City, N.Y.: Doubleday, 1987.

Cohen, Naomi W. *Jews in Christian America: The Pursuit of Religious Equality.* New York: Oxford University Press, 1992.

Cohen, Steven M. *American Assimilation or Jewish Revival?* Bloomington: Indiana University Press, 1988.

———. "The American Jewish Family Today." *American Jewish Yearbook* 82 (1982).

———. "Are Reform Jews Abandoning Israel." *Reform Judaism* 16 (Spring 1988).

———. *Content or Continuity? Alternative Bases for Commitment: The 1989 National Survey of American Jews.* New York: American Jewish Committee, 1991.

———. "Trends in Jewish Philanthropy." *American Jewish Yearbook* 80 (1980).

———. *Unity and Polarization in Judaism Today: The Attitudes of American and Israeli Jews.* New York: American Jewish Committee, 1988.

Cohen, Steven M., and Leonard J. Fein. "From Integration to Survival: American Jewish Anxieties in Transition." *Annals of the American Academy of Political and Social Science* 480 (July 1985).

Cohen, Steven M., and Paul Ritterband. *The Jewish Population of Greater New York: A Profile.* New York: Federation of Jewish Philanthropies of New York, 1981.

———. "The Social Characteristics of the New York Area Jewish Community, 1981." *American Jewish Yearbook* 84 (1984).

———. "Will the Well Run Dry? The Future of Jewish Giving in America." *Response* 12 (Summer 1979).

Danzger, M. Herbert. *Returning to Tradition: The Contemporary Revival of Orthodox Judaism.* New Haven: Yale University Press, 1989.

Davidman, Lynn. "Accommodation and Resistance to Modernity: A Comparison of Two Contemporary Orthodox Jewish Groups." *Sociological Analysis* 51 (1990).

———. *Tradition in a Rootless World: Women Turn to Orthodox Judaism.* Berkeley: University of California Press, 1991.

Davidson, Aryeh, and Jack Wertheimer. "The Next Generation of Conservative Rabbis." In *The Seminary at 100,* edited by Nina Cardin and David W. Silverman. New York: Rabbinical Assembly, 1986.

DellaPergola, Sergio, and Uziel O. Schmelz. "Demographic Transformations of American Jewry: Marriage and Mixed-Marriage in the 1980s." *Studies in Contemporary Jewry*, vol 5. New York: Oxford University Press, 1989.

Dolan, Jay P. *The American Catholic Experience: A History from Colonial Times to the Present.* Garden City, N.Y.: Doubleday, 1985.

Dubb, Allie A., and Sergio DellaPergola. *First Census of Jewish Schools in the Diaspora, 1981/83.* Jerusalem: Institute for Contemporary Jewry, 1986.

Duker, Abraham G. "The Emerging Patterns in American Jewish Life." *Publication of the American Jewish Historical Society* 39 (1950).

———. "On Religious Trends in American Life," *YIVO Annual* 4 (1949).

Elazar, Daniel, and Rela Geffen Monson. "The Synagogue Havurah: An Experiment in Restoring Adult Fellowship to the Jewish Community." *Jewish Journal of Sociology* 21 (June 1979).

———. "Women in the Synagogue Today." *Midstream* 27 (April 1981).

Ellenson, David. "Representative Orthodox Responsa on Conversion and Intermarriage in the Contemporary Era." *Jewish Social Studies* 47 (Summer–Fall 1985).

Endelman, Todd. "The Legitimization of the Diaspora Experience in Recent Jewish Historiography." *Modern Judaism* 11 (May 1991).

Fein, Leonard, et al. *Reform Is a Verb: Notes on Reform and Reforming Jews*, New York: UAHC, 1972.

Fishman, Sylvia Barack. "The Impact of Feminism on American Jewish Life." *American Jewish Yearbook* 89 (1989).

Friedman, Menachem. "Life Tradition and Book Tradition in the Development of Ultraorthodox Judaism." In *Judaism from Within and Without: Anthropological Perspectives*, edited by Harvey Goldberg. Albany: SUNY Press, 1987.

———. "The Lost *Kiddush* Cup: Changes in Ashkenazic Haredi Culture—A Tradition in Crisis." In *The Uses of Tradition: Jewish Continuity in the Modern Era*, edited by Jack Wertheimer. New York and Cambridge, Mass.: Jewish Theological Seminary and Harvard University Press, 1993.

Friedman, Peter, and Mark Zober. *Factors Influencing Synagogue Affiliation: A Multi Community Analysis.* North American Jewish Data Bank, Occasional Papers no. 3 (May 1987).

Friedman, Theodore, and Robert Gordis, eds. *Jewish Life in America.* New York: Ktav, 1955.

Gallup, George, Jr., and Jim Castelli. *The People's Religion: American Faith in the 90's.* New York: Macmillan, 1989.

Gillman, Neil. "Mordecai Kaplan and the Ideology of Conservative Judaism." *Proceedings of the Rabbinical Assembly* 48 (1986).

Glazer, Nathan. "New Perspectives in American Jewish Sociology." *American Jewish Yearbook* 87 (1987).

Goldscheider, Calvin. *Jewish Continuity and Change: Emerging Patterns in America.* Bloomington: University of Indiana Press, 1986.

Goldstein, Sidney. "The Jews in the United States: A Demographic Profile." *American Jewish Yearbook* 81 (1981).

———. "Jews in the United States: Perspectives from Demography." *American Jewish Yearbook* 81 (1981).

———. "American Jewry, 1970: A Demographic Profile." *American Jewish Yearbook* 72 (1972).

―――. "Profile of American Jewry." *American Jewish Yearbook* 92 (1992).

Goldstein, Sidney, and Calvin Goldscheider. *Jewish Americans: Three Generations in a Jewish Community*. Englewood Cliffs, N.J.: Prentice-Hall, 1968.

Goldy, Robert G. *The Emergence of Jewish Theology in America*. Bloomington: Indiana University Press, 1990.

Gordon, Albert. *Jews in Suburbia*. Boston: Beacon Press, 1959.

Greeley, Andrew W. *Religious Change in America*. Cambridge, Mass.: Harvard University Press, 1989.

Greer, Bruce A., and Wade Clark Roof. "'Desperately Seeking Sheila': Locating Religious Privatism in American Society." *Journal for the Scientific Study of Religion* 31 (1992).

Gurock, Jeffrey S. *The Men and Women of Yeshiva: Higher Education, Orthodoxy, and American Judaism*. New York: Columbia University Press, 1988.

―――. "The Orthodox Synagogue." In *The American Synagogue: A Sanctuary Transformed*, edited by Jack Wertheimer. New York: Cambridge University Press, 1987.

―――. "Resisters and Accommodators: Varieties of Orthodox Rabbis in America, 1886–1983." *American Jewish Archives* 35 (1983).

Heilman, Samuel. *Jewish Unity and Diversity: A Survey of American Rabbis and Rabbinical Students*. New York: American Jewish Committee, 1991.

Heilman, Samuel, and Steven M. Cohen. *Cosmopolitans and Parochials: Modern Orthodox Jews in America*. Chicago: University of Chicago Press, 1989.

Heilman, Samuel, and Menachem Friedman. "Religious Fundamentalism and Religious Jews: The Case of Haredim." In *Fundamentalisms Observed*, edited by Martin E. Marty and R. Scott Appelby. Chicago: University of Chicago Press, 1991.

Heimowitz, Joseph. "A Study of the Graduates of the Yeshiva of Flatbush High School." Ph.D. diss., Yeshiva University, 1979.

Helmreich, William. *The World of the Yeshiva: An Intimate Portrait of Orthodox Jewry*. New York: Free Press, 1982.

Herberg, Will. *Protestant, Catholic, Jew: An Essay in American Religious Sociology*. Garden City, N.Y.: Doubleday, 1955.

Hertzberg, Arthur. "The American Jew and His Religion." In *The American Jew: A Reappraisal*, edited by Oscar I. Janowsky. Philadelphia: Jewish Publication Society, 1964.

―――. *The Jews in America: Four Centuries of an Uneasy Encounter—A History*. New York: Simon and Schuster, 1989.

Himmelfarb, Harold S. "The Impact of Religious Schooling: The Effect of Jewish Education upon Adult Religious Involvement." Ph.D. diss., University of Chicago, 1974.

―――. "The Solace of Sociology." *American Jewish History* 74 (June 1985).

Hoge, Dean R. *Division in the Protestant House: The Basic Reasons Behind Intra-Church Conflicts*. Philadelphia: Westminster Press, 1976.

Horowitz, Bethamie, and Jeffrey R. Solomon. "Why Is This City Different from Other Cities: N.Y. and the 1990 National Jewish Population Survey." *Journal of Jewish Communal Service* 68 (Summer 1992).

Hunter, James Davison. *Culture Wars: The Struggle to Define America*. New York: Basic Books, 1991.

―――. *Evangelicalism: The Coming Generation*. Chicago: University of Chicago Press, 1987.

Hyman, Paula E. "The Introduction of Bat Mitzvah in Conservative Judaism in Postwar America." *YIVO Annual* 19 (1990).

Jackson, Kenneth T. *Crabgrass Frontier: The Suburbanization of the United States.* New York: Oxford University Press, 1985.

Joselit, Jenna W. "'Merry Chanuka': The Changing Holiday Practices of American Jews, 1880–1950." In *The Uses of Tradition: Jewish Continuity in the Modern Era,* edited by Jack Wertheimer. New York and Cambridge, Mass.: Jewish Theological Seminary of America and Harvard University Press, 1993.

Karp, Abraham. "A Century of Conservative Judaism." *American Jewish Yearbook* 86 (1986).

Kaufman, Debra Renée. *Rachel's Daughters: Newly Orthodox Jewish Women.* New Brunswick, N.J.: Rutgers University Press, 1991.

Kelley, Dean M. *Why Conservative Churches Are Growing.* New York: Harper and Row, 1972.

Kennedy, Eugene. *Tomorrow's Catholics, Yesterday's Church: The Two Cultures of American Catholicism.* San Francisco: Harper and Row, 1990.

Kosmin, Barry A., et al. *Highlights of the National Jewish Population Survey.* New York: Council of Jewish Federations, 1991.

Lazerwitz, Bernard. "Past and Future Trends in the Size of American Jewish Denominations." *Journal of Reform Judaism* 26 (Summer 1979).

Lenn, Theodore, et al. *Rabbi and Synagogue in Reform Judaism.* New York: CCAR, 1972.

Lerner, Anne Lapidus. "'Who Hast Not Made Me a Man': The Movement for Equal Rights for Women in American Jewry," *American Jewish Yearbook* 77 (1977).

Liebman, Charles S. "Changing Social Characteristics of Orthodox, Conservative and Reform Jews." *Sociological Analysis* 27 (Winter 1966).

———. "Extremism as a Religious Norm." *Journal for the Scientific Study of Religion* 22 (March 1983).

———. "Orthodoxy Faces Modernity." *Orim* 2 (Spring 1987).

———. "Orthodoxy in American Jewish Life." *American Jewish Yearbook* 66 (1965).

———. "Reconstructionism in American Jewish Life." *American Jewish Yearbook* 71 (1970).

———. "Religion, Class, and Culture in American Jewish Life." *Jewish Journal of Sociology* 9 (December 1967).

Liebman, Charles S., and Steven M. Cohen. *Two Worlds of Judaism: The Israeli and American Experiences.* New Haven: Yale University Press, 1990.

Magnus, Shulamit S. "Reinventing Miriam's Well: Feminist Jewish Ceremonials." In *The Uses of Tradition: Jewish Continuity in the Modern Era,* edited by Jack Wertheimer. New York and Cambridge, Mass.: Jewish Theological Seminary of America and Harvard University Press, 1993.

Martin, Bernard, ed. *Movements and Issues in American Judaism.* Westport, Conn.: Greenwood Press, 1978.

Marty, Martin E. *A Nation of Behavers.* Chicago: University of Chicago Press, 1976.

———. "Religion in America, 1935–1985." In *Altered Landscapes: Christianity in America, 1935–85,* edited by David W. Lotz. Grand Rapids, Mich.: Eerdmans Publishing, 1989.

———. "Transpositions: American Religion in the 1980s." *Annals of the American Academy of Political and Social Science* 480 (July 1985).

Marty, Martin E., and R. Scott Appelby, eds. *Fundamentalisms Observed.* Chicago: University of Chicago Press, 1991.

Masaryk, Fred. *Jewish Identity: Facts for Planning.* New York: Council of Jewish Federations, December 1974.

Matusow, Allen J. *The Unraveling of America: A History of Liberalism in the 1960s.* New York: Harper and Row, 1984.

Mayer, Egon. *Children of Intermarriage: A Study in Patterns of Identification and Family Life.* New York: American Jewish Committee, 1983.

———. *From Suburb to Shtetl: The Jews of Boro Park.* Philadelphia: Temple University Press, 1979.

———. "Gaps between Generations of Orthodox Jews in Boro Park, Brooklyn, N.Y." *Jewish Social Studies* 39 (Spring 1977).

———. *Intermarriage and Rabbinic Officiation.* New York: American Jewish Committee, 1989.

———. "Jews by Choice: Their Impact on the Contemporary American Jewish Community." *Proceedings of the Rabbinical Assembly* 45 (1983).

———. *Love and Tradition: Marriage between Jews and Christians.* New York: Schocken, 1985.

Mayer, Egon, and Chaim I. Waxman. "Modern Jewish Orthodoxy in America: Toward the Year 2000." *Tradition* 16 (Spring 1977).

Medding, Peter, et al. "Jewish Identity in Conversionary and Mixed Marriages." *American Jewish Yearbook* 92 (1992).

Meyer, Michael A. *Response to Modernity: A History of the Reform Movement in Judaism.* New York: Oxford University Press, 1988.

Moore, Deborah Dash. *At Home in America: Second Generation Jews in New York.* New York: Columbia University Press, 1981.

Parsons, Arthur S. "The Secular Contribution to Religious Innovation: A Case Study of the Unification Church." *Sociological Analysis* 29 (Fall 1989).

Perrin, Robin D., and Armand L. Mauss. "The Great Protestant Puzzle: Retreat, Renewal, or Reshuffle." In *In Gods We Trust: New Patterns of Religious Pluralism in America,* edited by Thomas Robbins and Dick Anthony, 2d rev. ed. New Brunswick, N.J.: Transaction Books, 1990.

Prell, Riv-Ellen. *Prayer and Community: The Havurah in American Judaism.* Detroit, Mich: Wayne State University Press, 1989.

Raphael, Marc Lee. *Profiles in American Judaism.* San Francisco: Harper and Row, 1984.

Reisman, Bernard. *Informal Jewish Education in North America.* Cleveland: Mandel Associated Foundations, 1990.

Ritterband, Paul. "The Determinants of Jewish Charitable Giving in the Last Part of the Twentieth Century." In *Contemporary Jewish Philanthropy in America,* edited by Barry A. Kosmin and Paul Ritterband. Savage, Md.: Rowman and Littlefield, 1991.

———. "The Social Basis of American Jewish Religious Organization." *Studies in Jewish Demography, 1989.* Jerusalem: Institute for Contemporary Jewry, forthcoming.

Robbins, Thomas, and Dick Anthony. *In Gods We Trust: New Patterns of Religious Pluralism in America,* 2d ed. New Brunswick, N.J.: Transaction Books, 1990.

Robinson, Ira. "Because of Our Many Sins: The Contemporary Jewish World as Reflected in the Responsa of Moses Feinstein." *Judaism* 35 (Winter 1986).

————. "That Marvelous Midos Machine: Audio Tapes as an Orthodox Educational Medium." In *Essays in the Social Scientific Study of Judaism and Jewish Society*, edited by Simcha Fishbane and Stuart Schoenfeld, vol. 2. Hoboken, N.J.: Ktav, 1992.

Roof, Wade Clark, and William McKinney. *American Mainline Religion: Its Changing Shape and Future.* New Brunswick, N.J.: Rutgers University Press, 1987.

Sarna, Jonathan D. "Interreligious Marriage in America." In *The Intermarriage Crisis: Jewish Communal Perspectives and Responses.* New York: American Jewish Committee, 1992.

————. "Reform Jewish Leaders, Intermarriage, and Conversion." *Journal of Reform Judaism* 37 (Winter 1990).

Schoem, David L. *Ethnic Survival in America: An Ethnography of a Jewish Afternoon School.* Atlanta: Scholar's Press, 1989.

Schoenfeld, Stuart. "Integration into the Group and Sacred Uniqueness: An Analysis of Adult Bat Mitzvah." In *Persistence and Flexibility: Anthropological Studies of American Jewish Identities and Institutions*, edited by Walter Zenner. Albany: SUNY Press, 1989.

————. "Ritual and Role Transition: Adult Bat Mitzvah as a Successful Rite of Passage." In *The Uses of Tradition: Jewish Continuity in the Modern Era*, edited by Jack Wertheimer. New York and Cambridge, Mass.: Jewish Theological Seminary of America and Harvard University Press, 1993.

Schorsch, Ismar. "Zacharias Frankel and the European Origins of Conservative Judaism." *Judaism* 30 (Summer 1981).

Shapiro, Edward S. "World War II and American Jewish Identity." *Modern Judaism* 10 (February 1990).

Sharot, Stephen. "Judaism and the Secularization Debate." *Sociological Analysis* 52 (Fall 1991).

————. *Judaism: A Sociology.* New York: Holmes and Meier, 1976.

Silber, Michael K. "The Emergence of Ultra-Orthodoxy: The Invention of a Tradition." In *The Uses of Tradition: Jewish Continuity in the Modern Era*, edited by Jack Wertheimer. New York and Cambridge, Mass.: Jewish Theological Seminary of America and Harvard University Press, 1993.

Silberman, Charles. *A Certain People: American Jews and Their Lives Today.* New York: Summit, 1985.

Silberman, Lou H. "The Union Prayer Book: A Study in Liturgical Development." In *Retrospect and Prospect*, edited by Bertram Korn. New York: CCAR 1965.

Sklare, Marshall. *America's Jews.* New York: Random House, 1971.

————. *Conservative Judaism: An American Religious Movement*, rev. ed. New York: Schocken, 1972.

Sklare, Marshall, and Joseph Greenblum. *Jewish Identity on the Suburban Frontier: A Study of Group Survival in an Open Society.* Chicago: University of Chicago Press, 1967.

Spickard, Paul R. *Mixed Blood: Intermarriage and Ethnic Identity in Twentieth-Century America.* Madison: University of Wisconsin Press, 1989.

Stark, Rodney, and Charles Y. Glock. *American Piety: The Nature of Religious Commitment.* Berkeley: University of California Press, 1968.

Tipton, Steven M. *Getting Saved from the Sixties: Moral Meaning in Conversion and Cultural Change*. Berkeley: University of California Press, 1982.

Urofsky, Melvin. *We Are One: American Jewry and Israel*. Garden City, N.Y.: Doubleday, 1978.

Vital, David. *The Future of the Jews: A People at the Crossroads*. Cambridge: Harvard University Press, 1990.

Warner, R. Stephen. "Change and Continuity in the U.S. Religious System: Perspectives from Sociology." Paper delivered at Princeton Theological Seminary, February 6, 1989.

————. *New Wine in Old Wineskins: Evangelicals and Liberals in a Small-Town Church*. Berkeley: University of California Press, 1988.

————. "The Place of the Congregation in the Contemporary American Religious Configuration." In James Lewis and James P. Wind, eds. *The Congregation in American Life*. Chicago: University of Chicago Press, forthcoming.

————. "Work in Progress Toward a New Paradigm for the Sociological Study of Religion in the United States." *American Sociological Review* 98 (March 1993).

Weissler, Lenore Eve. "Making Judaism Meaningful: Ambivalence and Tradition in a Havurah Community." Ph.D. diss., University of Pennsylvania, 1982.

Wertheimer, Jack. "The Conservative Synagogue." In *The American Synagogue: A Sanctuary Transformed*, edited by Jack Wertheimer. New York: Cambridge University Press, 1987.

————. "Recent Trends in American Judaism." *American Jewish Yearbook* 89 (1989).

————, ed. *The Uses of Tradition: Jewish Continuity in the Modern Era*. New York and Cambridge, Mass.: Jewish Theological Seminary of America and Harvard University Press, 1993.

Winer, Mark L., Sanford Seltzer, and Steven Schwager. *Leaders of Reform Judaism: A Study of Jewish Identity, Religious Practices and Beliefs, and Marriage Patterns*. New York: UAHC, 1987.

Woocher, Jonathan. *Sacred Survival: The Civil Religion of American Jews*. Bloomington: Indiana University Press, 1986.

Wuthnow, Robert. *The Restructuring of American Religion: Society and Faith since World War II*. Princeton, N.J.: Princeton University Press, 1988.

————. *The Struggle for America's Soul: Evangelicals, Liberals, and Secularism*. Grand Rapids, Mich.: Eerdmans, 1989.

GLOSSARY

aliyah (Hebrew). Literally, "going up"; refers to being called up to offer a benediction during the reading of the Torah.

amidah (Hebrew). Literally, "standing"; refers to the silent prayer that is central to the traditional liturgical structure of every prayer service. The *amidah* prayer is uttered while standing.

baal/baalat teshuvah; Pl. *baalei teshuvah* (Hebrew). Literally, "master, mistress of return"; refers to a Jew who has returned to religious tradition. Although used in the Orthodox community solely as a term for new recruits to Orthodox Judaism, it can be used to refer to a Jew who has become newly involved with any version of Judaism.

Bar/Bat Mitzvah (Hebrew). A rite of passage at the onset of puberty, for boys at the age of thirteen, for girls generally at the age of twelve. It is usually celebrated in a synagogue when the celebrant is called to the Torah for the first time and is accorded synagogue honors as an adult.

Beit Din (Hebrew). A Jewish court of law. Among its other functions, it decides upon the fitness of prospective converts to Judaism.

brit milah (Hebrew). The rite of circumcision, which symbolizes the entry of a male into the covenant of Israel. It is usually performed when a boy is eight days old.

Central Conference of American Rabbis (CCAR). The organization of Reform rabbis; founded in 1889.

Conservative Judaism. A movement of Judaism founded in the United States in the late nineteenth century as an alternative to the extremes of American Reform and the traditional Judaism imported from Europe. It was only in the second and third decades of the twentieth century that Conservative Judaism developed its own institutional identity and severed its ties with Orthodoxy.

Core Jewish Population. A term used in the 1990 National Jewish Population Survey to denote American Jews who identify with the Jewish religion or with a secular Jewish identity. It numbers approximately 5.5 million individuals.

daven (Yiddish). To pray.

Haggadah (Hebrew). A liturgical compilation of reflections on the Exodus account, which is read at the seder on the first evening/s of Passover.

halakhah (Hebrew). Literally, "the way"; the traditional Jewish law and its structure.

Hanukkah. A Jewish holiday commemorating the victory of the Maccabees over Syrian and Jewish Hellenists in the second century before the common era. Candles are lit on each of the eight nights of Hanukkah.

Hasidism, Hasidic. Refers to a pietistic version of Judaism developed initially in Poland and Russia during the eighteenth century by Israel Baal Shem Tov and his disciples. The movement subsequently spread throughout Eastern Europe; it achieved strength and prominence in the United States with the arrival of refugees from Nazism in the middle of the twentieth century. Adherents are called Hasidim.

havurah; Pl. havurot (Hebrew). Fellowship; a term appropriated from ancient rabbinic groups to refer to contemporary communities that engage in prayer and study.

High Holy Days. The ten-day penitential period beginning with the Jewish New Year (Rosh Hashanah) and concluding with the Day of Atonement (Yom Kippur).

Hebrew Union College—Jewish Institute of Religion (HUC-JIR). The rabbinical seminary of the Reform movement, which has campuses in Cincinnati, Jerusalem, Los Angeles, and New York; founded in 1875.

kaddish (Hebrew). An Aramaic prayer sanctifying and praising the name of God. It is recited by mourners, as well as the leader of prayer services.

kosher, *kashrut* (Hebrew). Pertaining to Jewish dietary laws concerning permissible and impermissible foods.

Jewish Theological Seminary of America. The educational "fountainhead" of the Conservative movement. Founded in 1886, its main campus is in New York; and it has affiliates in Buenos Aires, Jerusalem, and Los Angeles.

Lubavitch Hasidism. Perhaps the largest sect of Hasidic Jews in the United States. The group takes its name from a small city in Russia, where disciples of the Hasidic teacher, Rabbi Schneer Zalman of Lyadi, settled. It has attracted attention due to the charismatic appeal of its Rebbe, Rabbi Menachem M. Schneerson, and its bold outreach programs to non-Orthodox Jews. Also known as **Chabad,** based on a Hebrew acronym for the motto of the movement.

mezuzah (Hebrew). An amulet that is affixed to the right post of doorways in the Jewish home; inside the amulet is parchment containing handwritten excerpts from biblical texts.

mikveh (Hebrew). A ritual bathhouse.

minyan (Hebrew). The quorum necessary for public prayer.

mixed seating. Refers to men and women sitting together during religious services.

Orthodox Judaism. A movement that views itself as the only authentic continuation of traditional Judaism. In the United States it organized itself institutionally only in the last decades of the nineteenth century in reaction to the challenges posed by Reform Judaism.

Rabbinical Assembly. The organization of Conservative rabbis; founded in 1900.

Rabbinical Council of America (RCA). The organization of centrist (formerly Modern) Orthodox rabbis; most members were ordained either by the rabbinical seminaries of Yeshiva University or the Hebrew Theological College in Skokie, Illinois; founded in 1923.

Reconstructionism. An approach to American Judaism pioneered by Rabbi Mordecai M. Kaplan in the 1920s and 1930s. Long regarded as the left wing of the Conservative movement, Reconstructionism gained independence as a "fourth movement" through the establishment of a rabbinical seminary (the **RRC,** Reconstructionist Rabbinical College) in 1968 and the development of **FRCH** (the Federation of Reconstructionist Congregations and Havurot) and the **RRA** (Reconstructionist Rabbinical Association).

Reform Judaism. The first Jewish religious movement to organize in the United States. Under the leadership of Rabbi Isaac Meyer Wise, Reform grew in the post–Civil War era into the largest movement among native-born Jews. The **Pittsburgh Platform** of 1885 codified the movement's affirmations and negations of traditional Jewish beliefs and practices.

seder (Hebrew). On the first evening/s of Passover, Jews participate in a feast commemorating the Exodus from Egypt.

siddur (Hebrew). Prayer book.

tallit (Hebrew). A fringed prayer shawl.

Traditional synagogues. Largely a midwestern phenomenon. Traditional congregations permit men and women to sit together and utilize a microphone during religious services; their rabbis identify with Modern Orthodoxy and they use Orthodox prayer books.

Torah (Hebrew). Refers to the parchment scroll that contains the Pentateuch: the books of Genesis, Exodus, Leviticus, Numbers, and Deuteronomy.

Union of American Hebrew Congregations (UAHC). The congregational body of the Reform movement in Judaism; founded in 1873.

Union of Orthodox Jewish Congregations of America (OU). The largest congregational body of Orthodox Judaism. Founded in 1898, it plays a major role in the certification of food as kosher.

Union Prayer Book (UPB). The traditional prayer book of the Reform movement first compiled in the 1890s and replaced in 1975.

United Synagogue of Conservative Judaism. The synagogue body of the Conservative movement. For much of its history its name was the United Synagogue of America; founded in 1913.

yarmulke. A skullcap.

yeshiva (Hebrew). An academy of study; the term is often used to refer to Orthodox day schools.

Yeshiva University. The largest educational institution of Orthodox Judaism in the United States. Founded in 1886, its main campus is located in New York; it has affiliates in Jerusalem and Los Angeles.

yeshiva world. A network of Orthodox day schools and academies of rabbinical and postrabbinical study that guides right-wing versions of Orthodox Judaism. This network was primarily created by immigrants who arrived in the United States in the 1930s and 1940s.

INDEX

questions of limits in, 109–12; religious expression among, 64; results of new directions set by, 112–13; rituals and, 10–11, 57; social action programs of, 9–10, 19–20, 203n7; synagogue membership and, 57; women's participation in, 105. *See also* Union of American Hebrew Congregations (UAHC)
Reines, Alvin, 111
Religion and religious life: changes during the 1960s in, 25–28; comparison between Jewish and Christian patterns for, 63; conversions to Judaism and, 82; divisions in, 28, 39, 189–90; feminist revolutions and, 190; individualism and, 44–45, 191–92; involvement of young people in, 26; Judaism in mainstream of, 15–17; overall current health of, 187–88; reemergence after the 1960s of, 43–44; religious identity and, 45–46, 209n8; resurgence of conservative forms of, 26–27; special–purpose groups in, 89–90; stability of patterns of, 64, 215n69, 216n70; tolerance of diversity in, 27–28. *See also* Jewish religious observance
Religious Action Center, 10, 19, 111
Religious institutions: educational level and attendance at, 27; protest movements and, 19, 26. *See also* Interfaith movement; Synagogues
Religious revival, 4–5, 14, 66–91; conversions to Judaism and, 81–84; day schools and Jewish identity and, 86; educational programs for unaffiliated Jews and, 84–85; feminist Judaism and, 72–75; gay synagogues and, 76; Humanistic Judaism and, 79; impulse for, 66–67; interfaith synagogues and, 79–80; Jews on the periphery and, 75–81; Orthodoxy and, 118–23; overlap of Jewish populations involved in movements in, 80–81; renewal movement and, 77–79; rural Jews and, 76–77; special-purpose groups and, 89–91; synagogue services and, 87–89; trips to Israel and, 85–86. *See also* Havurah movement
Renewal movement, 77–79, 83, 220n51
Responsa Committee, 96, 109
Response (journal), 23, 141, 142
Richmond, 60
Riskin, Steven, 128, 134
Ritterband, Paul, 51, 65
Rituals: counterculture and, 23; feminist Judaism and, 72–73, 218n24; growth in American Judaism and observance of, 15, 202n58; Humanistic Judaism and, 79; intermarriage and, 61–62, 214n56;

Reform movement and positions regarding, 10–11, 95–96, 102–9; religious revival and, 66; surveys on participation in, 46, 47, 49–51, 57, 64, 211n17
Rochester, 49
Roe v. Wade, 182
Roof, Wade Clark, 44, 191
Roosevelt, Franklin, 29
Rosenthal, Erich, 32–33
Rosenthal, Gilbert, 156
Rosh Chodesh, 73, 74, 218n31
Rosh Hashanah, 104
Roth, Joel Rabbi, 151, 157
Routtenberg, Max, 140
Rubin, Saul, 69
Rural Jews, 76–77, 121

Sabbath and Festival Prayer Book, 8, 22n27
Sabbath observance, 50–51, 57, 118
Sabbath Prayer Book (Kaplan), 12
Sandmel, Samuel, 31–32
San Francisco, 32–33, 60, 76
Sarna, Jonathan, 62
Schachter-Shalomi, Zalman, 77–78
Schindler, Alexander, 105, 108, 109, 112, 178
Schneerson, Menachem M., 119–20, 121
Schools. *See* Colleges and universities; Day schools; Education; Students; Sunday schools; Synagogue schools
Schorsch, Ismar, 138, 143, 151, 158–59
Schulweis, Harold, 69, 148–49, 167
Schwarz, Sidney, 166
Seattle, 47
Second Jewish Catalogue, The, 67–68, 142
Secularism, 24, 43, 111
Seders, 47, 49, 57, 73–74
Seltzer, Sanford, 111
Seminario Rabinico Latinoamericano, 8
Separatist ideology, 12, 13, 121, 125, 179, 201n47
Sha'ar Zahav, 76
Shalom bat, 72
Shankman, Jacob, 5
Shapiro, Saul, 141
Shtiebel services, 128, 231n49
Siddur Sim Shalom, 152, 154, 155
Siegel, Richard, 142
Siegel, Seymour, 8
Simchat bat, 72
Simchat Torah, 105, 132
Six-Day War (1967), 25, 30, 31
Sklare, Marshall, 14, 33, 36, 50, 138, 140–41, 144
Social Action Center, 10, 195
Social action programs, and Reform Judaism, 9–10
Social conditions: antiwar movement and, 18–19, 20, 21, 25–26; changes during